MW00654113

Working Lives and in-House Outsourcing

This book offers a sociological account of the process by which companies instituted and continue to institute outsourcing in their organization. Drawing on qualitative data, it examines the ways in which internal outsourcing in the information technologies and human resources professions negatively affects workers, their work conditions, and working relationships. With attention to the deleterious influence of outsourcing on relationships and the strong tendency of market organizations to produce social conflict in interactions – itself a considerable "transaction cost" – the author challenges both the ideology that markets, rather than hierarchies, produce more efficient and less costly economic outcomes for companies, and the idea that outsourcing generates benefits for professional workers in the form of greater opportunity. A demonstration of the social conflict created between employees working for two separate, proprietary companies, *Working Lives and in-House Outsourcing* will be of interest to scholars with interests in the sociology of work and organizations and the sociology of professions, as well as those working in the fields of business management and human resources.

Jacqueline M. Zalewski is Associate Professor of Sociology at West Chester University of Pennsylvania, US.

Routledge Studies in the Sociology of Work, Professions and Organisations

This series presents the latest sociological and social scientific research on professions, work and organisations, welcoming studies of careers, professional motivations, organisational change, entrepreneurship, workplace issues, working lives and identities, labour relations and the transformation of work in a changing economy.

Titles in this series

Identity, Motivation and Memory
The Role of History in the British and German Forces
Sarah Katharina Kayss

Working Lives and in-House Outsourcing
Chewed-Up by Two Masters
Jacqueline M. Zalewski

For more information about this series, please visit: www.routledge.com/socio logy/series/RSSWPO

Working Lives and in-House Outsourcing
Chewed-Up by Two Masters

Jacqueline M. Zalewski

Routledge
Taylor & Francis Group

LONDON AND NEW YORK

First published 2019
by Routledge
2 Park Square, Milton Park, Abingdon, Oxon OX14 4RN

and by Routledge
711 Third Avenue, New York, NY 10017

Routledge is an imprint of the Taylor & Francis Group, an informa business

British Library Cataloguing-in-Publication Data
A catalogue record for this book is available from the British Library

Library of Congress Cataloging-in-Publication Data
A catalog record for this book has been requested

ISBN: 978-1-138-60631-9 (hbk)
ISBN: 978-0-429-46774-5 (ebk)

Typeset in Times New Roman
by Apex CoVantage, LLC

This book is dedicated to working-class kids who follow their dreams to things they can't yet imagine.

Contents

Tables

Acknowledgments

Most important, to all the subjects who shared your experience about inO and outsourcing with me, thank you! This book is about your perspectives on outsourcing, using a sociological lens. This book is not possible without you.

From the first time I heard "it takes a village," I understood and respected its meaning. Without my village, this book would not have been possible. Thank you for your contributions to this project – either directly and indirectly – my wife Anteaus M. Rezba, my parents Shirley and Frederick Zalewski, my sister Yvonne Zalewski and her partner Russell Stollenwerk, my father-in-law Godfrey Rezba, my friends David Ventura, Lisa Crowley, Susan Brudvig, Julie Wiest, and Lisa Huebner.

Jeffrey Zalewski, my loving brother, you helped me write this book. You left your family too soon to see it (tears). To the rest of my extended family, thank you for your support and pride now and through all the years.

Thank you to the faculty mentors and students in higher education who have shaped me and my scholarship. My faculty mentors include: Peter Whalley, Lauren Langman, Marilyn Krogh, Gerhard Schutte, and Leigh Shaffer. Students from West Chester University who have contributed to this manuscript either through transcribing interviews, finding literature, and annotating it for me include: Jackie Drumheller, Christine Caria, Zachary Schagrin, Molly Byrne, Zachary Kline, Joey Maysky, Collin Cunningham, Jessica Herling, Heather Welsh, Laura Sposato, Stephen Falance, Rebecca Chapnick, Jessica Tullie, and Sarah Kratz. Thank you.

A special thank you goes to Sarah Kratz, who in the past year has helped me with her excellent copyediting skills and sense of responsiveness.

1 "Trading in human beings on behalf of cost reduction"

An introduction to in-house outsourcing (inO) and why companies outsource

Introduction: how did I get here?

My journey with "in-house outsourcing" (inO) began in May 2002 on my best friend's porch in the Midwest. I was visiting George in a big city and a number of his local friends were there for a barbecue. They are all white-collar professionals with successful careers. Like my friend George and his friend Melissa,[1] many had jobs with companies who had excellent reputations as "good employers." From past conversations, I was well aware that both George and Melissa's firms used contingent workers (i.e., temporary workers). For example, George's employer Foreign Motors Inc. extensively used temporaries in production jobs in one form of contingency. Per Melissa, Concerto Inc. regularly employed consultants who worked on special projects in professional roles in another form of contingency work.

This time, however, Melissa told us that her employer Concerto Inc. had recently decided to outsource all of their information technology (IT) infrastructure, hardware, software, and most of their support to another company. Yet most of the hardware, business processes, and the people doing the work would continue to remain onsite at the physical location of Concerto Inc. While Melissa was not personally affected – she was part of a small group of IT development staff retained to work on special projects related to Concerto Inc.'s core product lines – hundreds of other IT professionals at her company would be outsourced. Per Melissa, rumors were rampant onsite and warned that this would not be the last large outsourcing deal Concerto Inc. employees would see at their company.[2] The rumors emphasized the CEO planned on shedding most of Concerto Inc.'s administrative operations to outsourcers so that the company could better focus on their "core competencies." In this case, those primary functions were developing home product remedies and marketing them to consumers.

I was dismayed by Melissa's news. My sociological understanding of organizational changes in the workplace and the effects of new technologies strongly implied that a developing outsourcing trend likely meant that the middle-class lifestyles white-collar professionals like Melissa had enjoyed because of their jobs in stable positions were becoming tenuous. Indeed, since our conversation, they have weakened.

After that gathering with friends through early 2018, I have extensively read news reports and scholarly studies that discussed the increased outsourcing of jobs. Most often, I found that the causes for its growth and the advantages of outsourcing were discussed in public media and academic sources. Only sometimes did media outlets discuss potential disadvantages of outsourcing for the companies and affected workers. A year after the barbecue, in 2003 at a family celebration, Russell – then the IT security director for Merchant Inc. – told me his employer was outsourcing a significant portion of their IT business processes, hardware, and support. Russell described the emotional anguish experienced by upwards of a 200-person IT department. At the time I heard of this case, Merchant Inc. had not decided which employees would be staying at Merchant Inc. as a direct employee (Russell included) or transferred to the outsourcing company. Furthermore, employees did not know if the new jobs with Master Technologies – the chosen outsourcing "vendor" – would remain onsite or be moved from their physical suburban location.[3]

In 2004, I chose to research business process outsourcing for my dissertation for several reasons. Foremost, in the public sphere, I felt Americans were missing an unfolding and important story about widespread changes to the company job. In 2004 and 2005 (when I started interviewing), the dominant theme in news reporting was the exporting of work and jobs to less industrialized countries. The outsourcing archetype seemed to be the movement of IT work and jobs to nations like India.[4] At the time, offshoring was the form of outsourcing that then presidential candidates Bush and Kerry were debating. Little else was being said about "business process outsourcing" as it is commonly called and – especially – the "in-house" kind of outsourcing affecting those close to me. There were occasional exceptions, such as small reports of deals in the business section of the local newspaper.[5] Ironically, the Bureau of Labor Statistic's (BLS) own estimates of job loss due to the domestic relocation of work to outsourcing provider firms in the US indicated that they accounted for two-thirds of the job losses in this category during the first quarter of 2004 (as reported by Hopkins 2004 for Reuters and MSN Money; BLS 2004).

> "In more than seven out of 10 cases (of layoffs at companies with at least 50 people), the work activities were reassigned to places elsewhere in the U.S.," The Bureau of Labor Statistics said in its report on mass layoffs for the January-to-March period.

More recently, in their mass layoff statistics, the BLS reports that a significant number of "separations" (i.e., layoffs) occurred in 2012 and 2013 because these jobs moved to a different US location. In 2012, their figures imply that layoffs preceding the shift of jobs to another US company were greater compared to those that moved out of the country. In 2013, the BLS data shows that this ratio reversed and the number of jobs and workers that "separated" and moved offshore was greater than those that moved to another US location. Per a recent inquiry I made to BLS on January 29, 2018, since 2013 the mass layoff statistics program has been discontinued. No more data has been collected or is available from the BLS on mass layoffs in the US.

It was clear there was – and still is – a lack of labor analysis and media coverage on the jobs that are being outsourced to provider firms who continue to deliver the work onsite or situate the job and provision of work within US borders. The result is that one in three US adults, according to a recent PEW research survey (Graf 2018), perceived the "increased outsourcing of jobs to other countries as the top trend they say has hurt their job or career." Compared to the predominant perception about outsourcing as the offshoring of jobs, since 2004, inO has been a significant trend in which the public has not been sufficiently informed. Labor economists, as do I, lament this lack of public awareness. For example, David Weil recently contributed to the *Huffington Post* an article (12/14/17) titled, "Millennial Employees Aren't the Problem. The Transformed Workplace Is: The Nature of Work Has Changed, and Millennials Are Getting Screwed."

I also have an ongoing interest in work and workplace changes because of my social location. I grew up in Kenosha, Wisconsin, a working-class community in the US Midwest. Kenosha's economy and jobs grew around the production of durable goods and most notably the automobile. Over the 20th century, Kenosha was home to Jeffrey Motors, then American Motors, and then Chrysler/Jeep manufacturing plants. Like industrial centers throughout the Midwest, economic recession, deindustrialization, and greater competition in these and most industries in the 1970s and 1980s led to considerable job losses in Kenosha. See, for example, Kathryn Dudley's (1994) excellent research on displaced automobile workers in Kenosha, Wisconsin in her award-winning book *The End of the Line: Lost Jobs, New Lives in Postindustrial America*. Job loss hurt many working-class families when they were forced from good paying jobs that afforded middle-class lifestyles into work that offered significantly lower wages, more instability, and fewer employment protections. Clearly, the economic and social landscape became more chaotic, competitive, and cut-throat. Peoples' lives and livelihoods across the US were increasingly at risk.[6]

In graduate school in the 1990s, I became interested in the growth of contingent work. Firms began instituting "just-in-time" inventory principles as a dominant labor strategy and making historically permanent jobs increasingly temporary. During the summer of 1998 – with the help of friends in the industry – for a master's thesis I completed field research as a temporary worker in a Chicago factory and experienced the degrading effects from the job conditions, the unstable working time, and witnessed the precarious effects on peoples' lives from this just-in-time and low-wage labor practice. After this, I completed comprehensive exams in the sociology of work and new technologies fields. Finally, in 2005, I started conducting qualitative research on the inO of information technologies (IT) and human resources (HR) jobs and work. I completed data collection 12 years later in early 2017. This book is based on the 51 interviews and – over the past 12 years – ongoing news reporting, emails from the Outsourcing Institute (OI) about their "roadshows," observations and subject contacts I made at two of their events, industry reports from the OI and other market analyst organizations, and academic research on outsourcing.[7]

The outsourcing of work

Many companies in the US and other advanced industrial societies and economies have been outsourcing work for some time (Abraham & Taylor 1996; Kalleberg & Marsden 2005; Pfeffer & Baron 1988). For example, as described by Abraham and Taylor, "over the period from 1972 to 1993, the Bureau of Labor Statistics shows that jobs in the business services industry grew by 288%" (1996:413). When I asked about the outsourcing of other jobs at their employers, most subjects in my study replied similarly to Russell and Barbara below. Their employers had been outsourcing functions such as sanitation, logistics, and heavily regulated (and standardized) tasks like payroll and benefits administration to third party suppliers for some time.

> Merchant Inc. outsources all of their logistics. In other words, the moving of products from a distribution center to stores. That's all outsourced to a trucking company. They don't have their own trucks. [*J: HR*?] People Solutions does some of their payroll processing. Benefits. . . . They don't outsource 100% of everything in a given area but they outsource chunks. Except for trucking, that's totally outsourced. Merchant Inc. has their own warehouses but they outsource all of the transportation to those warehouses.
>
> (Russell, former IT Security Director at Merchant Inc.)

> Rapture Hospital's rationale was their expertise is patient care. . . . Rapture Hospital had always outsourced what they considered their non-expertise type functions to outside companies. They had outsourced their food service, their security, their housekeeping, their engineering services, building services, all that kind of stuff. That's all farmed out.
>
> (Barbara, former IT Manager at Right Technology Solutions)

The inO of IT and HR jobs in this book are similar to the traditional outsourcing in more routinized (e.g., sanitation) and heavily regulated (e.g., payroll and CDL drivers) job functions identified above. Although, similarly to economists Hira and Hira in their analysis of the outsourcing of jobs in America (2005), most people would characterize the workers in these professional fields as embodying higher-level skill sets. In Zuboff's terms, the IT and HR work outsourced in cases here required "intellective skills" involving theoretical knowledge, and inferential and procedural reasoning (1988).

To understand what outsourcing is, it helps to note how it differs from other forms of nonstandard work like employment in the temporary help industry or jobs in contracting. Importantly in jobs working for temporary agencies or consulting for a company, the customer retains control and ownership of the work. Because of this, within legal parameters, customers also have the power to direct workers in these types of contracted jobs (Henson 1996; McNally 1979; Osnowitz 2010; Parker 1994; Rogers 1995; Smith 1994). In contrast, per industry insiders – for example Peter Bendor-Samuel (2000) below – and the subjects in this research, the key difference with outsourcing is that "the control and ownership of the work gets transferred" to the vendor company. The customer of an outsourcing agreement determines the end results of the business process, i.e., the configuring of "measurable performance metrics" (Gartner Inc. 2005). However, the provider firm chooses the best means of accomplishing this outcome because they own and control the work. Legally, the customer no longer has the power to direct the work of employees working for outsourcing companies.

> Outsourcing takes place when an organization transfers the ownership of a business process to a supplier. The key to this definition is the concept of transfer of control. This definition differentiates outsourcing from business relationships in which the buyer retains control of the process or, in other words, tells the supplier how to do the work. *It is the transfer of ownership that defines outsourcing and often makes it such a challenging, painful process* [my emphasis]. In outsourcing, the buyer does not instruct the supplier how to perform its tasks but, instead, focuses on communicating what results it wants to buy; it leaves the process of accomplishing those results to the supplier.
>
> (Bendor-Samuel 2000:25)

Bendor-Samuel has been an active proponent in the outsourcing industry since the 1960s. He is currently CEO at Everest Group, a company that markets itself as a "consulting and research firm focused on strategic IT, business services and sourcing." Sourcing is a popular way for identifying traditional outsourcing; i.e., the kind represented in this book. Similar to my discussion in Chapter 3 of the problematic social relations typically involved in "reworking a new arrangement" in the cases here – it is interesting that Bendor-Samuel notes the process of transferring ownership over the work from a customer to the vendor is fraught with "challenges" and is "painful."

To understand why outsourcing has grown, academics generally identify economic and technological causes. According to economist scholars, economic conditions in the US began changing in the 1960s because of the "unbalancing of institutional circuits that connect production and consumption" (Piore & Sabel 1984:4). Essentially the Fordist system of mass production, utilized by many large US manufacturers during the mid-20th century, became unsustainable. It was untenable because of the customized consumer preferences that were beginning to characterize the American public's buying patterns (DiTomaso 2001; Harrison 1994; Reich 1992). Along with this, US manufacturers began feeling pressure from foreign competitor companies (Hollister 2011). This was most obvious in the automotive industry, as manufacturers such as Toyota utilized tiers of suppliers and flexible systems of lean, specialized production to produce more customized automobiles to better match the consumer preferences of the American public (Womack, Jones, & Roos 1990).

Japanese companies posed serious challenges to US based manufacturers, as they began whittling away at their market share in the automobile industry. As a result, greater uncertainty in markets and increased economic globalization from the growing presence of foreign competition produced greater volatility in most US consumer markets. This uncertain economic environment led many companies to strategically begin instituting a variety of cost reduction strategies to reduce their risk and sustain the profitability of their companies (Kalleberg 2000; Pfeffer & Baron 1988; Powell 1990). Economically then, these realities have preceded the dismantling or externalization trend of vertically integrated organizations and they have directly affected the growth in the outsourcing of jobs.

Scholars examining the growth in nonstandard or contingent work and the externalization of jobs also highlight the importance of technology changes over time to explain these patterns (Hollister 2011; Pfeffer & Baron 1988; Piore & Sabel 1984; Powell 1990; Sennett 1998). For example, Pfeffer and Baron identify the "meterability of computers and the decreased cost of computing power" as interacting with the economic pressures discussed above (1988:281). Their combination led economic firms to emphasize the measurement and collection of increasing amounts of information about the various parts of their production and service work systems.

Firms began taking greater interest in managing and controlling their business processes to maintain and increase their profitability. To accomplish this, computerized technologies and their evolution have helped them transform work to make it more transparent. Especially illustrative research on this process is Shoshanna Zuboff's analysis (1988) of the adoption of early computerization technologies in the production and management processes within eight firms between 1981 and 1986. Computers have an informating function that gives managers important tools of control and provides a strong sense of the transformation process that has taken place over several decades to reengineer the social organization in firms by adopting flexibility strategies that lower the costs of producing work (Pfeffer & Baron 1988:281; Zuboff: 396, 414). As a result, technological change has also allowed firms to more efficiently externalize noncore functions to business suppliers, and it has helped produce a concentration of financial capital and power among large multinational firms (Harrison 1994; Sennett 1998).

Both academics and industry analysts describe the primary benefits and results companies seek when they contract with a vendor in an outsourcing deal. They correspond with the economic and technology causes for greater externalization of various noncore functions by firms, and they shape the reasons for the inO of IT and HR jobs and workers examined in this study. Most academic research on organizational decisions to outsource, including offshoring, emphasizes primary causes as firms' strategic interest in leveraging flexibility, more efficiencies in work processes, and greater profitability from the lower margins market suppliers take in the transaction (see, e.g., Adler 2003; Diomande 2017; Kalleberg 2000). As scholars previously found, this also corresponds with the rationale commonly used by organizations to support the growth of temporary workers in their operations. Per Peck and Theodore (1998), for example, the temporary help industry in Chicago grew through the 1980s and 1990s in large part because employers perceived strategic benefits from utilizing temporary workers for numerical and qualitative (or functional) flexibility (658). With numerical flexibility, costs are incurred by contracting firms only when necessary and as the demands of the customer's work warrants. In theory and in practice, labor is perceived as a commodity and it is typically contracted by customers in a "just-in-time" manner. With functional flexibility, organizations gain financial benefits from lower costs as a result of the rebundling of tasks, standardization and other efficiencies in the work, and a flexible social organization.

Since 2000, industry analyst companies have consistently reported economic reasons for why the firms in their research have outsourced job functions. For example, in 2000 an Outsourcing Institute/Spherion study of firms who outsourced found they did so for cost reduction reasons and the ability to focus on their core revenue-generating operations. More recently, a 2016 Deloitte Global Outsourcing Survey similarly found that the first and second reasons for outsourcing among companies in their sample were cost cutting and the ability to focus on their core competencies (Carillo 2018). These same surveys also found that technology – specifically its ability to improve "capacity" through the application of an outsourcing company's expert ways for accomplishing the work, improving the efficiencies within it, and reducing the costs of producing it – continue to be important reasons to outsource IT, HR, and other noncore functions. Per business commentary, in several recent examples, the global growth in e-commerce, social media use by people, and the increased emphasis firms give to data analytics have prompted firms to utilize outsourcing companies for their expertise in these emerging technology fields, including data security. Customer companies want to institute these new capabilities in their firms to financially benefit from this emerging consumer and online social behavior (Ammachchi 2013; Bradbury 2015; CIOL.com 2013; Masters 2015; Orem 2018).

Getting a sense of the scope of outsourcing generally and the number of people it affects is difficult because it is challenging to find consistencies across data measures and findings. Collectively, however, the information does give a sense of the size of the outsourcing industry and the fact that it has grown over time. For example from their academic analysis of a 1996/7 National Organizations Study, Kalleberg and Marsden (2005) found that 54% of companies surveyed used temporary help agencies or contracted with another company to deliver business services. In the mid-1990s, they especially used markets for "separable activities like repair, janitorial and security," but Kalleberg and Marsden found the use of intermediaries for computers and information systems was also significant at 23% (404).

In 2000, an Outsourcing Institute Survey estimated outsourcing expenditures in the US were $340 billion. Similarly, in 2013, Gartner reported that the global outsourcing market would reach $288 billion (Overby). Per quarter and year, the industry also reports numbers on the purported value of signed outsourcing deals. In first quarter of 2005, according to TPI Index (Nelson), IT outsourcing deals totaled 10.8 billion. This had increased 68% from the year prior. In 2014, ISG (formerly TPI Index) – reported that IT outsourcing deals were significant at 23.1 billion total contract value, up 19% from the year prior (Overby 2015b).

In yet another measure, *Computer Economics* found that large organizations responding to their survey spent 7.8% of their IT budgets in 2015 on outsourcing work, and this increased to 11.9% in 2017 (Violino 2017). Finally, a recent *Wall Street Journal* news story reported that five outsourcing companies now appear on the list of the 20 largest US companies (Weber 2017). While estimates give some concreteness to the scope of the outsourcing industry, because of the inconsistencies across and within measures, these figures only provide a relative ballpark size. However, the numbers strongly suggest that the global and US outsourcing industry are both significant and expanding.

Industry figures and experts identify the industries where organizations most often source. They also portray that the common types of outsourcing are shifting in new directions. For example, in a 2016 Deloitte Global Survey, the dominant sectors in outsourcing included: IT, defense and government, media, healthcare and pharmaceuticals, telecommunications, retail, travel and transport, and energy. Most of these sectors are represented in this study of outsourcing cases. When I began this research, IT and HR represented the most common and the fastest growing industries in outsourcing respectively (Capgemini 2005; *Outsourcing Essentials* 2003). Since 2013, many sources report that cloud (e.g., application hosting services) and data center outsourcing represent significant types of outsourcing that are growing today (Everest Group 2018; Overby 2016; Wright 2018). As data security concerns continue to persist (e.g., the security breach of customer data at Yahoo, other nations meddling in the 2016 US presidential election process) spending on IT security services is expected to increase in 2018 by 8% according to consulting and research firm Gartner (Schott 2017).

Lastly, as a sociologist, I am highly interested in knowing how many people have been affected by the outsourcing of jobs and their work. Unfortunately, valid data on the number of American working people affected by outsourcing is very limited. In 2005, the Bureau of Labor Statistics (BLS) found the proportion of US workers employed in contingent and alternative work arrangements (i.e., independent contractors) were 2 to 4% and 7% respectively. The BLS estimated that workers provided by contract firms were .6% of total employment. Per the BLS, these figures represented little change from a previous study conducted in 2001. The BLS conducted another study of contingent and alternative work arrangements in the US in May 2017. Compared to past surveys, the findings were consistent at 1.3 to 3.8% and 6.9% of US workers, respectively (2018). The proportion of workers provided by contract firms was continued at .6% of total employment.

Intrigued by a news and BLS report in 2004 that suggested the size of domestic outsourcing exceeded that of offshoring, I examined BLS published data on mass layoffs in the US from 2004 to 2013. The BLS reports on the number of employee layoffs where jobs migrated to either another domestic location or an offshore location. The data reflects gaps within quarters in some years but, foremost, it depicts the fact that separations persist and the movement of work has continued. For example, the number of separations that led to either the movement of jobs domestically or offshore was 9,422 in 2004 and 2,219 in 2012. The drop in separations supports one recent notion in the industry: outsourcing contracts are getting smaller and affecting fewer people in each instance (as reported in *CIO*, Overby 2015a and

2016). Finally, the pattern of domestic to offshoring relocations from 2004 to 2012 suggests that the former has consistently been greater. For example, in 2004 the number of domestic relocations was 5,477 compared to 3,292 relocations offshore. For the first time in the first quarter of 2013, the number of separations where work moved offshore was greater at 170 compared to 111 separations domestically.

In the system of waged labor, outsourcing is said to represent a dominant form of "fissuring," a well-regarded theory that describes labor markets today that continue to progressively degrade the working conditions for people in more and more jobs (Weil 2014). Jobs once part of the core labor markets of good employers have been shifted outside of firms to peripheral labor markets. Importantly, jobs become more insecure because they are predicated upon strategic practices of instituting flexible and more contingent relationships to spread the risks and liabilities of the company and cut costs. Thus, in the inO cases presented here, the effects of competitive and risky markets and the "mean" business practices of firms (Sheldon, former CIO for an outsourcing company) got transferred onto the backs of laborers before even they disappeared in organizational restructuring and the externalization of business processes. There can be no doubt that this understanding is reflected in the minds of outsourcing executives, who routinely carried out its corresponding job actions (e.g., layoffs) as Jay explained below. Invoking a market philosophy of "shedding people on behalf of cost reduction," corporations show the "brutal" ideology and outcomes (JB) that occur when labor becomes hyper-commodified in the fissured workplace.

> So, I didn't deal with a lot of the stuff that people deal with, which is the shedding of people and the *trading in of human beings on behalf of cost reduction* [my emphasis].
>
> (Jay, former Executive Vice President of a
> division at Sourcing Central)

This study's contributions

When I began actively researching inO in 2004, with the exception of studies on temporary work and one study on inO by Vicki Smith, little sociological research – quantitative or qualitative – had been completed. Thus, in 2004 historically studied foci in the sociology of work – for example the organization of work and its sociological effects – represented gaps in understanding how inO was instituted and what comprised its social effects. Unfortunately, most gaps still remain today. The research questions for this study focus on the process of internalizing a market organization within the physical structure of customers, how social relations among workers on the front line of both firms were affected, what comprised culture with the inO of work, and what characterizes professional careers with outsourcing companies. Specifically, my research questions were: 1. With inO, how is a market instituted within the same physical context of a customer company and how are professionals rebadged to an outsourcing company? 2. How does the market relationship work in practice on the employee front lines, and how do markets affect social relations there? 3. What are the common effects of inO on the work and jobs of professional IT and HR workers? Chapter findings addressing these broad research questions follow this same order.

Findings from this research on inO contribute to scholarly debates in several areas. Below, I discuss each of the areas and briefly describe how this study of inO of IT and HR workers contributes new information that advance our understandings of the historic problems with markets and the effects of inO on social relations in the workplace, the work, working conditions, and professional lives.

Markets and transaction costs

Several concepts are commonly used to characterize the interconnected organization of the outsourcing relationship. Terms include the networked organization, strategic partnerships, and the flexible firm. These terms describe the externalizing of once internal parts of the firm or hierarchy and, therefore, seem appropriate for use here. As is the case of IT and HR, externalization involves the outsourcing of these noncore functions to another organization with expertise in this area. But, in my book I prefer discussing the outsourcing cases and relationships using the term market from Williamson's market versus hierarchy approach (1975). This is my preference for several reasons.

Foremost, per most subjects in this study, outsourcing relationships had problems that raised the financial costs of executing the relationship. Transaction costs, as these problems are named in Williamson's approach, historically have stemmed from the environmental, contractual, and human factors in markets (1975:9). Environmental factors producing transaction costs include economic uncertainty, contractual factors include their tendency to be incomplete, and human factors include bounded rationality and opportunism. By taking advised steps to prepare for an outsourcing deal (e.g., "doing due diligence"), organizations here recognized that markets can and do produce transaction costs. They expected that companies embrace the market logic of self-interest toward their own separate financial goals and toward working out their relationships in markets (Thornton, Ocasio, & Lounsbury 2012). The companies in this study attempted to subvert the incongruent goals in markets and the sources of transaction costs by taking steps to build flexibility into outsourcing contracts and in their new social organizations. Like Bryan suggested at Industrial Solutions Inc., the ability to modify contracts, outsourced services, and labor supplies was a benefit for customers in the market relationship. But Bryan's position at the customer – Director of Outsourced Services – and the conflicts he handled regularly with his vendors (discussed in Chapter 3) underscore that both firms had separate financial interests that needed legal safeguards. In addition to flexibility in contracts, structurally this occurred by establishing costly administrative mechanisms and resources (like a whole job function of governance of the outsourcing contract) to do just that.

> J: *Okay. So then modifications can be made to the contract, the services that are being provided,* [B: Yeah, right.] *the staff levels can . . .*
> B: As a matter of fact, (Bryan takes a 3-ring notebook from his shelf, which is at least 2 ½ inches thick and begins leafing through it) this is our IT

Dynasty Co. contract. [*Wow.*] You know this is our renewal. This is all the things that we outsource right? And starting in the back here, we do formalized changes. There is a formalized change request and a formalized process to go through. Here's all the change requests that we've done just since 2003. Plus these that I haven't put in here yet (he motions to a pile of paper on his desk).

(Director of Outsourced Services at Industrial Solutions Inc.)

Secondly, according to scholars (Doz 1996; Powell 1990; Uzzi 1996), the network organization and strategic partnership terms emphasize trust, cooperation, and learning between the two contracting firms in the relationship. Per my interviews with subjects, this was not an appropriate characterization for many outsourcing deals and, in fact, was often the opposite. The adversarial structure and nature of the outsourcing relationship produced problems for organizations and for front-line workers in the course of everyday work. For these reasons then – the incongruent goals of two separate companies, the adversarial structure and nature of the relationship, and the lack of trust this engenders between employees of the two companies, the most suitable conceptual characterization for the cases here, and the term that is used throughout the manuscript, is "market organization."

Reports of the early termination of contracts (e.g., after one year in the Merchant Inc. and Master Technologies deal here) or the nonrenewal of contracts by large customer firms supports an approach highlighting the use of the market concept in this analysis.[8] To explain the problems and the failure in some deals, scholarly research has found customer dissatisfaction with outsourcing for reasons related to discord in relationships, not achieving the expected cost savings, and other factors (see Kakabadse & Kakabadse 2002:196, for a list of causes). Reported conflict in many outsourcing cases here provides a better understanding of the social causes for some transaction cost problems.

In Davis-Blake and Broschak's research on outsourcing, they found customer companies made few investments toward training their staff on the new relationship and how to interact with vendors appropriately and effectively (2009: 328). As a consequence, Davis-Blake and Broschak assert, problematic social relations in the coordination and production of the work commonly arose in the outsourcing cases they examined. By analyzing the new social arrangements from the position of multiple vendors, in part, this study of inO reaffirms that customers failed to recognize the importance of educating their staff on their proper role, perspective, and the new processes to work in outsourcing markets. This produced recurring social conflicts – in some cases over years – between professionals who interfaced between the two organizations at all levels (e.g., from analysts to executives). This study, using an interactionist approach in the analysis of social interactions in markets, shows why and how these conflicts persist between front-line workers.

Invisible social relations in the workplace

Scholarship on the invisible nature of social relations in the workplace is useful because of its call for more recognition, value, and analysis of the social relations and interactional mechanics needed to produce work in any institutional context (Brodkin 1988; Daniels 1987; DeVault 1991; Fletcher 1999; Zelizer 2012). Historically, this scholarship has highlighted the invisible work that women do to support and produce economic organizations and other important institutions like family. Their social relational work is neither recognized in public discourse, nor by the women whose relational support is manifest throughout institutional life. And, it is not the standard to give financial compensation for doing this type of work. Rather, the pattern of doing social relational work is perceived as an essential or natural trait of femininity and not a characteristic that is learned (DeVault 1991). Feminist scholars say, as a consequence of the association of social relational work with women and the understanding that it results from essential displays of femininity, social relational work is undervalued in our culture and by institutions.

In this study of inO, I found that employers gave little recognition or compensation for the new social relational work that employees negotiated on the front line of markets. Because of the incongruent expectations of customers and vendors regarding the ownership and control of outsourced work and the market logic that quickly pervaded the context for the new relationship, work on the front line between the two firms was very political. Customer companies, on the one side of markets, prepared for the outsourcing deal by doing their "due diligence." They attempted to document every aspect of the work being outsourced to develop appropriate service level agreements and accountability measures to guarantee service they wanted at a preset cost. On the other side of the market relationship, employers trained outsourced professionals on the new ticketing and change management processes that would structure their work. However, both companies failed to account for and prepare their employees for transitional issues related to the working-out process with outsourcing. Instead, outsourcing companies largely left their employees alone to duke it out on the front line with customers and change their incorrect expectations. For many outsourced subjects, the greater political nature to work in markets was described as its biggest drawback. Outsourced professionals were neither prepared nor compensated for the added political work in markets. Still, it was added work – I call it market labor – that outsourced professionals had to contend. By examining the relational aspects to outsourcing and showing that markets produce adversarial work relations and conflict between employees of customers and vendors, this study contributes to the literature on the structure and nature of social relations in this new organizational context.

The social effects of nonstandard employment

Literature detailing the growth of nonstandard employment and its effects on workplace culture, the work, job conditions, workers' identity and meaning, and professional careers is very useful for my analysis here. Foremost, scholarship on nonstandard employment, such as temporary work and contracting, shows that jobs in these labor markets are more precarious or contingent (Barley & Kunda

2004; Henson 1996). This study shows that the context of outsourcing across cases was designed to reduce the costs of producing the work. Because the realization of most cost reductions came from reducing labor costs and adding corresponding value from standardizing the work, in most cases, jobs with inO were inherently contingent. As Pedulla (2013) defines,

> Contingent employment is distinguished from standard employment by two key characteristics. Contingent work implies that the employment relationship is conditional on some other factor, such as time, and it indicates a lack of attachment between the worker and the employer, such as the employee being paid by a separate agency than where he or she works.
>
> (693)

Per subjects' experiences, my findings show that work with outsourcing was always contingent. Contracts were conditional and the number of professionals working onsite at customers was always purposefully reduced.

Addressing the effects on culture, scholars find that adding contingent workers into the same physical context has a strong tendency to lower the morale of permanent workers (Davis-Blake & Broschak 2009; Pedulla 2013). From the perspective of the onsite vendor with inO, however, little has been said about the existence of any culture that gets developed and supported by employers of nonstandard workers. Unfortunately for them, my study explains this general gap in scholarly discussion. In general, subjects were lost for words when asked about the outsourcing company's culture working onsite at customers. When they did express a culture, they described one of hyper-commodification. Management at both companies focused only on the "numbers" related to the costs of producing work, upselling, and meeting the service requirements in contracts as the primary constitution for the work and its outcomes. As such, many subjects in this sample lamented the empty meaning of work and jobs in outsourcing.

In the case of temporary work and contracting, studies find the externalization of work has implications for material benefits like pay because "externalization ties wages to the general labor market" (Pfeffer & Baron 1988:295). Other research suggests that externalization "reduces incentives to provide internal training and promotion opportunities" (Kalleberg & Marsden 2005:411). Indeed, the recent theory of a fissured workplace – where jobs and work are pushed into peripheral labor markets as they are with outsourcing and inO – is predicated on declining work and job conditions (Weil 2014). Earnings fall with contracting work outwards to supply vendors, there are diminished opportunities for training, and access to important social networks that convey mobility opportunities are cut off. In this book I explain that outsourcing companies – driven by the market logic (Thornton et. al. 2012) – have masterfully organized professionals to work flexibly with the goals of lowering the costs of producing the work through standardization, centralization of the work, and automation. The result on the work, jobs, and professional lives of employees is often negative. Dominant results in cases here included degradation from work speedup, more insecurity in jobs, invisible political work, and broken careers because of outsourcing.

Finally, this research contributes to scholarship on the effects of nonstandard, contingent employment on working identity. Early in the growth of nonstandard jobs, scholars such as Pfeffer and Baron speculated that externalized jobs do not provide the same benefits for social identities as jobs in hierarchies (1988:294). Qualitative research on onsite temporary clerical workers, more recently, found that people in these jobs often experience alienation from permanent staff, the work and job, and the self (Henson 1996; Rogers 1995). Other studies find that higher skilled contract workers can identify with employers or customer firms, depending on characteristics of the organization and social relations (George & Chattopadhyay 2005). This study contributes new knowledge of how professional identity was impacted by inO.

The research

I chose to research the in-house outsourcing (inO) of information technologies (IT) and human resources (HR) work because, in 2004, they were the biggest job sectors according to industry analysts TPI, Everest Group, and the Outsourcing Institute. IT outsourcing, the largest sector in 2003, was a "$115-plus billion industry" (*Outsourcing Essentials* 2003:4). Furthermore, HR outsourcing was the fastest growing sector at that time and had "estimated revenues of $46 billion" (*Outsourcing Essentials* 2003:4). By focusing on inO's two largest sectors in the US, IT and HR, my intention was to be able to generalize the effects of outsourcing on many professional workers.

Both inO cases I knew of early on involved IT work and jobs. Using my contacts, I tried to obtain access from both Concerto Inc. and Merchant Inc. to do participant observation of inO. After their denials, I spent the 2004 summer emailing and calling HR departments trying to find a local company that would grant me access to do qualitative research on inO. When no interest or agreement with a company materialized, my graduate school advisor Dr. Peter Whalley and I agreed that I could research inO using interviews and a purposive sampling approach (Gilbert 1995). I should find subjects affected by the inO of their jobs and interview them.

In the first two inO cases and in most cases since, social networks of friends, family, students, and colleagues have been instrumental in locating subjects. Furthermore, these close relationships have been important intermediaries for the establishment of swift trust, leveraging subjects' voluntary support to be interviewed. In a few cases, subjects were obtained with no network intermediaries but by advertising on listservs of HR and IT professional organizations and attending Outsourcing Institute Roadshows, or they happened randomly (through jury service).

For this research, I wanted subjects who knew how outsourcing affected the work, working conditions, and social relationships of IT and HR professionals in the workplace. To qualify for the study, then, I sought research subjects who had intimate experience with outsourcing. Subjects had to have experienced the outsourcing of their job and become directly employed by an outsourcing company. Or, if they had not directly experienced the outsourcing in their own position, they had to have worked alongside people whose position was outsourced or decided, facilitated, and/or managed an outsourcing agreement(s).

I completed the first phase of interviews from 2005 to 2006, conducting 22 with IT and HR professionals. From 2008 through 2017, I interviewed 29 more professionals for a total of 51 subjects as my sample. Geographically, all research subjects were obtained from the Midwest and the Eastern Mid-Atlantic regions of the US, with the exception of one subject from the South.

Outsourcing companies directly employed or had employed most subjects in the sample (N = 42). Most onsite vendors worked in positions of front-line specialist and manager, with some subjects in director and executive-level positions at outsourcing companies. In interviews, these subjects were asked questions about their former employer's (the customer's) decision to outsource, the "rebadging process" (i.e., the process of changing employment from a core firm to an outsourcing company), and the effects of inO on the work, their social relations, jobs, and professional careers. Other subjects in the sample had worked in executive and administrator roles deciding, negotiating and/or managing one or more outsourcing contracts, and/or working directly with professionals who got outsourced (N = 9). I asked these subjects about the core firm's decision to outsource, what preparations were involved, how the outsourcing relationship was managed, and what the effects were on the work environment and professionals directly affected by the outsourcing deal. Interview subjects are mostly IT professionals (N = 45) with a smaller group of HR professionals (N = 6).

Finally, the number of interviews with subjects in each outsourcing case varied. For example, there were a few cases where I interviewed only one professional. This compares with the mode of other cases, where three to five interviews were more often obtained. Although there is variation in the number of interviews across cases, the consistencies in outcomes described across cases have assured me of the reliability of the findings presented here. As is customary in human subjects' research, pseudonyms are used for names of all subjects and all of the employer companies to protect the privacy and employment of individuals interviewed (See Table 1.1 The Subjects).

Collectively, subjects gave information on 20 separate outsourcing deals, 16 cases in IT and four cases in HR, each beginning sometime between the late 1980s and 2012. "Core or customer companies" – references for the customer company deciding to outsource work and jobs – represent global, national, and regional competitors in various markets for goods and services. It is highly probable that the vast majority of US people have purchased goods and services from several of the multinational, core companies (e.g., Titan Inc., Concerto Inc., Foreign Motors Inc., and Digital Services Inc.). The industries of the core companies in the sample include: chemicals, hospitals, telecommunications, retail, pharmaceuticals, technology, banking, product development and marketing, media, and automotive manufacturing. The industries of companies who were outsourcing at the highest levels over the period of this study are represented by 15 of the 20 customers in this sample, supporting generalizability of the findings for outsourcing during this time period (Carillo 2018). Core companies operate in the industries of: hospitals

Table 1.1 The subjects

Case no.#	Interview no.	Interview date	Pseudo name	Pseudo outsourcing co	Pseudo core co
1	1	1/25/2005	Hope	Accessible Hardware	Accolade Hospital
1	2	4/9/2005	Rob	Accessible Hardware	Accolade Hospital
2	3	4/28/2005	Barbara	Right Technology Solutions	Rapture Hospital
2	4	5/12/2005	Nadia	Right Technology Solutions	Rapture Hospital
2	5	5/12/2005	Rosemary	Right Technology Solutions	Rapture Hospital
2	6	5/12/2005	Kathleen	Right Technology Solutions	Rapture Hospital
2	7	5/29/2005	Doris	Right Technology Solutions	Rapture Hospital
3	8	5/5/2005	Paul	Circuit	Concerto Inc.
4	9	5/17/2005	Mike	Tech Leader	Technologies/ Apex Inc.
4	10	5/25/2005	JB	Tech Leader	Technologies/ Apex Inc.
4	11	6/7/2005	Fred	Tech Leader	Technologies/ Apex Inc.
4	12	6/12/2005	Fran	Tech Leader	Technologies/ Apex Inc.
5	13	5/25/2005	Maria	Master Technologies	Merchant Inc.
5	14	5/29/2005	Davetta	Master Technologies	Merchant Inc.
5	15	6/6/2005	Keith	Master Technologies	Merchant Inc.
5	16	6/8/2005	Brad	Master Technologies	Merchant Inc.
5	17*	10/15/2005	Russell		Merchant Inc.
6	18	9/21/2005	Sandy	First Class Resource Mgmt.	Foreign Motors Inc.
7	19*	10/5/2005	Bryan	IT Dynasty Co.	Industrial Solutions Inc.
8	20	11/29/2005	Gerri	People Solutions	Peoples Banking Inc.
8	21	12/2/2005	Franca	People Solutions	Peoples Banking Inc.
9	22	11/28/2005	Lynette	Web Tech	Wireless Inc.
10	23	10/21/2008	Lisa	Ballast Group	Bravado Hospital
10	24	1/22/2009	Donald	Ballast Group	Bravado Hospital
10	25	9/9/2008	Will	Ballast Group	Bravado Hospital
10	26	1/22/2009	Tony	Ballast Group	Bravado Hospital
10	27	3/26/2009	Chuck	Ballast Group	Bravado Hospital
10	28	4/2/2009	Joan	Ballast Group	Bravado Hospital
10	29	2/19/2009	Mary	Ballast Group	Bravado Hospital
10	30	3/12/2009	Ross	Ballast Group	Bravado Hospital
10	31	2/5/2009	Steve	Ballast Group	Bravado Hospital
10	32	9/25/2008	Brandon	Ballast Group	Bravado Hospital
10	33	3/12/2009	Ken	Ballast Group	Bravado Hospital

(*Continued*)

Table 1.1 (Continued)

Case no.#	Interview no.	Interview date	Pseudo name	Pseudo outsourcing co	Pseudo core co
10	34	11/9/2012	Morgan	Ballast Group	Bravado Hospital
11	35	10/7/2008	Dominic	Sourcing Central	St. Francis Hospital
11	36	11/7/2008	Salma	Sourcing Central	St. Francis Hospital
11	37	3/9/2009	Taylor	Sourcing Central	St. Francis Hospital
	38*	9/11/2008	Ishan		IT Advisory Group (offshore)
12	39	5/20/2010	Dwayne	Default Systems	Digital Services Inc.
13	40	8/5/2010	Tanya	Tech Leader	Titan Inc.
14	41	1/22/2011	Carson	Tech Leader	Trading Inc.
15	42	9/10/2012	Courtney	Circuit	Cloud Inc.
16	43	1/9/2013	Sally	Master Technologies	Mammoth Inc.
17	44*	6/12/2013	Frazier	Indian IT Co	International Tech Inc.
17	45*	6/12/2013	Ruth	Indian IT Co	International Tech Inc.
18	46	6/13/2013	Christina	Digitize	Drug Developer Inc.
19	47	8/13/2013	Hillary	Dynasty Co. Affiliate	Diagnosis Hospital
	48*	8/27/2013	Jay		Sourcing Central
	49*	8/29/2013	Sheldon		Sourcing Central
	50*	9/10/2013	Norm	System of Local Transportation	ChemRegional Inc.
20	51*	1/11/2017	Beverly	Sourcing Central	Cedar Point Hospital

* Signifies an "industry insider": she or he helped either: plan or facilitate an outsourcing deal(s), manage the deal, was an executive who made decisions to outsource job functions, or remained as a direct employee when colleagues were outsourced.

(N = 6), technology (N = 3), telecommunications (N = 2), banking (N = 2), media (N = 1), and manufacturing (N = 1). The five leading American multinational companies in IT outsourcing and the leading company in HR outsourcing in 2005 are also represented in this sample. They were: Tech Leader, Digitize, Circuit, Master Technologies, IT Dynasty Co, and People Solutions. There are more competitors in the field today and the outsourcing industry has had its ongoing share of mergers. As of 2018, several of these five companies remain prominent and are landing the largest outsourcing contracts and/or being awarded elite recognition in the outsourcing field. They include: Tech Leader, Digitize, and Master Technologies.

Table 1.2 gives information on each outsourcing case in my sample and includes: the year the outsourcing deal began (timing for the first two deals are estimated by subjects), the name of the core company, what work and jobs were

Table 1.2 The in-house outsourcing cases

Deal began	Core company	Work and jobs outsourced	Number of staff rebadged if known	Outsourcing company	Contract cost and duration if known
1990s^ renewed 2004, some insourced	Rapture Hospital	IT Ancillary Clinical Applications		Right Technology Solutions	
1990s^ 1996	Accolade Hospital Technologies Inc./ Apex Inc.	IT Network and Call Center IT Data Centers and Custom Software	N = 700	Accessible Hardware Tech Leader*	
1997	Mammoth Inc.	Entire IT Department: infrastructure and 50+ applications	N = 2,600	Master Technologies*	$4 billion, 10 years
1998	Industrial Solutions, Inc.	Entire IT Department: network, web-hosting, help –desk, applications	N = 0 (all quit)	IT Dynasty Co.*	5 years
2000	Titan Inc.	IT Billing and Ordering Applications	N = 3,500	Tech Leader*	$4 billion, 10 years
2001	Bravado Hospital	Entire IT Department: help desk, applications, support, network	N = 179	Ballast Group	
2002	Drug Developer Inc.	Data Operations for Clinical Drug Trials	N = 135	Digitize*	
2003	Diagnosis Hospital	Entire IT Department: applications, network, data center, help desk, desktop support	N = 200	Dynasty Co. Affiliate	
2003	Concerto Inc.	IT Delivery Side	N = 1,800	Circuit*	$3 billion, 10 years

Year	Client	Function	N	Vendor	Deal Value
2003	Wireless Inc.	HR: Call Center, Benefits Administration, HRIS, Training, EAP, Relocation, Testing	N = 600	Web Tech*	$650 million, 10 years
2003	Trading Inc.	IT Data Center and Technical Support	N = 75%	Tech Leader*	$600 million, 7 years
2004	Merchant Inc.	IT Operations	N = 200	Master Technologies*	$1.6 billion, 10 years
2004	Peoples Bank	HR: Recruitment, Benefits Administration, Compensation, Evaluation	N = 15	People Solutions*	
2004	St. Francis Hospital	Entire IT Department	N = 30	Sourcing Central	
2005	Foreign Motors Inc.	HR Temporary Recruiting and Selection	N = 3	First Class Resource Mgmt.	
2009	International Technology Inc.	HR Applications and Call Center** (The work went to India, but the affected people @ International Technology Inc. were redeployed internally)		Indian IT Co.*	
2010	Digital Services Inc.	IT Data Center and Billing Software	N = 89	Default Systems*	
2012	Cloud Inc.	IT Desktop Support	N = 5	Circuit*	
2012	Cedar Pointe Medical Center	IT Hardware and Clinical Support	N = 3	Sourcing Central	

Shading = Immediate job losses occurred in deal onset

* = Industry Leader in 2005

** = Special note

^ = Exact year of outsourcing deal unknown

outsourced, (if known) the number of people who rebadged to the outsourcing company in the deal, and the name of the outsourcing company. One industry – hospitals – is obvious in the naming convention for core companies. Otherwise, core companies are signified in the chart and in all text by "Inc." Job loss, with the onset of a particular deal, is duly noted in the table by shading of the cell in the "work and jobs outsourced" column. If known, either from subjects or public news sources on deals, the number of staff who rebadged, the contract cost, and its duration are noted.

Overview of chapters

Chapter 2, "Betrayed, Sold, and Rebadged" to Outsourcing Companies, describes the process that began when employees were told about the outsourcing deal and it followed their experiences up until they received new badges and began jobs as outsourced professionals. I begin the chapter with a feature describing Christina and her colleagues' experiences when her former employer Drug Developer Inc. publicly announced the outsourcing of most of their IT development jobs to the vendor Digitize. Announcements like these trigger an emotional roller coaster, where feelings of stability get ripped away and replaced first by angry foment from subjects' perceptions of employer betrayal and job uncertainty. Many subjects were critical of the hand that was forced on them – they felt forced to take the jobs offered with outsourcing companies. Before the outsourcing takes place, social divisions usually developed in job functions where some professionals rebadged and others remained. Professionals who were outsourced began feeling unwanted by employers and colleagues that were staying in jobs with customers. Because of various push and pull factors, outsourced professionals usually accepted new jobs and began learning about their new employers' processes and contracted work. As they received their new employment badges, professionals were told to expect work as usual the next time they reported to the job site as a vendor.

Chapter 3, "Chewed-Up": The Adversarial Nature of Work Relationships in Markets, describes the common social conflict that subjects say characterized the outsourcing relationship. I theorize why this typically occurs. I feature Paul, one subject who best characterized and summarized the cause for social conflict in the new market relationship. To understand why the new work process was problematic, I begin by describing a symbolic interactionist theory – the articulation of work through interaction – that helps to conceive and understand why social relations in markets promote social conflict. Next, I describe the new structural conditions of governance and ticketing systems to both account for the work produced by outsourcing companies and also to root out work being requested that isn't currently being paid for by customers. New social statuses, symbols, and restrictions on space, technical systems, and conversations with former colleagues helped management at both firms paint an adversarial message about the relationship among their employees. As a result of adversarial structural and interactional conditions, most outsourced subjects described social conflicts that regularly occurred in their interactions with employees of customers. Employees of customers tended toward authoritative stances in interactions with outsourced professionals to receive the work that they wanted. Outsourced employees, on the other hand, used procedural stances with their customers to break their expectations for continuing control over the work. Conflict, per subjects' descriptions, continued indefinitely because of the inherent contingencies in contracts and market relations. I argue that the political haggling with contracts and markets represents added political work and requires related skills that I call "market labor."

Chapter 4, "It All Revolved around Numbers": Greater Commodification of the Work and Culture with Outsourcing, reflects findings on the effects of inO on the work, culture, meaning, and professional identity of subjects. Beginning features of two professionals, Salma and Tanya, help establish that work and culture with outsourcing had less to do with the technical work and problem-solving that subjects were passionate about. It mostly involved greater commodification of the work. The rationalization with numbers and greater commodification were present in all the parts to outsourcing including justifying it through cost, documenting all of the work that is produced by vendors for customers, always looking to upsell services to customers, procedurally working toward standardizing the work, flexible organization, and steadily reducing the human labor to produce it. With great emphasis on commodification of the work and culture with outsourcing, work speedup was usually the result. Subjects in many cases described the absence of doing work that made a difference, the lack of professional recognition for work well done, and loss of care and commitment from employers for their professional well-being. As a result, work and jobs with outsourcing were generally perceived as less meaningful and less amenable for casting a professional identity.

Chapter 5, "(Only) Better for Some": Consent, Resistance, and Professional Careers with Outsourcing Companies, I discuss traditional issues in the sociology of work including the consent and resistance of subjects to the work and the effects of inO on their professional careers. I begin with a section that describes how outsourcing companies' approaches to manufacturing consent changed from hegemonic to despotic forms over time. I argue that the learning opportunities, at least initially, functioned to generate consent to jobs and the intense working conditions at outsourcing companies. In cases post-2000, outsourcing companies cared very little if people accepted the substandard jobs they offered. Because of labor market actualities, most professionals offered a job with outsourcing companies had to take it. Following this argument, I describe the high tendency to quit jobs at outsourcing companies as the dominant form of resistance. Professionals also resisted by limiting their level of cooperation and commitment to the work and to customers, which is significant for explanation rooted in economic theories about the failure of market organizations. Next, I discuss the few subjects who experienced mobility at outsourcing companies. I theorize possibilities for this mobility using scholarly findings and the perspectives of these subjects. Finally, I discuss how the focus on standardization and automation of work has implications for the ongoing deskilling of professional work in fields with heavy outsourcing, for future job losses there, and for abetting an increase in "portfolio careers."

Chapter 6, Conclusion, I discuss the key research findings on inO. Based on the outcomes for subjects from 20 cases here, overall outsourcing did not revitalize professional careers in IT and HR. Foremost, the lack of revitalization of their jobs was because of the cost rationale for most outsourcing deals. Outsourcing companies, especially the large ones, were very adept at instituting lean and flexible social organization that led to work speedup. New arrangements of a market organization had to be worked out and this caused added political labor in outsourced professionals' everyday work. In addition, the hyper-commodified work and culture in outsourcing emphasized the quick transition from the customer's unique tools and processes to the vendor's standard and automated ones. This work emphasis, subjects report, was not as meaningful for IT and HR professionals here and it was challenging to identify with distant employers. While the economic signs are disparate, they do suggest that outsourcing – and the job insecurity and inequality it fosters – will continue to grow. These findings have implications including calls for more research on outsourcing by reliable sources and the public dissemination of these findings. My study, over time, suggests that the effects of outsourcing on people and jobs are becoming increasingly despotic and mean. And, per industry insiders, it is expected that more and more professional jobs and workers become targets for outsourcing. Finally, I recommend that further research address our lack of knowledge on the breadth and depth of outsourcing, the effects of markets on social relations in outsourcing, and how the more degraded and political nature of work in outsourcing markets may be helping shape the divisiveness in public discourse today.

Notes

1 As the protocol for research on human subjects requires, pseudonyms are used throughout the book to protect identities of subjects and the companies that employ(ed) them.
2 Concerto outsourced most of its human resources function a year later in 2003.
3 Russell introduced me to the term rebadging. I did a database search and the results showed dual uses. Though the term can be used to refer to changing a product's brand name after one company buys another, in this usage it refers to employees who have had their position outsourced. Their employment relationship ends with one firm and they become reemployed by the outsourcing company, thus receiving new badges or rebadging to another company.
4 This was especially apparent when outsourcing became a leading topic of debate in the 2004 presidential race. When "outsourcing" was used in presidential debate forums, it was synonymous with the exporting of white-collar IT work to other countries. The issue of outsourcing – really the offshoring – of work became such a hot-button political issue that several articles in the local newspaper said Indian outsourcing companies and the Indian government were worried about "protectionist" policies being proposed at the state and federal levels of US government. See, for example, an article that appeared in the *Chicago Tribune* on February 8, 2004, entitled "India Feels Backlash on Jobs." Anecdotally, for a while at the beginning of my conference paper presentations on my developing research (circa 2006 to 2008), I did word association of the term "outsourcing" and the dominant image among all audiences was the offshoring of IT jobs to India.
5 The report about Merchant Inc.'s decision to outsource their IT jobs and staff, for example, took up just two inches of print in the local newspaper and the article was buried inside of the business section. This compared to two lengthy biographical pieces on the company CEO at Merchant Inc. that appeared around the same time as lead stories on the front page of the business section and the biographical stories filled entire pages on the inside.

6 Job displacement produced "grave" changes in communities like Kenosha, Wisconsin. After the final automotive engine plant closing there in 2010, there were no more automobile production jobs left in Kenosha. Former Kenosha plant workers, like my brother Jeffrey, either lost jobs or they relocated to Chrysler facilities in other states several months after the engine plant closed. Communities like Kenosha lost good jobs, their economies were adversely affected, and neighborhoods physically and socially deteriorated because long-standing citizens had to leave to follow adequate family wage levels. See a discussion of the outcomes from the loss of jobs in Kenosha, WI in *The Fall of Wisconsin* (2018), by Dan Kaufman, recently published by W.W. Norton & Co. If they didn't follow the work, like my brother Jeffrey Raymond Zalewski, it led to serious mental health problems (that go untreated because of a lack of medical insurance), drug and alcohol addiction, and in some cases death.

7 My neighbor Marcie Hull, a technology expert at her school, showed me Google Alerts and we set up an alert on "outsourcing" around 2011. Every day since, I have received my daily briefing on the top ten plus stories on outsourcing on the Internet. Per Marcie, the Google Alert filters the entire Internet using "meta-info and keywords" to present daily results on outsourcing news.

8 For example, in 2012, General Motors reversed most of their IT outsourcing and hired back 3,000 people (see Savitz, Eric, *Forbes*, October 18, 2012). In other examples, Sainsbury Grocery and Santander Bank both reversed outsourcing deals and rehired workers (see Baldwin, Howard, *ComputerWorld*, July 18, 2013).

References

Abraham, Katherine G. and Susan K. Taylor. 1996. "Firms' Use of Outside Contractors: Theory and Evidence." *Journal of Labor Economics* 14(3): 394–424.

Adler, Paul S. 2003. "Making the HR Outsourcing Decision." *MIT Sloan Management Review*: Fall.

Ammachchi, Narayan. 2013. "Infographic: Outsourcing Firms Look to Monetize Social Media Wave." *Nearshoreamericas.com*: August 12.

Barley, Stephen R. and Gideon Kunda. 2004. *Gurus, Hired Guns, and Warm Bodies: Itinerant Experts in a Knowledge Economy*. Princeton: Princeton University Press.

Bendor-Samuel, Peter. 2000. *Turning Lead into Gold: The Demystification of Outsourcing*. Provo, UT: Executive Excellence Publishing.

Bradbury, Danny. 2015. "IT Outsourcing Remains Healthy but the Functions Being Outsourced Are Changing." *ITworldcanada.com*: August 31.

Brodkin, Karen. 1988. *Caring by the Hour: Women, Work, and Organizing at Duke Medical Center*. Urbana, IL: University of Illinois Press.

Bureau of Labor Statistics. 2004. "Extended Mass Layoffs Associated With Domestic and Overseas Relocations, First Quarter 2004 Summary." June 10.

Bureau of Labor Statistics. 2005. "Contingent and Alternative Employment Arrangements." February.

Bureau of Labor Statistics. 2013 and 2012. "Movement of Work Actions by Type of Separation Where Number of Separations Is Known by Employers." In *Mass Layoff Statistics*. Washington, DC: US Department of Labor.

Bureau of Labor Statistics. 2018. "Contingent and Alternative Employment Arrangements." June.

Capgemini. 2005. "Companies Look Beyond Cost Reduction When Choosing an Outsourcing Partner, According to Capgemini/IDC Bi-Annual Survey." April 25.

Carillo, Dianne. 2018. "The Ultimate List of Outsourcing Statistics." *Customerthink.com*: February 3.

CIOL.com. 2013. "Data Analytics Outsourcing to Grow at 31.68 pc CAGR." October 7.

Daniels, Arlene K. 1987. "Invisible Work." *Social Problems* 34(5): 403–415.

Davis-Blake, Alison and Joseph P. Broschak. 2009. "Outsourcing and the Changing Nature of Work." *Annual Review of Sociology* 35: 321–340.

DeVault, Marjorie. 1991. *Feeding the Family: The Social Organization of Caring as Gendered Work*. Chicago: University of Chicago Press.

Diomande, Sarah. 2017. "Why Outsourcing Doesn't Have to Be a Dirty Word." *Fox School of Business Idea Marketplace*: November 28.

DiTomaso, Nancy. 2001. "The Loose Coupling of Jobs: The Subcontracting of Everyone?" In *Sourcebook of Labor Markets: Evolving Structures and Processes*, edited by Ivar Berg and Arne L. Kalleberg. New York: Kluwer Academic/Plenum Publishers.

Doz, Yves L. 1996. "The Evolution of Cooperation in Strategic Alliances: Initial Conditions or Learning Processes?" *Strategic Management Journal* 17: 55–83.

Dudley, Kathryn M. 1994. *The End of the Line: Lost Jobs, New Lives in Postindustrial America*. Chicago: University of Chicago Press.

Everest Group. 2018. "Global Offshoring and Outsourcing Market – What's Hot, What's Not: Everest Group Highlights 2017 Trends, 2018 Predictions in Feb. 15 Webinar." *PR Newswire*: February 13.

Fletcher, Joyce K. 1999. *Disappearing Acts: Gender, Power, and Relational Practice at Work*. Cambridge, MA: MIT Press.

Gartner Inc. 2005. "Gartner Says Increased Demand for Business Process Outsourcing to Create a Seller's Market in 2005; Analysts to Show How To Implement and Manage a Successful Outsourcing Partnership During the Gartner Outsourcing Summit." *Businesswire*: March 29.

George, Elizabeth and Prithviraj Chattopadhyay. 2005. "One Foot in Each Camp: The Dual Identification of Contract Workers." *Administrative Science Quarterly* 50: 68–99.

Gilbert, Nigel (ed). 1995. *Researching Social Life*. Thousand Oak, CA: Sage Publications.

Graf, Nikki. 2018. "Americans See Both Good and Bad in Trends That Are Changing the Workplace." *PEW Research Organization*: January 23.

Harrison, Bennett. 1994. *Lean and Mean: The Changing Landscape of Corporate Power in the Age of Flexibility*. New York: Basic Books.

Henson, Kevin. 1996. *Just a Temp*. Philadelphia: Temple University Press.

Hira Ron and Anil Hira. 2005. *Outsourcing America: What's Behind Our National Crisis and How We Can Reclaim American Jobs*. New York: American Management Association.

Hollister, Matissa. 2011. "Employment Stability in the U.S. Labor Market: Rhetoric Versus Reality." *Annual Review of Sociology* 11: 305–324.

Hopkins, Andrea. 2004. "Outsourced Jobs Rarely Leave U.S., Feds Say." *Reuters and MSN Money*: June 10.

Kakabadse, Andrew and Nada Kakabadse. 2002. "Trends in Outsourcing: Contrasting USA and Europe." *European Management Journal* 20(2): 189–198.

Kalleberg, Arne. 2000. "Nonstandard Employment Relations: Part Time, Temporary, and Contract Work." *Annual Review of Sociology* 26: 341–365.

Kalleberg, Arne L. and Peter V. Marsden. 2005. "Externalizing Organizational Activities: Where and How US Establishments Use Employment Intermediaries." *Socio-Economic Review* 3: 389–416.

Masters, Greg. 2015. "Outsourcing IT Security Continues to Grow, Study Finds." *SCMagazine.com*: August 20.

McNally, Fiona. 1979. *Women for Hire: A Study of the Female Office Worker*. New York: St. Martin's Press.

Orem, Tina. 2018. "Understaffing Has Many Credit Unions Outsourcing IT." *CUTimes*: February 7.

Osnowitz, Debra. 2010. *Freelancing Expertise: Contract Professionals in the New Economy*. Ithaca, NY: Cornell University Press.

Outsourcing Institute. 2003. "Preparing for Lift Out: How Recent Outsourcing Deals Are Shaking Up Career Paths." *Outsourcing Essentials*: Fall.

Overby, Stephanie. 2013. "Gartner Predicts Limited IT Outsourcing Growth and Increased Volatility." *CIO*: August 2.

Overby, Stephanie. 2015a. "IT Outsourcing Deal Values Hit 10-Year Low." *CIO*: May 1.

Overby, Stephanie. 2015b. "Buyers' Market Led to Strong 2014 for IT Outsourcing Deals." *CIO*: February 13.

Overby, Stephanie. 2016. "How Long Can IT Outsourcing Deliver More for Less?" *CIO*: February 26.

Parker, Robert E. 1994. *Flesh Peddlers and Warm Bodies: The Temporary Help Industry and Its Workers*. New Brunswick, NJ: Rutgers University Press.

Peck, Jamie and Nikolas Theodore. 1998. "The Business of Contingent Work: Growth and Restructuring in Chicago's Temporary Employment Industry." *Work, Employment, and Society* 12(4): 655–674.

Pedulla, David S. 2013. "The Hidden Costs of Contingency: Employers' Use of Contingent Workers and Standard Employees' Outcomes." *Social Forces* 92(2): 691–722.

Pfeffer, Jeffrey and James N. Baron. 1988. "Taking the Workers Back Out: Recent Trends in the Structuring of Employment." *Research in Organizational Behavior* 10: 257–303.

Piore, Michael J. and Charles F. Sabel. 1984. *The Second Industrial Divide: Possibilities for Prosperity*. New York: Basic Books.

Powell, Walter W. 1990. "Neither Market Nor Hierarchy: Network Forms of Organization." *Research in Organizational Behavior* 12: 295–336.

Reich, Robert B. 1992. *The Work of Nations: Preparing Ourselves for 21st-Century Capitalism*. New York: Vintage Books.

Rogers, Jackie Krasas. 1995. "Just a Temp: Experience and Structure of Alienation in Temporary Clerical Employment." *Work and Occupations* 22(2): 137–166.

Schott, Paul. 2017. "Gartner: IT Security Spending to Increase in 2018." *Fairfield Citizen*: December 8.

Sennett, Richard. 1998. *The Corrosion of Character: The Personal Consequences of Work in the New Capitalism*. New York: WW Norton and Company.

Smith, Vicki. 1994. "Institutionalizing Flexibility in a Service Firm: Multiple Contingencies and Hidden Hierarchies." *Work and Occupations* 21(3): 284–307.

Spherion Corporation. 2000. "Dramatic Growth Expected in U.S. and International Outsourcing Marketplace; Survey Conducted by the Outsourcing Institute Sponsored by Spherion." *PRnewswire*: August 28.

Thornton, Patricia H., William Ocasio, and Michael Lounsbury. 2012. *The Institutional Logics Perspective: A New Approach to Culture, Structure, and Process*. Oxford: Oxford University Press.

Uzzi, Brian. 1996. "The Sources and Consequences of Embeddedness for the Economic Performance of Organizations: The Network Effect." *American Sociological Review* 61(4): 674–699.

Violino, Bob. 2017. "Rising Data Security Threats Drive Growth in Outsourcing." *Heathdatamanagement.com*: August 24.

Weber, Lauren. 2017. "Some of the World's Largest Employers No Longer Sell Things, They Rent Workers: Outsourcing Firms' Workforces Grow as More Companies Look to Cut Their Headcounts." *Wall Street Journal*: December 28.

Weil, David. 2014. *The Fissured Workplace: How Work Became So Bad for So Many and What Can Be Done to Improve It.* Cambridge, MA: Harvard University Press.

Weil, David. 2017. "Millennial Employees Aren't the Problem. The Transformed Workplace Is. The Nature of Work Has Changed, and Millennials Are Getting Screwed." *Huffington Post:* December 14.

Williamson, Oliver E. 1975. *Markets and Hierarchies: Analysis and Antitrust Implications.* New York: The Free Press.

Womack, James, Daniel Jones, and Daniel Roos. 1990. *The Machine That Changed the World.* New York: Rawson Associates/Harpers.

Wright, Tom. 2018. "Why Are Outsourcers Such as Capita and BT Struggling?" *CRN.com:* February 13.

Zelizer, Viviana A. 2012. "How I Became a Relational Economic Sociologist and What Does That Mean?" *Politics and Society* 40(2): 145–174.

Zuboff, Shoshana. 1988. *In the Age of the Smart Machine.* New York: Basic Books.

2 "Betrayed, sold, and rebadged" to outsourcing companies

Christina (2013)

In the summer of 2013, I fortuitously met Christina at a barbeque and then later interviewed her in her suburban home. Similar to other subjects forced to change employers because of outsourcing deals, Christina expressed resolute feelings about the experience. She was deeply angry at her former employer Drug Developer Inc. for selling her off to another company without any forewarning or her informed consent. At the extreme in my sample, Christina repeated she would never, ever consider a job working for Drug Developer Inc. again.

Outsourcing forever changed the expectations and outlook Christina and most other outsourcing professionals had about the probability for stable jobs. They accepted that a job for life – even with "good employers" – could not be expected anymore. In Christina's case, it was the way the outsourcing decision and planning were handled by Drug Developer Inc. that festered her deep anger towards them. Compared to subjects who quickly brushed over the all-hands IT meeting when employers first shared their plans for outsourcing with affected employees, Christina's description of the event went into far more detail and was deeply critical and emotional. The public scene where Drug Developer Inc. announced the outsourcing to their employees compared to scenes commonly seen in "reality shows" like (the former) *American Idol*. As Christina shared her story of the outsourcing announcement, I pictured the raw emotion arising when a reality show's power-brokers separate contestants into two or more rooms only to blindside most of them and cause personal heart-break and anger for the primary purpose of public consumption and generating revenues for large corporations.

Meet Christina

Christina is a single mother with a comfortable model home for her and her son located in the suburbs of a large metropolitan area. Her residence was just "blocks" from Drug Developer Inc., her employer from 2000 to 2002. After obtaining her job with this "good employer," Christina had confidently bought her home in an adjacent neighborhood. At Drug Developer Inc., Christina was employed in IT and developed protocols for clinical research trials. Important to the disparate effects with outsourcing (Zalewski 2015), Christina's job required higher-level and higher-valued analytical skills and technical knowledge.

Early one morning in 2002 an email popped up in the inboxes of 250 people in the IT department at Drug Developer Inc., urgently calling the staff to a meeting in the auditorium just later that morning. The email emphasized the meeting was mandatory; no one was exempt from attending it. Christina said the email immediately got people talking. Their chatter revolved around the question, "What was so important that the entire IT department was being called to a mandatory meeting?"

IT employees responsible for "scrubbing data and doing the tedious manual work in clinical research trials" were directed to Room One on one side of the auditorium. Employees in this room were told their jobs were terminal, and they were being offshored to a company in India. As consolation, severance packages of two years of wages and benefits were forthcoming. Plus, the employees in this room could choose to extend their jobs for six months with Drug Developer Inc. by training the staff who would be replacing them at the Indian outsourcing company. This would include travel to India. Employees who chose this option would earn a salary and a bonus during this time, but to repeat, at the end of the six-month term they would be out of a job at Drug Developer Inc. Of course, employees in this group were not obligated to extend their jobs with Drug Developer Inc., but some of them ended up doing this.

In contrast to the first group, IT employees in Christina's room – the "subject matter experts" (SMEs) – were told of the plan to outsource all of IT but staff in this room were given the choice to keep jobs. However to keep them, professionals had to "rebadge" to Digitize. In a separate "near shore" outsourcing deal, Digitize (a large outsourcing company headquartered in the US) was assuming ownership of Drug Developer Inc.'s IT development work related to the protocols and records for testing of their new pharmaceutical drugs. If Christina or any of the other SMEs decided not to rebadge to Digitize, they effectively resigned from jobs at Drug Developer Inc. when the outsourcing deal began. Clearly, compared to staff in Room One the offer of long-term jobs was a more positive outcome for SMEs. Yet, as Christina adamantly affirmed, the offer was – from her perspective – a forced decision constructed by Drug Developer Inc. In her words, "It was an ultimatum! You got two weeks to make a decision, either you're with us or you're gone!" Christina called out senior leaders at Drug Developer Inc. for recognizing that people like her "needed the damn job!" They were using their greater power to force their employees to take jobs with the outsourcing company. Like Christina, subjects across the cases of outsourcing reported they were forced to rebadge to outsourcing companies because they too needed their jobs. Personal well-being, families, neighborhoods, and other community institutions depended heavily on incomes from stable jobs at core companies.

For the group of SMEs, there was an added rub. The two-year severance offered to the first group was not part of any voluntary resignation package offered to the second group. With this added inducement, executives at Drug Developer Inc. better ensured that most of the SMEs in the second group would rebadge to

Digitize to help smoothly transition the research protocol work to the new supplier. In sum, Drug Developer Inc. caused the problem, circumscribed the choices, and then used their power to ensure that employees in each group would choose the option that was in the best interest of the company.

Christina's deep anger toward her former employer Drug Developer Inc. underscored the power employers increasingly exercise over human lives. In sociological terms the consent of workers to new jobs with outsourcing companies was obtained despotically because of the coercion by senior leadership in creating and framing the context of personal choice for their employees. Professionals on Christina's side of the auditorium had two weeks to accept the offer made by Digitize or resign from their jobs at Drug Developer Inc. To Christina and many other subjects, it felt like two big bullies were pushing them around, and the reality was they had little recourse in the matter.

Christina repeatedly said she was incensed about how the choice she was forced to make was constructed by her employer. Yet when leaving the auditorium, she was confronted by the fortunes of colleagues in the other room. They were exiting their side of the auditorium at the same time, and they had not been given the choice to keep long-term jobs like she and the other SMEs. Their jobs were terminal. "They were just plain shocked!" Christina said of the other group. "They couldn't really talk about it for the next two weeks."

Christina was livid about the disrespectful and callous way senior leadership at Drug Developer Inc. treated their IT workers by intentionally throwing their lives into debilitating states of chaos and uncertainty. Demonstrating her only means of labor power given the circumstances, Christina said "I waited until the very last second" to say yes to the new job with Digitize.

Introduction

One of the broad research questions I had regarding in-house outsourcing (inO) was the process by which it was typically instituted. Specifically I asked: how was inO instituted and how were decisions to force a job change experienced by the professionals it affected? Because of academic training and my own personal experiences in workplaces, I presumed the outsourcing of jobs and work unfolded in a lengthy and highly emotional process. Emotions became engaged when unsuspecting employees were first told about the outsourcing of their jobs. It hit one emotional note after another all the way through the final day at customer companies, when employees turned in their badges and obtained new ones signifying the change of employment affiliation to the outsourcing company. "Rebadging" was the industry term for the employment change from outsourcing. To catch the nuances in the process from the public announcement to rebadging, I asked subjects a series of questions to tease out probable stages in their feelings.

Surprisingly even when the road had been financially tumultuous for employers prior to outsourcing, most subjects expressed "shock" when first learning about it in an all-hands meeting for workers in the affected department. Subjects perceived the outsourcing of their work as a betrayal by the core company, and they quickly became angry. In cases like Christina's, employers were an anchor institution for entire suburban neighborhoods. In Drug Developer Inc.'s case, the public decision to outsource IT jobs exposed their lack of commitment and care toward their employees and to the communities that had helped the company achieve a competitive advantage in markets for their goods and services (Porter 1985). For most subjects, the outsourcing of jobs revealed that their past loyalty to employers was significantly misguided in a "meaner" economic context. From that day forward, many subjects acknowledged that they would not presume any employers would act in a manner reminiscent of the paternal labor market practices of the past. The pendulum was moving in the opposite direction from the traditional social contract in post-war America. Powerful employers were becoming meaner to the working classes so as to render their resistance – by quitting increasingly degraded jobs and working conditions – increasingly challenging. Many subjects here felt forcibly stuck in their jobs because of families, mortgages, and other established financial and moral commitments. Employers used this actuality to their advantage when they extended job offers to affected employees.

From the public outsourcing announcement to the time old employee badges were handed in and new ones were obtained, outsourced professionals commiserated in shock, anger, sadness, and – because of the inevitability of outsourcing – finally showing acceptance of their imminent job change. Emotional reactions through the whole process, therefore, were marked by an evolution in feeling. These stages correspond to Kubler-Ross's (1969) theoretical model of grief in mourning the terminal diagnosis in one's own life. Kubler-Ross's (KR's) model includes five emotional stages in the dying process: 1. denial, 2. anger, 3. bargaining, 4. depression, and 5. acceptance. These stages may not occur sequentially, and they oftentimes overlap. But from a social psychological perspective, KR's model implies a complex and deeply emotional experience in mourning the loss of someone close.

Losing jobs with "companies you could retire from" and decimating relationships with "the colleagues you were close to and sat with every year at the company holiday party" were devastatingly similar to losing a close family member or friend, an intimate and valued part of oneself. In their grief over impending material and social costs, subjects in outsourcing typically described a comparable evolution: 1. ignoring the signs of economic, organizational, and technical changes at employers that increased personal insecurity in jobs; 2. feeling deep anger toward employers because they purposefully hid their planning and decision to outsource from their employees; 3. attempting to maintain normalcy by bargaining for internal job transfers at employers; 4. feeling depressed that work and jobs were changing and they had no control over it; and finally 5. accepting the inevitability of a new job with the outsourcing company.

Kubler-Ross's (KR) stages of grief are useful for structuring the narrative headings in this chapter. In a first section entitled "rumblings of outsourcing," I describe environmental contexts of greater economic uncertainty, recent downsizing, and other strategies such as reengineering business processes to eliminate redundancies and lower costs of operations at customer companies. Failed "remediation projects" in IT, continuing job cuts, the growing use of consultants, and the presence of other contingent workers especially raised employee suspicions about the growing insecurity of more jobs and about the possibility of outsourcing their own work. In a few cases, suspicions surfaced in department meetings and were fodder for a rumor mill, although employers generally denied allegations of impending cuts and reorganizing strategies like outsourcing. Rumblings of outsourcing represented the first stage in the grief cycle – the denial stage. It comprised subjects' growing recognition that the economic environment and the actions of companies were changing; they were less committed to acting paternally toward their employees. Yet subjects and their colleagues usually chose to ignore the growing possibility that job changes at good employers could occur, and these job changes could affect them.

In a second section "Betrayed! It will never be the same again," I describe the public announcement of inO at an all-hands meeting for employees in the affected departments. In many of the outsourcing cases in this sample, knowing what and who would be outsourced were not determined when the first announcement was publicly made. Some employees reacted angrily at the initial announcement to feelings of company betrayal. This was especially true in cases where employees had brought outsourcing up before at meetings and executives had rejected the idea outright. Anger parallels the same stage in KR's theory of grief.

After the announcement, management at customer companies began an intense planning phase conceived of as "doing due diligence." A schema of the work to be outsourced, an understanding of how it interfaces with work that will remain at the customer company, deciding what roles and people will continue to be directly employed, and which jobs within the company would move to an outsourcing environment were all developed in a breakneck working and emotional period. Doing due diligence on how the work with outsourcing would be reorganized usually took several months, which was unfortunate for employees uncertain if it would be directly affecting their job. In this stage, subjects often discussed former colleagues with long tenure at good employers as trying to bargain for an internal transfer to keep excellent pensions and lifetime medical benefits that were only retained when employees retired from the customer company. The bargaining by these employees parallels the same stage in KR's framework.

After learning they would rebadge to outsourcing companies, in the section "Sold! Unwanted but I needed the damn job!" I discuss how professionals often compared their forced job transfer by companies to feeling like a bought and traded commodity. In the only way they could resist, subjects mostly were highly critical of the increased commodification of labor markets signified by the growth of outsourcing whole job functions. Despotic elements set the tone and circumstances for the terms of the outsourcing change. Subjects like Christina had to take job offers from outsourcing companies because of their hardwired ties to families, property, and communities in physical space. Adding insult to injury, in cases where employees were split up in departments – where some employees were outsourced and others were retained by customers – social divisions between the two groups of workers materialized very quickly. Subjects felt sold, unwanted by employers and once close colleagues, and depressed enough – paralleling the depression stage in the grief cycle – to purposefully carve out time on or off the job to commiserate with other affected colleagues sharing the emotional ride with them. During this time, many subjects said it was difficult focusing on anything but the animosity and anguish they had from feeling sold by employers – like a piece of property – and without their knowledge or consent. In cases like Mammoth Inc., the commiseration and depression among IT professionals went on for months.

To conclude, I describe "rebadging," the stage where subjects accepted jobs at outsourcing companies and participated in the necessary steps to change employers. Here, I describe the effects of outsourcing on material benefits such as pay and seniority. Similar to a comparable study of outsourcing at a government office (Kessler, Coyle-Shapiro, & Purcell 1999), the "pull" of jobs at outsourcing companies – especially the material offers – helped outsourced professionals begin to look ahead and accept rebadging to another company. Before the start of the contract, at customers, time was set aside each day so that subjects could train on the outsourcing company's procedures and systems for completing work and making strategic changes to it. Most described training as helping people begin to identify with the outsourcing company. Departing the evening before the outsourcing deal begins, customer companies reassured outsourced professionals that they would work the next day as if nothing was changed. This, outsourced professionals learned quickly, was a sad irony with no basis in the empirical facts here. Established social relationships with old colleagues at customer companies and the nature of the work had to change because of the new market organization.

Rumblings of outsourcing

The majority of outsourcing cases in this sample began between 1996 and 2005. Before this time, economic changes affecting US companies had been widespread and were transforming the structure of organizations, workers and their work, and the quality and stability of jobs (Harrison 1994; Reich 1992). For US firms, economic globalization meant more competition from foreign firms. Greater competition was occurring in industries US companies once dominated. For example in the 1970s, Japanese manufacturers significantly increased their share in US automobile markets because of economic globalization. The Japanese production model also excelled because of other factors including their less costly systems of: lean, just-in-time inventory (including labor); flexible specialization; and decentralized network forms of production (Womack, Jones, & Roos 1990). These systems produced less expensive and more customized cars and trucks that supported a US economy increasingly based on conspicuous consumption, individual choice, and freedom.

Digital technologies have abetted the lean, low-cost systems firms have instituted since the 1970s including: the flexible, networked organization; increased standardization, automation, and job loss in professional work; and more contingencies in jobs. Labor economists describe fissuring – the shedding of peripheral activities in the organization – and skills-biased technology change (i.e., greater standardization and automation with technology) as important factors in the growing contingencies in jobs, large scale and ongoing job losses across occupational categories, and increased income inequality over the past decades (Weil 2014; Autor & Dorn 2013). These economic and job trends were precursors for the outsourcing in the cases here. Many subjects in the sample contextualized the outsourcing by referring to economic changes and their effects on labor organization and practices, especially the adoption of lean and flexible organization at their employers. In the view of many subjects, with Carson and Courtney from two separate deals featured below, there were definite precursors of outsourcing that suggested something was changing in their employer's strategic approaches to their brick and mortar organization and to their labor force.

It wasn't long, it was only a year after I started, that *the rumblings of outsourcing* [my emphasis] started . . . about 2001, there were already rumblings. Trading Inc. actually ended up spending about $3 million on a study to determine whether or not they were going to outsource, which basically told me they're gonna outsource. You don't spend that kind of money without finding a way to get it back.

(Carson, former Desktop Support Supervisor at Tech Leader)

The last year [2011] I could see the writing on the wall. I could feel it coming. . . . And then all of a sudden, our boss John, he asked us to start documenting things, that's when we were like, "Ah, God, here it goes. We gotta document everything we do. We gotta document this and that. Cloud Inc. is not big on documentation or instructions or anything."

(Courtney, Desktop Support at Circuit)

In this section, before making the decision to outsource, I describe a few strategies customer companies had taken to offset the new economic realities challenging them and to leverage the information and automation possibilities of new technology environments. New institutionalism theory argues that because companies are embedded in the same organizational environments, they will value and act in increasingly homogeneous ways (Powell & DiMaggio 1991). Core companies in this sample were doing what other companies were doing to best establish, maintain, and grow in markets for their products or services. Similar doctrines shaped the reengineering of their organizations and work, which were namely: increasing organizational flexibility, cutting operating costs, and instituting new technologies to better coordinate, centralize, further standardize, and automate work processes and systems.

From the 1970s on, cutting costs had been a central prerogative for large established companies in industries like telecommunications (Technologies Inc. and Titan Inc. in this sample). They faced new competition from alternative telecommunication technologies such as mobile phones and their markets. To cut costs, they focused on reducing them through large downsizings of employees. In the early 1990s Technologies Inc. significantly reduced staff in a company-wide job action called "CREST." Managers in this case – JB, Mike, and Fred – described their participation in "absolutely brutal" meetings to assign a value to subordinates' job performance and then institute the mandated number of layoffs of managers and front-line workers in data centers located across a large Midwest city (LMC) and the region. Workers identified as low performers in the data center operations were released through this job action, and the best performers continued in their jobs at Technologies Inc.

> It was 1991 that Technologies Inc. did a thing called CREST where, it was absolutely brutal! We had to go into a meeting, a room full of ten, 12 managers with a list of people. You had to collectively rank everybody on this list from 1 to 25 or 30. And then they drew a line, so it became a real cut throat kind of environment. But then they decided, after we went through all that that, we don't want to let all these technicians go so we're just going to let everybody go on the list that's from operations. And so that was really brutal and we let a lot of good people go! I think that changed everything. People were more, "Okay you're not a valued employee anymore, you're just somebody here to do a job and then when they're done with you, you're done."
>
> (JB, former Network Manager at Tech Leader)

The downsizing was one instance of a broad company strategy to centralize the work and jobs from the surrounding townships into only one Technologies Inc. data center located in the central business district of the LMC. Data centers were being consolidated because they could run through WANs, wide area networks, that centralized and standardized the work. Centralization eliminated jobs, labor, and other costs from physical property and its ongoing maintenance needs. Tanya, a self-described "fire-jumper" and featured in Chapter 4, referred to similar job actions at her large telecommunication employer Titan Inc. as opportunities to eliminate "deadwood." Her moniker for job actions – reducing "deadwood" and "heads" and "headcount" – signified the market business logic prompting many organizations to eliminate human and process redundancies in their operations for efficiency and cost purposes (Thornton, Ocasio, & Lounsbury 2012).

> Now there were some people that I worked with that were just insanely great to work with. Don't get me wrong! But there were just *so* [she stressed] many that you're thinking, you know? For example, when a round of layoffs would come down and people would get a hit, you'd be like "Eh, I'm not that surprised" when you'd hear who some of the people were. Unfortunately that term "deadwood," not that people weren't doing anything. But, you weren't that surprised.
>
> (Tanya, Project Manager at Tech Leader)

Organizations were also involved in job actions because of the particular economic environment in industries. One industry example was healthcare.

Worsening economic forecasts for health providers in the public sector led to round(s) of employee layoffs, preceding the outsourcing, at several of the hospitals in this sample. In the 2012 case involving Cedar Pointe Medical Center – a 200-bed facility located in a sparsely populated part of a northern state – Beverly described "three layoffs over her eight year" tenure that decreased staff significantly and affected the salaries and benefits associated with most of the other staff positions.

> During my time at Cedar Point there was a lot of financial stress, I was there through three series of layoffs, and overall it ended in about a 10–15% staff reduction over those three layoff periods. Step increases and 401k employer matching funds were suspended almost through my entire time there, and I was there eight years.
>
> (Beverly, former IT analyst at Cedar Pointe Medical Center)

New communication and information technologies and their "informating and automating" functionalities enabled significant organizational restructuring and employee downsizing in the 1980s and 1990s, affecting most industry sectors (Zuboff 1988). As a result, good labor markets were transformed as job losses became a planned strategy of employers and a common result. Wireless Inc. was one example here showing the informating and automating capabilities being leveraged to lower the company's labor and other material costs. I spoke with Lynette, a former VP of HR for the company. Before the outsourcing, Lynette had helped Wireless Inc. open a "shared services" center for all of their employee records. To do this, she developed and facilitated the plan that digitized all of Wireless Inc.'s paper records on 75,000 employees from 50 locations nationwide. Lynette emphasized the cost benefits of this for the company. Redundancies in the work processes were removed and employees' records were accessed and kept up to date by HR workers in one physical location now for the company. The reduction in transaction costs per employee was realized through the information, networking, and automation capabilities from the then emerging information and communication technology systems (e.g., enterprise-wide systems like Peoplesoft or SAP). They were also realized by reducing the labor costs from maintaining employee records in the company's various physical and electronic locations.

> Wireless Inc. said they wanted to do shared services as a whole Alrich Model. Center of Excellence tapped me in October to open a shared services model for all US, like 75,000 employees, service them, and you have to open up in January also. Picked four people to be part of the team. Off for a week in a small room and plotted how to roll out shared services for all US. Told the Executive VP of HR, "here's the plan. #1, we're not going to be able to open the doors day one for everybody. We're going to do a cascading type roll-out, every 45 days I will take on anywhere from 15–20,000 new people. I guarantee everyone will be onboard 100% by June 1." Came up with a ten-step marketing strategy, took the theme of "life just got a little bit better at

Wireless Inc." Had portfolio presentations. Went on road trips. Before you came on you would have already seen us. "These are the services, this is what's changing, these are the tools you will now have through SAP. This is E-net, front end tool. These are the transactions that are going to be done automatically, the moment you put them in. These will be updated immediately. These are the ones that are going to take a little longer." We gave them an 800 # that they could call. We had the EVP of HR send letters home to everybody. Debit cards, mouse pads, we came up with a variety of different things. The team held ourselves very much accountable. Within the June time frame everybody was brought into the service.

(Lynette, former VP of HR at Wireless Inc.)

Through the 1980s and 1990s, firms instituted strategies to gain flexibility in their social organization and in obligations to direct employees. Many companies in this sample utilized contingent workers. In the automotive industry, Foreign Motors Inc. was known for incorporating a permanent layer of temporary workers in their production processes. Sandy, an HR specialist from the case, worked on the hiring, development (through learning opportunities), and evaluation of the temporary work population while employed by Foreign Motors Inc. Per Sandy, Foreign Motors Inc. contracted with several temporary help agencies to supplement their core production capacity with temporary workers as necessary, or just-in-time. As has been described about the tiered suppliers working for large Japanese automobile manufacturers (Womack, Jones, & Roos 1990), agencies working for "big clients" like Foreign Motors Inc. were willing to do "whatever [the client] felt was necessary . . . to please [them]." Usually this meant contracting and increasing temporary automotive production staff to closely correspond with current production needs. This action is known in management terms as lean and flexible production.

I think most temporary agencies, well ones we've [Foreign Motors Inc.] worked with anyway, they're all about how to supply their client with what they want and so they're pretty much unstructured, very flexible about what they'll do for the client. So that was my experience anyway, 'cause we were a big client for them and we could request pretty much whatever we felt was necessary. And they would usually be amenable to do it. It was something that they would want to do to please us, to get our business. I think with the agencies, that they're mostly not well managed [she laughs]. They're so interested in pleasing the client that they're not as structured as a normal human resources department. A normal human resources department is very structured, you have your policies. But, the temporary agencies are more prone to adapt to whatever their client wants.

(Sandy, formerly HR Specialist at Foreign Motors Inc.)

In another changing social organization in companies, many in the sample had employed technical consultants to help them prepare for the challenges posed by "the Y2K problem." To save money in the early development of digital language and memory, a two-digit year (e.g., 68) had become the technology standard. As a result, all companies had to convert all of their technology applications and systems to accommodate the shift to a new century and design and institute a four-digit date convention beginning on January 1, 2000. Here, most technicians on-the-job during Y2K said the preparations for it took several years. Increasingly, too, consultants were becoming normative to customer companies across most industries for helping transition or upgrade complex changes to technology environments. Like Bravado Hospital below, this was apparent in most of the hospitals here, who were either contracting with consulting companies or outsourcing companies to implement new clinical systems and electronic medical records applications. This capital investment in technology was guaranteed to improve healthcare outcomes while also reducing costs, and future jobs, for the organization.

> The Chief Administrative Officer at the time felt that we were trying to compete in the dot.com era for highly skilled IS [information systems] resources on a budget of a hospital, and there was no competing with trying to attract and retain top talent to work in IS in the healthcare environment. And the thought, the notion that a company whose core business was to deliver IS-type services was in a better position to provide top shelf talent because that was their core business. That was the primary reason because we were about to explode in terms of IS system development in the very late '90s spilling over into the year 2000 and on, that the proliferation of our systems was really starting to get its legs under them. And in this environment, we, at that time, we had historically always been a "best of breed" purchaser and we were fearful that we would not be able to compete for really, really smart talented IS people. So that was one of the reasons that . . . I think it was the primary reason that we outsourced.
>
> (Ross, Clinical Systems Director at Bravado Hospital)

Through the 1990s to today the use of consultants and the outsourcing of cost centers were increasingly common among the core companies in this sample. The dominant theory most organizations began adopting was to build larger markets and increase revenues and profits for the company their material and human resources should be directed toward the "core competencies" of the firm. Cost centers, in contrast, were tasks companies increasingly outsourced to some company who – in this theory – had "top talent" for the work that needed to be accomplished.

An established chemicals supplier, Industrial Solutions Inc., had outsourced numerous cost centers in their operations by the time I spoke with Bryan, their Director of Outsourced Services, in 2005. Industrial Solutions Inc. had outsourced: document management, accounts payable, information technology, and multiple human resource functions like benefits administration. Bryan discussed how Industrial Solutions Inc. was examining whether to outsource other job functions currently internal to the core company. He explained that the difference between deciding to outsource something or not depended on whether the function "was key to our business rather than core to our business." Functions core to the business of delivering chemicals to customers were activities kept in-house. For a chemicals company that distributed this resource to customers, accounts receivable (a function that is commonly outsourced) was kept in-house because Industrial Solution Inc.'s chemical market had "low [profit] margins" or markups.

> We're having a real struggle right now from an AR standpoint. Our cash flow, because of our low margins, is really important. You know we need to have that cash flow. We know from benchmarking that our AR department is typically better than "best in class." "Best in class" is something like 71% of your AR is current, and we're in the '90s range for current on AR. But that's from a collections' standpoint. From a credit standpoint, making credit decisions things like that, we can't seem to get our credit managers beyond transactional thinking, and so, we struggle internally as to "Okay well is this really core? If we were able to take the collections efforts away, or add a layer or something, can we get our people to focus on credit risk and really make it even more efficient?" So, it's considered a back-office, it's considered something we may want to outsource, but because it seems to be so key to our business, its one that's almost never going to touch. Whereas other things, you know like document management, payables, you know our HR. HR is outsourced. . . . We consider it key to our business, we just don't consider it something we need to keep employees to do. Because it's not core to our business. It's key to our business but it's not core to our business.
>
> (Bryan, Director of Outsourced Services at Industrial Solutions Inc.)

Finally, subjects in some cases explained the "rumblings of outsourcing" by invoking a company experience where a tipping point happened. Commonly, a plan to remediate or improve the IT environment for the firm had failed. According to Sally, an IT project manager, this was the case for Mammoth Inc. Prior to deciding to outsource, their internal IT department failed to coordinate and deliver on a major IT initiative. This also happened at Merchant Inc. prior to outsourcing. Digital Services Inc., a company with a very large market in media services, was another example when multiple efforts to build a new billing system internally failed. Per Dwayne, a network manager for billing, the IT (hardware) department was outsourced after that.

> From 2000, Digital Services Inc. wanted their own billing system. They didn't want third party venders. They had a couple different venders. They were going to take a part from each one, and they were going to develop it themselves, maintain it, and then run it themselves. So, that's what the last ten years has been about, development of this! This guy named Barry White came in. Digital Services Inc. is really pretty tight with their money. How he got full rein, no one ever knew. He changed everything. They built the new building, there were three of them. He hired so many people. . . . He

would say, "I need this done." You would say, "It's not tested." He would say, "I need it now!" If you didn't, you would get canned. People started just snapping to it. Everything put together just wasn't working. It wasn't tested, it wasn't timed, it just wasn't working with all the other peripherals it had to work with, so it was a big failure. He had a five year contract, so around his fourth year he was nowhere near success, and he was running out of contract time and he had spent so much money.

(Dwayne, formerly the Network Manager at Digital Services Inc.)

From the 1990s, more large companies made decisions to outsource some of their internal cost centers like IT and HR. Big cases were covered in local newspapers. Subjects often said to me they felt that outsourcing could happen to their positions and companies before it did. In some cases, employers did inform workers – well in advance sometimes (e.g., Trading Inc., Diagnosis Hospital) – that they were researching the option. But for the most part, employers preferred keeping their exploration into the possibility of outsourcing secret from their workers. In most cases, subjects recognized that the economic environment and the actions of employers were changing. While wary, they mostly ignored any suspicions that change could happen to them. It is for this reason that the rumbling of outsourcing stage was similar to KR's denial stage.

Betrayed! It will never be the same again

Most subjects reported hearing about the decision to outsource at an all-hands meeting for affected employees and departments. While there was some variance across the cases, mostly, subjects said the outsourcing deal was unexpected and a highly emotional experience. Usually subjects and their colleagues were shocked and reacted angrily at feeling they had been "betrayed" by employers. Similar to Christina, in the featured circumstance, for many of the subjects, employers were an important anchor institution in their neighborhoods, townships, suburban, and urban cities. Decisions to outsource jobs exposed their lack of commitment and care (i.e., paternalism) to their employees and the communities that had helped give them a competitive advantage in markets for their goods and services (Porter 1985). In the past, employers and subjects participated in a social contract characterized by reciprocal obligations and good treatment toward each other. With the announced outsourcing of their jobs, subjects felt deceived by core companies. Many were angry because their formerly confident choices regarding decisions that might affect their families – for example, committing to a 30-year mortgage on a costly home in an adjacent neighborhood to employers and/or deciding the family could survive solely on one income – were misguided, possibly disastrous, personal decisions. Fred gave an emotional account of how the Technologies Inc. outsourcing decision affected employees, like him, and their families in this case.

You just don't know what's gonna go on. Okay, and you have all this responsibility. So you have the pressure of that, that's there. People don't talk about it. When you have personal things in your own life you mask it, everybody does. And especially being a man I think, you probably mask it even more at times. I mean my [stay-at-home] wife was upset! She didn't know what was going on! And I just tried to tell her, "Don't worry about it at this point because I can't control it." I'm a believer that if you can control things in life then you worry about 'em. But if there's certain things you can't control, if you have no control over those, just let it go.

(Fred, former Network Manager at Technologies Inc.)

Two immediate effects of outsourcing are explored in this section. First, professionals (potentially) affected by outsourcing quickly became upset because the understanding they thought was mutual with employers was now retracted without their knowledge and consent. It was interpreted as underhanded and perceived as setting new (and lower) standards of employer transparency, disclosure, and overtures of care toward their employees. They were now in unfamiliar territory and placed in a potentially bad socio-economic position. Some tried to bargain for other jobs internal to employers. Second, because of the emotional chaos set off from the employment uncertainty that now existed, subjects usually said that – from that time forward – their expectations of job permanency changed forever. Both themes correspond with KR's anger and bargaining stages in the grief cycle.

A particularly emotionally charged announcement was the 2010 case of Digital Services Inc. outsourcing of their IT data center and billing software functions. Dwayne conveyed explosive images of a public scene where the CEO of a very large media company came to make the outsourcing announcement to the people it would be affecting. As Dwayne noted, the focus and concern of executives at the companies who make decisions to outsource have relatively little to do with the people they affect. In this case, Digital Services Inc. was dominating a media market and doing well financially. They were in the enviable position of having the financial power to purchase other companies to expand their dominance to other markets for goods and services. Yet, their CEO sauntered past the legions of workers affected by the outsourcing without an outward sign of care about the emotional effects this news was having on them or how their collective feelings might negatively impact his own personal safety.

The anger was there when [the CEO] had his presentation. I was so surprised, I mean, I literally expected him to have a bodyguard and he didn't. People were sooo angry! Having worked in mental health I'm used to bodyguards and security and stuff. I was shocked when I saw him. I was in the parking lot with tons of people and he walked out, went and got in his car. He isn't often [at the suburban location]. He didn't have a clue of how these people were feeling about him. These people were just angry! If I had to come tell them what he did, I would have the bodyguards! Digital Services Inc. has bodyguards. They have security. I looked, I was amazed. Anyway, it made me realize that he didn't have a clue about what he was doing to people's lives.

(Dwayne, former Network Manager at Digital Services Inc.)

At St. Francis Hospital, a local community health center, the entire IT department was outsourced in 2004. Salma's description of the outsourcing announcement was archetypical of the sentiment that many subjects expressed when they learned about their own case. Most were blindsided by outsourcing. They were "shock[ed]" by the first announcement. (Notice how often subjects used this word in cases featured below.) Betrayal quickly replaced shock. First, subjects questioned the decision to outsource, and then they became deeply critical of the plan. "Why had [the employer] not shared the possibility or the intention to outsource their jobs" before then? Instead, they "led their employees along" into thinking everything was okay. Anger followed as subjects began challenging their employers' logic, like Salma does below.

> It was a complete shock when they told us that we were being outsourced. It felt like, I guess the best word to describe it is *betrayal* [my emphasis]. Like, why would you lead everybody along? And to then just have the rug basically – that's what it felt like – to have the rug ripped out from underneath of you that, you know, "by the way we're outsourcing your whole department." It felt like "How are you trying to explain that this is good for us?!" It wasn't just me.
> (Salma, former IT Manager at Home Nurse Care Inc./St. Francis Hospital)

In many of the cases, at the time the decision to outsource was made by employers, there was no indication of what and who was going to be affected. This period of job uncertainty and anxiety produced a highly emotional work context for subjects in these cases. Unfortunately, these feelings endured for time spans from one month to one year before details about the business process(es) to be outsourced and the human resources this would affect were established, finalized in contracts, and shared with the departments and people. The shock and chaos that emerged from employment uncertainty deeply affected most subjects and their colleagues. Subjects often said they and their colleagues used chunks of work time to process the betrayal and the possibility of imminent and forced job changes or large job losses among staff in the IT or HR area. Subjects like Brad below, a charismatic 26-year-old working in IT security at Merchant Inc., described the emotional roller coaster he and his colleagues felt surrounding the initial 2004 outsourcing announcement.

> I was shocked! I was shocked because we had a perfect organization with the managers getting their deliveries met. Everything was working out really perfect. I couldn't see why we needed to outsource what was already good. . . . But I was shocked, everyone was shocked, and then we immediately started getting nervous. "What's gonna happen?!" And they couldn't give us anything for a month, about our jobs or if we were gonna be moved, if we're gonna be let go? People were saying . . . "We're going to lose our jobs!" All these rumors started circulating. I mean tons and tons of rumors! They said that they were bringing in their own work force and not keeping Merchant

Inc. work force. So immediately after the announcement rumors just started. Everybody was uncertain about "Well what's gonna happen to us?! Are we moving to Master Technologies?" I only ever worked at Merchant Inc. in a corporate environment, so I was comfortable with that. I didn't know what to expect with another company. So I was nervous!

(Brad, former IT Security Specialist at Merchant Inc.)

In some cases, such as Diagnosis Hospital, the period of unknowing could go on for a year. Here Hillary, a Senior IT Manager, described the "angst" the outsourcing immediately produced among employees there. Besides wrestling with her own personal turmoil, during the entire year Hillary had to manage the IT work that needed to be done. *And* she had to address the emotional needs of her staff, who were worried about the real prospect of losing jobs. Because of the prolonged time of uncertainty in this case, IT staff ended up finding other jobs either internal to Diagnosis Hospital or at an industry competitor. Because of the significant job losses in this case, successful attempts by affected workers to obtain other jobs definitely served both the employee and employer interests.

Oh everybody was afraid for their jobs. So I was outsourced in September 2003. Our fiscal year was October through the end of September. They announced it in October of 2002, and then signed the contract in the summer of 03, and they wanted us off the Diagnosis Hospital books as expenses, meaning salaries, by the end of the fiscal year. So by September 30th of 2003, we had to have transitioned to the outsourcer. They had a couple of false starts. It's a county hospital, government, so they had to send out an RFP [request for proposals] first, and when the scores came back, the scores were miscalculated so they had to redo the RFP, so then in the summer they did it again. And so all of this was adding to the angst of the employees. We were trying to do an upgrade, for example to our pharmacy system. . . . People were leaving. I was a program manager, trying to hold everybody together. I had projects due. I had a line out my door every morning. "What have you decided to do? Are you going to stay?" I had those kinds of questions all the time.

(Hillary, former Senior Manager at Diagnosis Hospital)

Even in cases where the period of uncertainty was short or details about what was being outsourced were clear from the beginning, subjects usually said some colleagues who had been with customer companies for decades and were close to retiring with good pensions tried to bargain for transfers to other internal departments in order to stay their planned course to retirement. Paul described this in the 2003 case of Concerto Inc., a large and very successful product development and marketing company.

Not everyone in my group rebadged. The majority of people did. There were some individuals who had been with Concerto Inc. for many years, for whom leaving Concerto would have also meant losing some rather nice retirement benefits. The ongoing profit sharing and retirement investing that Concerto Inc. had done for its employees over the years, and it would have been a financial impact on some of them. Some of them scrambled for jobs within the company. Very difficult though because Concerto Inc. put a moratorium on any hiring at that point. Because they didn't want to lose qualified IT people to non-IT jobs just because they didn't want to go to the strategic partner Circuit. So then the choice really became, "You either go to Circuit or you can leave the company altogether. Because we aren't going to create space back in the company that might take resources away from the outsourcing."

(Paul, former Workplace Services Manager at Concerto Inc.)

It was very clear, from the beginning to the end of my interviews, subjects experienced what many called a "betrayal" by employers for changing their expectations for lifetime jobs and secure employment contracts. To subjects and their colleagues, the outsourcing decision revealed that the old loyalty and commitment employees gave to employers was misguided in the new economic context. The possibility of outsourcing put them in a potentially harmful financial and social position that led to feelings of self-doubt, especially when confronting their families. This created deep anger in subjects. For those few who were able – meaning they were in a position to leverage some luck from the position of uncertainty – bargaining created alternative job opportunities internal at core companies or at competitors in the industry. These dominant feelings with the inO of jobs parallel the psychological outcomes in the anger and bargaining stages in Kubler-Ross's grief cycle (1969).

Sold! Unwanted but I needed the damn job!

In a majority of the cases in this sample, many people in jobs to be outsourced received job offers. Comparatively and generally speaking, getting a job offer is financially (and most likely qualitatively) better than losing one. Yet just like critical scholarship has said about the working classes through time, subjects here mostly felt the inO decision by management and the job offer with outsourcing companies showed them what little power they had. From management's perspective, a pretty good choice had been given to subjects whose jobs would be outsourced. Either take the job or don't take the job. But from the position of subjects, this was a real misnomer. They were constrained by financial and familial obligations to real communities and the varied prospects in job markets. Because of the despotic control of employers, many subjects explicitly described or alluded to "feeling sold" and treated as if they were property of employers. For subjects who were especially critical, they blamed employers for manufacturing the problem for them and then leveraging their greater power to force the hand of employees to take the offered job. To them, it amounted to nothing more than a constructed choice.

In a thorough examination of interview transcripts, interestingly, women seemed more outwardly critical of the forced choice they had to make as a result of their employers' decisions to outsource. This is probably the result of different factors. Given the recent women's marches and #metoo movements across the US, it probably reflects a more critical perspective being expressed by increasing populations of educated and experienced females who see and experience inequities in professional labor markets. The IT and HR professionals here are a segment of the population most likely to have the understanding and the power to identify and express personal experiences reflective of socio-economic inequality on the basis of their gender. Because of gender socialization, females are also more likely to show a greater ease with talking about feelings related to their emotional experiences, in this case those related to outsourcing. In other words, it is part of the cultural domain of girls and women to show emotion and discuss the provision of care to others (Daniels 1987). And finally, because of my own identity as female, more critique probably emerged because of a shared gender with my female subjects. It was most likely a combination of these elements and probably others. The point being that women in the sample expressed stronger criticism of their past employers for the constructed choice they forced them to make.

Fran, a subject in an earlier deal between Technologies Inc. – a local phone company – and Tech Leader, was typical of the feminine critique targeted at employers who outsourced once secure jobs. Fran felt that, because of the outsourcing decision and the constrained choices Technologies Inc. uncaringly manufactured for her and her colleagues, they were "sold like property." One of the few tools she had in the working class was simply "quitting" the job with her employer. However, because of Fran's financial obligations to a home, family, and her community, she determined this was not a viable option. Instead, in her case and in most others, outsourced professionals' perspective on long-term jobs and company loyalty forever changed.

> It felt like you were being *sold* [my emphasis]. It felt like you were just a piece of property. I was very upset. I was very upset! I mean at that point in time I was thinking of just quitting. The manager from Tech Leader who ended up as my manager, he was very good. He tried to help, they tried to help you ease the transition but, you can't transition stuff like that! I mean you still, you're sitting in the same desk, doing pretty much the same job, and you just get a new badge. In your head it doesn't click! You don't go from one, it's not like a train switch where you're "Okay today now I work for this company, and fine I'm with this company." Because nothing really changed! Your paycheck said Tech Leader, but in your function, I mean in mine, nothing changed. At that point in time, I lost all my loyalty to the corporation that I worked for.
>
> (Fran, former Data Center Manager at Technologies Inc.)

Among subjects, Fran has uniquely shown the ability to take that critical attitude and leverage it in a continuously progressive career at Tech Leader. From information on social media sites and as measured by her improved job status at Tech Leader through 2017, of all my subjects, Fran had the most ascension and cases of longevity over an employment career in outsourcing.

Regardless, in the vast majority of cases, despotic elements set the tone and circumstances for the terms of the forced job change. Most subjects had to take offers with outsourcing companies because of their obligations to families, property, and local communities. In my view, Christina – featured in the introduction to this chapter – was the quintessential critic in this regard. Two years prior to the outsourcing, Christina had "relocated to be close to the company" and her job at Drug Developer Inc. With the long-term job outlook historically good at many of the customer companies in this sample, she and other subjects had made financial decisions that "mortgaged" their future and cemented ongoing ties – at least in physical proximity – to employers. With their significant, long-term, financial commitments, subjects like Christina saw little alternative but to accept the position offered by employers as part of the outsourcing deal.

> I knew I was going to take the job, I needed the damn job! I had just bought this house and relocated here because the company's just up the street. So I bought this house. I got a mortgage now that's *a lot more mortgage than I had before* [she emphasized]! And I'm like, "I have to take this job, I know I have to!"
>
> (Christina, former IT Developer at Drug Developer Inc.)

To add insult to injury, in many of the outsourcing cases, employees in the department were split between the two companies with some or most scheduled to rebadge to outsourcing companies and a few or some to stay back. For example, some of the IT staff remained directly employed by Merchant Inc. and they were assigned the role of overseeing the provision of contracted services and the work of their former colleagues. Several senior managers at customers, like Bryan, referred to them as their "subject matter experts" (SMEs), giving a strong sense of their future role and their economic value to the company.

In contrast, professionals rebadging to outsourcing companies were both figuratively and socially moved from an insider position within a customer company and forced into the status of a "stranger" (Wolff 1964) because of the new cast from a changed employment identification. Per subjects like Brad below, this identification and the general "unknowing" of what lay ahead had immediate social consequences for the once "perfect team[s]" in these cases. A social division materialized quickly between professionals who would be rebadging and those staying back at customers. (After rebadging to outsourcing companies, this social division between employees of the two companies becomes the focus of the next chapter, "Chewed Up.") With a forced job change and the altered and "more demanding" attitudes and "different treatment" of former colleagues, these feelings added up to feeling "unwanted" by employers and their soon-to-be former colleagues, according to subjects like Maria below.

> After they made the announcement that they're gonna split the sides, immediately two groups began to form, they just separated, it completely cut in half our perfect team. We had the Merchant Inc. team and the Masters Technologies team. We would see the Merchant Inc. team go into meetings, and

our team would be "Well what are they talking about?! What do they know that we don't know?!" They can't tell us any information like that. So their attitude immediately changed. They felt that they were on Merchant Inc. now, and not Master Technologies. And people on Master Technologies I mean the same thing happened on our side! So immediately, it was separated. And it just immediately started going downhill from there. And then, the Merchant Inc. team, the team that stayed, started having more demands.

(Brad, former IT Security Specialist at Merchant Inc.)

It was real difficult for quite a while, going from February to June because our group [IT security] in particular split up. Half stayed at Merchant Inc. and half went to Master Technologies, so there were some animosities about who was chosen to go where and what side and that type of thing. There was a feeling of, I know on the Master Technologies side, that Master Technologies felt like they were the unwanted ones, you know, the ones that were pushed over to the outsourcing. We weren't the chosen ones was the feeling overall, that they don't want me, Merchant Inc. doesn't want me. So that was definitely there initially. That caused a lot of separation in our group, a lot of different relationships, different feelings, different attitudes, treated differently, you know?

(Maria, former IT Security Analyst at Merchant Inc.)

During the transition but before the outsourcing, some subjects attributed the commiserating among the people who were being outsourced to the "need" to understand an "uncertain" event. Either at "happy hours" or during the work day, they "commiserated" with others "in the same boat" to see if they "knew more" information that would help them with their own feelings of personal uncertainty and self-doubt. Commiserating helped subjects and their colleagues exercise some personal control over a general information void made by the less than transparent manifestations of upper management at customer companies. Informal gatherings among professionals affected by the outsourcing helped employees "talk and share" their feelings about the impending forced employment separation and the growing animosity from colleagues who would be continuing as direct employees at customers. Fran and Sally, IT professionals who worked at large employers in the region, discussed this commiseration tendency below in the Mammoth Inc. and Technologies Inc. outsourcing cases.

As we were going through this I actually started this happy hour. Because everybody was part of this change, we felt like we needed to get together and talk. We had so many people go to these happy hours! No lie. There were so many people always at the happy hours, and I would schedule them once a week or every other week. And then after we moved over, you couldn't get anybody together. But there was a need for them at that time. Because everybody needed to talk and vent and share and just, "Hey, what's going on there?! What are you doing?" Because some of the people were going to

Digitize. Most were going to Master Technologies. So it was a pow-wow with everybody and they, you know, obviously they needed it. Everybody went.

(Sally, former IT Specialist at Mammoth Inc.)

We were all in the same boat though. We just all felt betrayed, we all felt sold. And it affected the work that we did during that period of time. Because there was a lot of conversations! I mean half your day you just sat there, you know? Sat at the coffee pot and just bitched at each other. "How could they do this?!" You know, the uncertainty, you just didn't understand what was going on. So so we're all in the same boat though so, we all commiserated with one another.

(Fran, former Data Center Manager at Technologies Inc.)

Thus, in the transition of knowing you and your position will be outsourced, across the cases subjects said professionals were critical of the employment change being forced upon them. Many professionals likened their situation to having "no control," feeling "sold" like a commodity, and "unwanted" by "perfect teams." A big change was coming, and they had no power to resist it by quitting their jobs. Most often, subjects took one of the only steps they could to help minimize the anxiety and depression that were caused from having little power or foresight into a forced job change. The one measure they could utilize was talking with others to try to make sense of a tenuous situation. Most subjects described the feelings of powerlessness, the impending loss of jobs, and the "need" to better understand the circumstances they faced by talking with others affected by outsourcing.

Rebadging and its sad irony

Similar to the acceptance stage in Kubler-Ross's grief cycle, subjects and colleagues who have been offered and accepted jobs with outsourcing companies begin to accept the forced job change. It is important to recognize the new context that developed during the transition to the general acceptance of outsourcing by professionals (Kessler, Coyle-Shapiro, & Purcell 1999). Similar to what other research has found on the subject of employee commitment preceding and after outsourcing, the subjects here said they had reduced personal commitment to employers from this time forward (Harris, Klaus, Blanton, & Wingreen 2009; Kennedy, Holt, Ward, & Rehg 2002; and Maertz, Wiley, LeRouge, & Campion 2010). They would be rebadging to outsourcing companies without giving their absolute consent. And especially in the cases where professionals in a job function were split between some staying and some going to the outsourcing company, changes to social interaction and gaps in the flow of information from management helped solidify the realization among those going with the outsourcing that they were outsiders at customers both now and for good.

Previous research on the impact of outsourcing on employees' attitudes and behavior found that the pull of jobs at outsourcing companies matter (Kessler,

Coyle-Shapiro, & Purcell 1999). In the case of a government office, the identity of the outsourcing company, continuous communication about the impending change to social organization, and material offers were most important in this regard. In the early IT cases especially, material benefits (pay level, vacation time, and seniority) transferred to outsourcing companies unchanged. The "pull" of jobs at outsourcing companies, especially the material offer and the fact that subjects and colleagues would be working directly for an established IT company (as compared to a retailer for example), helped some outsourced professionals begin to look ahead and accept the idea of rebadging.

In most earlier IT cases, both customers and outsourcing companies made "gestures" to assuage "concerns" professionals who would be outsourced had about benefits like immediate job security, "vacations, pensions, and accumulated sick time." For example, in the large IT outsourcing deal Mammoth Inc. negotiated with Master Technologies, professionals would maintain jobs for a set number of years and would have comparable pay and vacation benefits. In another smaller deal between St. Francis Hospital and Sourcing Central, where the customer represented an important employer in a locale and most employees had been in jobs for long periods of time, outsourcing companies agreed to carry over accumulated sick time to reduce concerns over the availability of this benefit in the event of a "sudden illness."

> I think some of the concern was, "Ok, we know how this works. You outsource and then you let us all go." But Mammoth Inc. actually made them put in stipulations that they would hold onto these people for so many years, you will also take their pension and pay into it. They will get their vacation that they already have, because Master Technologies does not give more than four weeks. If someone already had five or six weeks they got to keep it, so they were grandfathered in. So there was a lot of things like that that made you feel comfortable.
>
> (Sally, former IT Specialist at Mammoth Inc.)

> The benefits were actually an improvement – health insurance. I was getting four weeks of vacation and I got five weeks when I came over. And what they ended up doing is a concession. There was one sticking point that concerned people, particularly the people like myself who had a long amount of time in the organization, is that I had accumulated sick time with the understanding . . . I had like 300 hours of sick time that was accumulated with the idea that if I had any sudden illness that I'd be covered with that until long term insurance kicked in. Well, when we moved over, St. Francis paid us our vacation. They didn't pay us our sick time. And what Sourcing Central did was give everybody a week's vacation. . . . They basically came up with an idea that said, "We'll carry your sick time that you earned, but it can only be used for that one contingency, a long-term illness." You couldn't dip into it because you had a cold. And that was a good compromise. That took care of

the fear that people had of losing that and they made a nice adjustment . . . it was a good gesture in moving that one point that was a concern.

(Dominic, former IT manager at St. Francis Hospital)

In all inO cases, professionals rebadging to outsourcing companies did lose symbolic benefits. Some examples of this included the loss of employee parking privileges and other restrictions on the access of physical space at customers, the loss of employee discounts at retailers, and significant financial discounts on cable and telephone services.

Over the period of outsourcing cases, however, this comparable pattern in the transfer of salary and benefits between customers and outsourcing companies does not hold. In most cases from 2003 forward, deals had immediate job losses, managers got demoted, and the timely elimination of jobs and people were a central part of outsourcing deals. In part, this is a consequence of the sharper focus both customers and outsourcing companies had on reducing costs in the later cases of outsourcing. Below, for example, Courtney describes the pay reduction and loss of "vacation" time she experienced with her new position at Circuit in 2012. In other cases, for example 2003 Trading Inc., subjects like Carson described immediate job losses and his own job demotion from an operations manager to a supervisor position in desktop support.

They docked me about 12 grand, which is not that bad considering what I heard other people got docked. Because Circuit is really low-balling people right now, because they're having problems. And I lost my vacation, and that's it. Yeah, my vacation hurts more than the money right now. With time with the girls and stuff and appointments.

(Courtney, former Desktop Support at Cloud Inc.)

When they walked in they cut off 25%. . . . First foot in the door, and their methodology was basically anyone with seven years or more was gone immediately, because they were the ones making the most, they had the most benefits. If you're talking about keeping costs down, they're the ones you get rid of first. Tech Leader changed my job from day one. When they came in they said, "One of the things we're gonna do is we're gonna take this fast operations team, and we're going to now move it to our holder operations center." So my team, was gonna go away. So they said, "Ok, you are now the team leader for desktop support."

(Carson, former Operations Manager at Trading Inc.)

In addition to material benefits, subjects in the early cases that involved the installation of new hardware technology and software were pulled to outsourcing companies like Tech Leader because of their then "world-class" status as an IT leader. This corresponds with the emphasis in early years by advocates that argued moving to outsourcing companies would help launch IT careers not possible back at customers involved in other industries like retail. JB below, a network manager for Technologies Inc. was one of the subjects who viewed the job change to a then predominantly IT outsourcing company as an improvement over his position at the regional telephone company.

> I can't say everybody was happy but, most people seemed to be happy because we were going to some place that seemed to be an IT-focused organization, is what you view Tech Leader as. And so it's like, "Alright. We're finally going to be able to go someplace, get some training, become part of a world-class IT organization" and those kinds of things.
>
> (JB, former Data Center Manager at Technologies Inc.)

Additionally, before contracts begin, time was set aside each day so that subjects could learn the outsourcing company's procedures and "systems" for completing work and making strategic changes to it. These meetings were also instances of socialization into the "culture" at outsourcing companies. "Town hall meetings" about changing employers, learning about their material benefits, and "business processes" helped people to identify with the outsourcing company, and it characterized an acceptance stage of the impending outsourcing change. As scholars of the reorganization of work have previously identified, some outsourcing companies – like Master Technologies below – worked at developing a "community of purpose" (Heckscher 1995) among "transitioning associates." A community of purpose involves bringing together "individuals with commitments to similar skills, goals, interests, and affiliations to an organization with a mission" (145). "A community of purpose lays the moral basis for mutual obligations and stable relationships and therefore for effective cooperation" (146). Ballast Group, below, seemed to especially embrace the idea that the outsourcing "change could be difficult" for employees. But they worked to positively reshape subjects' "approach" to the changes with outsourcing. Master Technologies, in another example, took a very "intense" approach to socializing associates into "how [individuals] at their company do business."

> So in our town hall meetings, they [Ballast Group] talked about change and how everybody adapts to change a little differently, and that's how it was laid out. I thought it was good though. And I thought it was something that was important for an outsource company to do, or even just a company in general, because change always happens. It's how you approach change. There were different books that they gave us. There was one book, *Who Stole My Cheese?*
>
> (Morgan, former IT analyst at Bravado Hospital)

Master Technologies they had intensive training sessions. Oh yeah they had meetings after meeting, after meeting, where they brought people in. It was a whole department that came in. And it was a good couple of weeks where we went through, they sent us the mailing alone. The stuff you got at home to go through, so you could be prepared on the day you came in and they taught us, they showed us here are the insurance, they used this company as opposed to what Merchant Inc. used. Here's our 401K, as compared to Merchant Inc. It wasn't just "oh okay, we'll send you something in the mail to figure it out." No they had very intensive, and not only on benefits but on their culture. And how they do business. And some of the things that were just non-negotiable, as far as practices within Master Technologies. So they trained, they did in-depth training on, these are the systems that we use, these are the processes that we follow, they are non-negotiable, if you don't follow them they can be reasons for termination in some instances. And it could be two, three hours, every other day. So yeah, they spent a lot of time working with the transitioned associates. They set up a special help-line, phone number, and website for you to go to if you had questions. It was great, they spent a lot of time with us. I don't know how other companies handle it, but Master Technologies they spent a lot of time with us. So, and you had to jump on the boat real quick. You learn it. If we send it to you, read it. Learn it.

(Davetta, former Identity Management Specialist at Merchant Inc.)

On the final day, subjects and their colleagues turned in one badge and accepted another. Across the cases, both customer and outsourcing companies reassured rebadging professionals that they would continue their work the next day as if nothing changed. Similar to JB's description below, outsourcing companies had the strategic imperative to "keep [the outsourced business processes and systems] running as they were." It was in their financial interests that the business process and the social organization around it continued in the "same" way that it had. Avoiding change in the move to an outsourcing environment would diminish possible costly work flow service disruptions with customers.

For the most part you went over as you were. There wasn't a lot of changing jobs. Because they wanted to keep the data center running. They wanted to make it as transparent as possible so actually what happened was the end of June, the beginning of July was when it took place. You went home a Technologies Inc. employee one day, you came back you're a Tech Leader employee the next day, and you had your same job, your same telephone number, you were just a different employee.

(JB, Data Center Manager at Tech Leader)

Unfortunately, outsourced professionals learned within days that the idea that nothing was "changing" was simply not true. As described in later chapters, their established social relationships with old colleagues at customer companies and the nature of outsourced work must change because of the new context of a market organization.

References

Autor, David H. and David Dorn. 2013. "The Growth of Low-Skill Service Jobs and the Polarization of the US Labor Market." *American Economic Review* 103(5): 1553–1597.

Daniels, Arlene K. 1987. "Invisible Work." *Social Problems* 34(5): 403–415.

Harris, Michael, Timothy Klaus, J. Ellis Blanton, and Stephen C. Wingreen. 2009. "Job Security and Other Employment Considerations as Predictors of the Organizational Attitudes of IT Professionals." *International Journal of Global Management Studies* 1(1): 32–45.

Harrison, Bennett. 1994. *Lean and Mean: The Changing Landscape of Corporate Power in the Age of Flexibility*. New York: Basic Books.

Heckscher, Charles. 1995. *White-Collar Blues: Management Loyalties in an Age of Corporate Restructuring*. New York: Basic Books.

Kennedy, James, Daniel Holt, Mark Ward, and Michael Rehg. 2002. "The Influence of Outsourcing on Job Satisfaction and Turnover Intentions of Technical Managers." *Human Resource Planning* 25(1): 23–31.

Kessler, Ian, Jackie Coyle-Shapiro, and John Purcell. 1999. "Outsourcing and the Employee Perspective." *Human Resource Management Journal* 9(2): 5–19.

Kubler-Ross, Elizabeth. 1969. *On Death and Dying*. New York: Palgrave Macmillan.

Maertz Jr, Carl P., Jack W. Wiley, Cynthia LeRouge, and Michael A. Campion. 2010. "Downsizing Effects on Survivors: Layoffs, Offshoring, and Outsourcing." *Industrial Relations* 49(2): 275–285.

Porter, Michael E. 1985. *Competitive Advantage*. New York: The Free Press.

Powell, Walter W. and Paul DiMaggio. 1991. *The New Institutionalism in Organizational Analysis*. Chicago: University of Chicago Press.

Reich, Robert B. 1992. *The Work of Nations: Preparing Ourselves for 21st Century Capitalism*. New York: Vintage Books.

Thornton, Patricia H., William Ocasio, and Michael Lounsbury. 2012. *The Institutional Logics Perspective: A New Approach to Culture, Structure, and Process*. Oxford: Oxford University Press.

Weil, David. 2014. *The Fissured Workplace: Why Work Became So Bad for So Many and What Can Be Done to Improve It*. Cambridge, MA: Harvard University Press.

Wolff, Kurt H. (ed) 1964. *The Sociology of Georg Simmel*. New York: The Free Press.

Womack, James, Daniel Jones, and Daniel Roos. 1990. *The Machine That Changed the World*. New York: Rawson Associates/Harpers.

Zalewski, Jacqueline M. 2015. "'It Worked Out Better For Some:' Consent, Resistance, and Professional Careers With Outsourcing Companies." *Eastern Sociological Society Conference*, New York City.

Zuboff, Shoshana. 1988. *In the Age of the Smart Machine*. New York: Basic Books.

3 "Chewed-up"

The adversarial nature of work relationships in markets

Paul (2005)

I had the good fortune of speaking with Paul early on in the course of this study. He was my fourth interviewee. Because Paul lived in another state, it was the first of several interviews I did using the landline telephone so that I could transcribe and analyze a tape recording later. Because I was relying entirely on audio in the interview, the emotional qualities in Paul's voice seemed magnified as he described the effects of in-house outsourcing (inO) on his interactions with former colleagues, the new way his work was organized, and his future career prospects at Circuit. Circuit was a major company in the IT outsourcing industry, one of the largest five outsourcing companies at the time.

Paul was enthusiastic and candid about sharing his 18 months of experience with an outsourcing company. At this early stage in my research I remember thinking that Paul was especially thorough at explaining key employment differences and the transformations in social interactions in the workplace to jobs at "vendors," like Circuit, from pre-outsourcing employment at "customers" like Concerto Inc. Paul proudly shared his concept for the latter form, the non-market or the direct employment relationship he once had in a vertically integrated hierarchy. Several times during our conversation he described it as, "working for the company I work for."

Paul's tone quickly became negative, sounding bitter when he described the work conflicts he commonly experienced with former colleagues because of the new outsourcing deal. He stated the conflicts with those still employed at Concerto Inc. began immediately upon the onset of the deal. When I interviewed Paul, I knew that he shared a compelling story of how the new market structure and market logic negatively impacts social interactions and how most established relationships between outsourced subjects and old colleagues deteriorate because of it.

Meet Paul

Paul was in his mid-thirties. He had worked for five and a half years as the Workplace Services Manager at the corporate headquarters for Concerto Inc., a Fortune 100 company. In this role, Paul managed the computer, technology, and network needs of other employees. In earlier years, Paul commented, "Concerto Inc. was considered a company you could retire from!" Yet in 2003, Concerto Inc. decided to outsource the majority of IT jobs and IT work at their corporate headquarters and all other physical locations of the company. Outsourcing IT was part of Concerto Inc.'s strategic plan to transfer the ownership of parts of their business – i.e., their "cost centers" – to a "strategic partner." Transferring the ownership of the work to Circuit allowed Concerto Inc. to focus their development and material resources, which they termed "core competencies," on the revenue-producing side of their business. With this transfer, Concerto Inc. could devote more resources toward internal departments like product development, marketing, and sales. These types of departments contributed directly to the profitability and financial position of the firm.

After transferring to the job at Circuit, Paul worked in a comparable role, at the same physical location as Manager of Workplace Services for Concerto Inc.'s corporate headquarters. After one year, Circuit expanded Paul's role to include three of Concerto Inc.'s other physical locations. Positively for Paul, the new job involved relocation closer to his family. Yet, Paul acknowledged that he was "working more hours for more stress" from the tripling of his work. He emphasized that the increased stress directly emanated from the way outsourced work was reorganized.

I asked Paul if the outsourcing had affected his relationships with former colleagues – the people who worked onsite in similar roles in Workplace Services but who continued on as direct employees of Concerto Inc. Paul carefully explained that the greater complexity of his work and the new social structure in an internal market caused high levels of conflict between them daily. Paul's voice pitch became low as he detailed how the division of labor changed in a market and – especially – how the new market roles of "customer" and "vendor" quickly reshaped interactions and relationships with his old colleagues at Concerto Inc.

In the new market organization, old colleagues at Concerto Inc. now represented "the customer." In part, customers were responsible for monitoring the delivery of work from "the onsite vendor" and for ensuring that other work in Concerto Inc.'s contractual and financial interests in the relationship were protected. This meant Paul's former colleagues now scrutinized his work and the work of other outsourced professionals to ensure that the services and service levels detailed in the outsourcing contract were delivered to the exact standards determined in the deal. Paul said, "Just two days after the contract was signed," old colleagues began demanding that the onsite vendor produce the new (and higher) contracted service levels. "They were making sure the contractor felt the heat!" Paul felt bitter toward the new arrangement because he and old colleagues had worked side by side for five years at Concerto Inc. They had shared the challenges of their work in their old roles, so they understood the added work burden they were demanding from Paul and other outsourced colleagues at the vendor. Yet, they lacked empathy toward the burdensome effects on former close colleagues like Paul from the added work, new processes, and high service levels in contracts.

Paul adamantly felt his old colleagues were not treating him with dignity, like established, committed, and (albeit once) collegial relationships usually warrant.

This feeling revealed itself very clearly to me through the telephone wire. Paul was livid about his former colleagues' unsympathetic behavior. The warm feelings Paul once had for his old colleagues – the ones who he had "sat next to every year at the Christmas party" – disappeared in the new market context. Because of the raised political nature of his social interactions in the internal market organization and the undignified treatment from old colleagues, Paul only felt resentment and alienation towards them.

Introduction: work relations in markets

In 2004, at the beginning of my qualitative study, the common rhetoric framing organizations' decisions to outsource their business processes and jobs was very positive. It dually highlighted the operational and financial advantages customers would gain from the support of a "strategic partner." For example at an Outsourcing Institute (OI) Roadshow I attended in Chicago that year, the program facilitators often used the term strategic partner to imply a positive nature to the outsourcing relationship and beneficial financial outcomes in the deals they featured in their program. The representatives from featured deals, as well as several attendees I lunched with at a round table, also used the term to imply that their company's outsourcing relationships were financially benefitting them. In the pro-business and pro-outsourcing environment of the 2004 OI Roadshow – as a critically oriented sociologist – I hesitated to explore the meaning of the strategic partner term or directly ask how a company's partnerships harmoniously developed between professionals on the front line of either organization to produce the positive economic benefits that the term implied.[1]

In interviews from 2005, some subjects also used the phrase strategic partner to explain why former employers decided to outsource their jobs. When Paul used the term in my fourth interview, I quickly responded, "What did Concerto Inc. mean by strategic partnership?" His explanation was similar to the meaning implied by people in the pro-business and pro-outsourcing camps. In their theory, strategic partners – both customers and vendors – are dedicated to "delivering better business [practices] to customers because of expertise in their respective [and complementary] fields." As Paul emphasized below, the outsourcing company's expertise in IT services is supposed to directly enhance the customer's business operations and financial position. In this ideology, the strategic partnership relationship was a win-win situation for both companies. Ideally, after declaring allegiance to each other, the allies "bring their full weight and expertise" to the work that helps the other to leverage more market share in their respective core industries.

> This concept of strategic partnership means, Circuit is going to bring the full weight and expertise of Circuit to the table. We're going to help Concerto Inc. deliver better Concerto Inc. business by making sure that we deliver better IT business. And we're going to do so because we, Circuit, are experts in that field.
>
> (Paul, Workplace Services Manager at Circuit)

This study's subjects shared their firsthand knowledge of how strategic partnerships worked at the employee interface, or "edge" (Spinuzzi 2015), between the two companies. Collectively, the experiences in a majority of the cases here stood in sharp contrast to the smooth market relationship implied by the strategic partnership theory. Instead and more often, while trying to articulate the work in outsourcing, subjects reported immediate and continuous conflict with their former peers while trying to "rework a new arrangement" (Corbin & Strauss 1993). The title for this chapter, "Chewed-Up," was a metaphor several subjects used to capture the adversarial, confrontational nature and angry emotionality of interactions they commonly experienced in inO. In practice, subjects say, the work by vendors at all levels of the market organization produces an added, everyday, political dimension that workers must contend.

When I began my project in 2005, little sociological research existed on inO arrangements; for example the new social organization, its nature, and its subjective outcomes (Davis-Blake & Broschak 2009; Schieman & Reid 2008; Vallas 2003). One qualitative case study of the inO of copy center services and staff (Smith 1994) described the flexible organization of the work and people onsite at their customers. Smith also mentioned the "hidden hierarchies and conflict" in the organization and onsite interactions between employees of the two companies. However, her research did not offer explanation for the social conflict, how, and why it arose. More recently and through the perspective of "lead firms," studies of outsourcing find that mechanisms for "command structures and dispute resolution" were necessary to coordinate and monitor relationships between firms (Davis-Blake & Broschak 2009:328). Recurring findings indicating the challenges of the market relationship and social conflict are supported by the high rates of failure in outsourcing deals.[2]

Specifically, the political dimension to the interactions and work produced in markets is missing from, or invisible in sociological and economic debates and public scholarship on inO (Zelizer 2012). Feminist scholars argue that the general lack of analysis and understanding of workplace interaction and relationships is because relational work and social dynamics are associated with femininity, and they are culturally understood as a natural attribute of women. Because of this, social relational work has historically been undervalued, infrequently studied, and poorly understood by most institutions (Daniels 1987; DeVault 1991; Schieman & Reid 2008; Zelizer 2012). To remedy this gap, my work contributes new knowledge on how inO (one form of a market organization) affects workplace interaction and established social relationships.

This study identifies the ways in which the social conflict in interactions among former colleagues was the direct effect of new arrangements, processes, and the roles of customer and vendor in the market organization. The recurring political interactions and social conflicts with customers, as described by Paul and other subjects, alienated them from formerly close colleagues. Further, findings from this study demonstrate that political and emotional work were a significant part of subjects' interactions with customers in market-organized inO.

In contrast to the smooth relationship invoked by the business management class and the strategic partnership theory, according to subjects in this study, the social interactions on the front-line or "edge" (Spinuzzi 2015) of the market organization were not as collegial as they had been told to expect before the outsourcing. In actuality, the new structural arrangement associated with the internal market produced regular social conflicts between outsourced professionals and their old colleagues at customer companies. The greater political nature and the social conflict with inO were commonly cited as its most significant drawback by professionals in this sample, including Paul introduced in the beginning of this chapter and in the quote below. Per subjects' testimonies, the market sets the context for the added politics workers like Paul experienced everyday with inO. Below, Paul acknowledged the emotional hardships that he and other employees faced when dealing with the politics of the inO of their work.

> Emotionally for me, this process has been both up and down. There are days when I feel good about it, I feel good about my job because my job went well that day. But, for the overall amount of emotional turmoil it puts people through, it's not been worth it for me. And the unfortunate truth is many of my peers that I speak with in the same work areas are all saying the same thing. I even hear my own upper management saying, "Look you oughta be putting together your resume, you could go get a better job." That's unheard of! You know at Concerto Inc. my managers were always saying, "Man, you could be with Concerto Inc. for the rest of your life, you could retire from here! You've got great opportunities!" Right? Now my management is saying, "Man, you're too smart to stay here." It's a big difference.
>
> (Paul, Workplace Services Manager at Circuit)

Based on the frequency that the social conflict topic arose in interviews here, political work and emotional labor were significant requirements and challenges, and produced personal and organizational costs for employees. Employees had to handle the relational work and its degrading personal costs with little recognition or reward by management. And by inference, companies also incurred added "transaction costs" from the effects of politics on the front lines of markets and the obstacles it poses for relational qualities of collegiality, trust, and cooperation and their effects on productivity between employees of the two companies (Williamson 1975).

The articulation of work through interaction theory

To understand why instituting markets often produced conflicts in the social interactions between employees of the two companies, I applied a symbolic interactionist (SI) theoretical framework in this analysis. A SI theoretical framework is suited for micro-level analysis. The assumption in SI is to understand "how work in organizations is carried out, research needs to examine social interaction and the structural and organizational conditions that bear upon the work" (Corbin & Strauss 1993:81). Corbin and Strauss's "articulation of work through interaction theory" (1993) emphasizes structural conditions, such as a market organization, which impact the stances of workers in their approach to the job and the interaction strategies they use in the process of articulating or coordinating the work. Also, the theory presumes that the articulation process is political. The power and control participants wield is contested. Therefore, outcomes are determined during the coordination of work process, and power and control will ultimately tip toward one participant position or the other.

Corbin and Strauss's theoretical framework (1993) for studying the articulation of work includes the concepts of articulation, arrangements, the working-out process, and stances. They define the concepts as follows:

- *Articulation*: "the coordination of lines of work, which is accomplished through the working-out process, to establish the arrangements" (72). This definition refers to the actual work performance itself.
- *Arrangements*: "agreements between people and units about policies, process, etc." (72). By this, Corbin and Strauss are referring to social arrangements between employees.
- *The working-out process*: "the interactional process of establishing and revising arrangements; subjects will strategize to shape arrangements and exert control by using interactional strategies" (73). This definition refers to the ways in which workers come to terms and adjust arrangements to suit their new environment.
- *Stances*: "the position taken by actors toward the working-out process; a stance will be shaped by a subjects' perceived power to influence organizational conditions, arrangements, and meanings; stances are expressed through interactional strategies" (73). Corbin and Strauss emphasize the common approach workers take in their interactions to control the definition and meaning of the situation during the working-out process.

I use Corbin and Strauss's interactional framework to identify and define the structural conditions that directly impact interaction with inO. In the next section, I describe how the market organizational context and its historical problems arise from the institutional logic of markets (e.g., resource competition, upselling, and growth) and the goal incongruency between the two companies (Thornton & Ocasio 1999; Williamson 1975). Then, I depict the social interaction in the working-out process and the stances and interactional strategies that were common in the inO cases described in my research. New structural conditions with inO/markets were competitive and adversarial in nature. They produced conflictual interactions by increasing the political maneuvering required by the employees of vendors and customers during the articulation work process. I call these interactional elements and requirements of jobs in inO *market labor*.

Corbin and Strauss make several statements that are pertinent to analyze the shift from a hierarchical to a market organization and they help explain why it leads to conflictual changes in social interaction. First, they contend that social arrangements will be affected by changes to structural conditions (80). With inO, the organization of work changed and, therefore, the social arrangements between former colleagues had to be renegotiated. Both companies established general rules and guidelines for engagement and interactions between them. But, professionals on both sides of the market organization had to work out new arrangements in their interactions to articulate the work.

Second, the authors explain that stances will change in response to variations in social structure. Subjects will access the power they have at their disposal and use it to influence the renegotiation of the social arrangements (73). At either company, foremost, management guidelines for conduct instructed their employees to protect their separate proprietary and financial interests.

Finally, Corbin and Strauss explain that the process of reworking new arrangements is difficult for professionals. This is because of the "complex lines of work and the webs of arrangements that each subject is involved in" (80). Every person in a work role is responsible for coordinating a multitude of tasks that tie into various parts of the organization. Changing any arrangement, according to the authors, will have a cascading effect on various parts, if not most, of the organization (73).

In my study of inO, the social organization in a single department (e.g., IT security in the Merchant Inc. case) was split, morphing from one employer into two distinct employers in the same physical space. Thus, in Corbin and Strauss's theory, the market inO organization will raise the complexity of "lines of work and webs of arrangements" (80) for professionals working on its front lines. Not only were outsourced professionals negotiating the work that was internal to their new company now, but they were also instituting and following different processes now because they were vendors. Finally, outsourced professionals have new constraints on how they negotiate work in their interactions with former colleagues, now their customer. Structurally the staff from the two organizations continued to co-exist in the same physical space, which probably exacerbated the opportunities and occurrences for social conflict in markets.

In markets, therefore, the complexity of arrangements multiplies. The social web of arrangements at the outsourcing company exists alongside and among the physical web of arrangements at the customer. Both arrangements connect in front-line physical and digital spaces at the structural "edge," separating the two organizations (Spinuzzi 2015). And as scholars in the SI tradition contend, working-out new arrangements with inO markets mandate "cognitive processes involving judgment, mediation skills, and emotion work" or articulation work (Hampson & Junor 2005:175).

"Drawing a line": new adversarial arrangements in markets

In economic terms, inO involves a market organization between two companies recognized by law as the "customer" and the "vendor." Customers purchase and receive goods and services, and vendors produce and/or deliver them. Customers and vendors have different proprietary investments and financial goals in the market transaction. The revenues from the operations of customers and vendors reflect their particular "core competencies" and, from an economic perspective, they are separated and competed. For example, for the six hospitals in the sample, effectively and profitably delivering medicine was the core source for their investment and revenue. This compared to the IT outsourcing companies in these cases, whose core investment and revenue came from delivering technologies and their "best practices" to their hospital clients at a minimum cost from labor and other overhead in order to make significant profits.

Scholars of economic organization call the issue of different proprietary goals in markets "goal incongruence" (Williamson 1975; Ouchi 2006). In theory and practice, goal incongruence exists in market organizations and has financial and social effects – known as "transaction costs." Based on Williamson's market failures theory (1975), these types of costs make a business operation less profitable. In practice, markets elevate the possibility or risk for transaction costs. For customers, there is added risk in markets because they may not get the quantity or quality of services they contracted from the vendor. For vendors, risk increases in markets because they may unintentionally add to the costs of delivering the work or "give work away for free" (Paul) to customers. To offset the new financial risks to either company in the market, new structural arrangements in the workplace were instituted.

To compensate for the risks in markets, outsourcing and core companies instituted a governance function and a "ticketing" system to make the work changes and requests from customers more transparent, centralize decision-making between customers and vendors, and document the resolution of issues for accountability purposes and cost reduction purposes. Importantly, ticketing systems allowed outsourcing companies to evaluate whether requests from the customer constituted new work and, therefore, a source of potential new revenue. But inO ticketing systems made work processes more complicated, as compared to the more informal and collaborative methods of hierarchies. Governance and tickets added extra steps to the work and mandated a central point of contact and mutual decision-making for customers and vendors. Lynette, a former account manager for Web Tech, discussed the added steps and politics she experienced in this governance role after an outsourcing deal with Wireless Inc. began.

> "Jacqueline, you can no longer look at it that way. You've got to look at it this way! And this is a customer, and every time they change their mind there's got to be a process and we have to fill out this paperwork." I mean trying to educate people about the difference between a client and the partnership and everything else was a real tough one! And so the first time that Wireless Inc. asked for something and we said, "Okay. Write down the requirements." They're looking at us and saying, "We never had to do that!" "I understand, but now you do."
>
> (Lynette, former dual Account Manager and Strategic
> Business Unit Manager for Web Tech)

In fact, governance and ticket systems eliminated much of the discretion that professionals used to have in comparable hierarchical professional roles (Zalewski 2007). With inO, decisions of any financial consequence were made by management in a shared governance function/department generally comprised of an account manager representing the vendor and designated managers representing the customer. One subject, Bryan, was a Director of Outsourced Services for Industrial Solutions Inc. and satisfied a governance role for the outsourcing deals the company had with vendors in the logistics, property management, records management, HR, and IT sectors. Per Bryan's account, his governance role involved making regular changes to the outsourcing contract as a result of his employer's changing needs. Yet a constant part of it, he carefully explained below, also involved the nitty-gritty political battles with his vendors. Conflict arose over missing deadlines, potentially negatively affecting Industrial Solutions Inc.'s operations and increasing cost overruns on their contracted projects with vendors.

J: *Okay. Do conflicts ever occur?* [B: Sure!] *Okay. Does this happen often, infrequently?*

B: A lot. Yes, frequently. A conflict recently. And this is with IT Dynasty Co. [the IT vendor]. IT Dynasty Co says, "Okay, you have contracted to have 10.5 people on your application side." We get a request from a customer that they want to be on EDI [electronic data interchange] and running by such-and-such time. And we say to them, "We'll get you the time. So we go over to IT Dynasty Co and we say, 'Okay IT Dynasty Co, tell us when you can get this customer completed?'" IT Dynasty Co says, "Well we can do it in six weeks." "Okay." So we tell the customer that its mid-July. Well, all of a sudden other things start impacting and now the scope gets pushed back, but yet we've told the customer, "Hey we're gonna be done by such-and-such time." We say, "You need to work on this!" They say, "Well gee we don't have enough people." That's a conflict! They're saying, "Even though we promised this date, we still have to put the other things as priority," and we say, "No we can't put those as priority." And then we have to sit there and renegotiate or argue about ah, "How are you gonna get this done in this amount of time? You don't understand! You're impacting our customer which could mean in the long term, that you as our supplier may not have a customer left, so you need to do something about that!" And, we have to talk about it, and, sometimes when that happens, that's where maybe we get an extra person in because it needs to be done. Well there's a question as to, "Well, who pays for the extra person?" "Well okay, you guys promised you'd have it done at this date. Why couldn't you get it done?" "Oh, well I see it's your person who got the flu, and he was off for a week that impacted it. Well if it's your person who is out for the week, that's not my fault." So then they have to argue about that. Or, "Well gee it was because you guys had something else that came up that impacted it from a business standpoint. We had no control over it." Okay, well then we have to sit there and negotiate, just on that level of the deal. But the conflicts occur, we resolve them.

(Bryan, Director of Outsourced Services at Industrial Solutions Inc.)

In markets and demonstrated in the cases here, the labels "customer" and "vendor" rested upon the employees of both firms constituting their identities. As compared to being part of the same hierarchy, employees of customers and vendors were at odds in various ways in the new social structure. Old colleagues at customers often functioned as internal "subject matter experts (SMEs)" for their management. In this role, employees of customers were responsible for identifying ways of improving the quality of the outsourced work, seeking bids for that work, and helping negotiate its purchase from vendors. More of the time, however, employees of customers were there to offset the added risk in markets by ensuring that vendors – their former colleagues in these inO cases – were delivering the contracted work services and not "slacking" on performing the tasks (Davis-Blake & Broschak 2009; Williamson 1975).

In markets, the vendor's role was responsible for producing only the purchased work in outsourcing contracts. Getting the purchased work in contracts accomplished – often in a lean and flexible labor organization at outsourcing companies – placed a heavy burden on onsite vendors. Lean organization and its effects are discussed further in the next chapters. The duty of delivering only contracted work corresponded with an equally burdensome problem and professional task barely recognized with resources by management with inO. To my surprise, the role of outsourced professionals – rather than the customer's employer – was "charged with limiting resources." This meant outsourced professionals were given the arduous work of changing old colleagues' "expectations" for continuing power and control over the work production and the response level that used to characterize hierarchies. Below, Hillary described this experience working with staff at Diagnosis Hospital, a community hospital who outsourced their IT department in an effort to "save money."

> You were charged with limiting the resources because we went from like 90 people in applications, down to 50. So of course, there was tightening of the pipeline for requests for things to change or for things to be implemented. That was part of the Diagnosis Hospital strategy to save money.
> (Hillary, former Senior Manager at Dynasty Co. Affiliate)

In addition to the burdensome stretching of resources and changing the expectations of customers for access to their "resources," employees of vendors were expected to help identify goods and services that customers did not already pay for that would enhance the work and could be sold to them. Upselling work was a significant expectation for account managers at each client, and it was the source for well-endowed bonus structures at outsourcing employers (I discuss bonuses in detail in Chapter 4). A robust layer of project managers located onsite at customers also augmented the upselling of the vendors' goods and services. Project managers (PMs) developed bids for new work and, if accepted by customers, they monitored the progress and costs on each of them. For example, PMs like Salma at Sourcing Central worked with two other PMs onsite at St. Francis Hospital to bid on new projects and follow each contracted project to satisfactory fruition.

Social interactions with customers changed because outsourced professionals' status shifted to a "vendor," or a "stranger" in the once familiar but now alien physical environment of the customer (Wolf 1950). Similarly to how the vendor is labeled in inO, Georg Simmel's archetype of the "stranger" is exemplified by the Jewish trader (402). The trader is someone who physically occupies a position within a social group for economic reasons, but she or he is not an indigenous member to that group. Simmel emphasizes that this alien quality of the stranger is an important feature in interactions, and social distance or difference is a point of frequent reference by the indigenous group members. As a result, strangers experience both nearness and remoteness in interactions and in relationships to the dominant group. With inO, members of the dominant group were professionals retained as direct employees by customer companies. Many outsourced subjects described their shared conversations, after converting to outsourcing companies, where old colleagues relabeled them with the new identity of "the vendor."

> That was one of the interesting things that some of the techs, or some of the approaches that Technologies Inc. [the customer] took was, "Well you work for us." Which was an interesting twist. You know the same people, "Oh wait a minute you're a vendor, you work for me now! And I say it's going to be this way." And so it's like, "Oh well, yeah I guess that is true. I guess I am a vendor now."
>
> (JB, former Data Center Manager at Tech Leader)

At the onset of inO deals, cultural symbols identified outsourced professionals as people who, although able to participate in the inO environment, were not a part of the customer organization anymore. Concluding the last chapter, I ended by describing the process of taking employees' old badges and reissuing new ones. Badges looked different and (in most cases) prominently signified the vendor or stranger status of the subjects who wore them. Professionals like Brad and Maria, for example, wore bright red badges as vendors for Master Technologies as compared to the green badges worn by Merchant Inc. employees. Because of this, they stood out as vendors in the physical environment of a company "that was not [their] own" (Fran). Many subjects like Fran, a seasoned Account Executive with Tech Leader, described the remote feelings of not "belonging" because of the symbolic, material reminders that were all around vendors while working onsite at customers.

> There's a big difference of walking into a building that is [the customer] Insurance Inc. I sit at their desk, I am a vendor. As much as they want to say I'm a partner, that's nice, but I'm a partner and I don't belong here. I don't! This is not mine. I get a different color badge, it says vendor on it . . . [the customer's] exterior around me is constantly everywhere I look!
>
> (Fran, Account Executive at Tech Leader)

Access to buildings, staff parking structures, and strategic meetings of customers were off limits to vendors too. These symbolic markers and physical constraints reinforced that subjects were "strangers" now to their old colleagues and no longer belonged as part of the customer company.

The new market arrangements impacted interactions between former colleagues. With inO, markets not only conveyed new statuses but they also placed new constraints on some of the interactions between employees of the two firms. Private information about the vendor or the customer company became privileged knowledge and could not be shared with old colleagues. These boundaries constrained subjects' once open and friendly interactions, and many professionals in this sample felt surprised by this because no one had psychologically prepared them for this interactional change.

Before the onset of the outsourcing deal, management assured employees at both firms that nothing about their working relationships would change. Yet, after the outsourcing deal began and subjects had rebadged to vendors, their managers' directives changed. Overseers stressed the new proprietary risks inherent in the market organization and the need to shield private company information about the vendor from the customer. Employees needed to refrain from "gossiping" about anyone in the other company and they needed to treat former colleagues at customers differently. The consequent changes in subjects' interactions with old colleagues seemed dramatic. The analogy of "drawing a line" was a way outsourced professionals described the halt to their casual hallway conversations with old colleagues because of the new internal market.

> You couldn't go to your buddy at Technologies Inc. [the customer] anymore because now you're a vendor. You couldn't talk as freely like, "Well this is what Tech Leader [the vendor] is planning to do." You had to *draw the line* [my emphasis], you know? It was different having to do that.
>
> (JB, former Data Center Manager at Tech Leader)

> So, where before you'd walk down the hall and you'd say to your friend in pathology or your friend in radiology, "Oh man, did you hear what the CEO said? Where is he coming from?!" Noooooooo! (while shaking her head). There was none of that corporate gossip because you weren't corporate anymore. You were a vendor.
>
> (Hillary, former Senior Manager at Dynasty Co. Affiliate)

From the perspective of subjects intimate with deals at outsourcing companies, for the most part however, employees at customers and vendors were expected to maneuver through the different social atmosphere on their own. Executives seemed to have few concerns over how outsourcing relationships would work out in practice on the "edge" of their organizations (Spinuzzi 2015). In this sample, Norm represented a former company division president who described to me his executive leadership's process in deciding to outsource. Below he discussed a logistics outsourcing deal (i.e., trucking and distribution) that he and his leadership team at ChemRegional Inc. decided upon. In this deal, Norm explicitly stated that the working-out process for articulating the new logistics arrangements were left for employees at their physical plants and the trucking employees from various vendor firms who were competing for their business to handle.

> Part of what my central group did [Norm was President and had eight direct reports in his executive team]. . . . We emphasized to the people who won the bids for us, "You need to build a relationship [with our plant managers and staff] because in another 1–3 years, we're gonna consider replacing you or not. We will see how good a job you're doing." So we would tell the plant manager who they were, would tell the local outsourcing company. We would leave it to them to work together.
>
> (Norm, former President of a global region at ChemRegional Inc.)

The big takeaway from Norm and other industry insiders in this sample was clear. In their budgets for outsourcing deals, companies were reluctant about planning and "paying for change management and its costs" (Sheldon). Both professionals who rebadged to vendors and those who were retained by customers were given little "change management" training on how to perceive the market relationship differently and act accordingly in a new social organization – what does outsourcing mean and how does it affect the social organization and the flow of the work? Yet, generally, the responsibility of working-out the new arrangements with inO was just dropped on front-line professionals, who had difficulty conceiving of their new roles without proper training. Subjects across the cases claimed the outsourcing transition, without important institutional guidance, was "very, very difficult" for employees across the new market organization.

> And 600 people all of a sudden ended up at Web Tech . . . it would have worked if those 600 people stayed doing what they were doing [when they were direct employees of Wireless Inc.]. But, unfortunately things changed so fast. . . . And, I think that that created a real issue. When you take people that are embedded in a corporation, and then you don't do any change management of any sort, what changes my behavior?! I mean, there's nothing there to help me in changing that. I'm gonna still think that I'm part of the other company. And that transition was very, very difficult. . . . I think we still have that same relationship right? And you might think I have that same relationship, only to find out I'm keeping your feet to the fire.
>
> (Lynette, former Vice President in human resources
> for Wireless Inc. and then dual Account Manager/Strategic
> Business Unit Manager at Web Tech as part of this deal)

Generally, and in the cases in this sample, many companies outsourced to reduce the costs from their operations. According to Sheldon, a former CIO at Sourcing Central who retired in 2013, any deal that had budgeted line items for change management "sticks out like a sore thumb." Because of the dominant corporate ethos to reduce costs, rarely – in Sheldon's 13-year experience with this company – did customers make decisions to raise their costs by including change management as part of the financial outlay of an outsourcing deal.

> "Here's what's gonna happen. Here's why it's happening. Here's what it means to you. Here's what's gonna happen to you." This is what is meant by change management. . . . Change management to me is helping people, and helping people prepare for and deal with the effect of the change. . . . That's the first thing that gets cut. And I think its penny wise and pound foolish. I used to be responsible for a 285 million budget annually, and change management is less than, it's nothing! It sticks out like a sore thumb if you put it there.
>
> (Sheldon, former CIO at Sourcing Central)

To concur with this large company's behavior, in a recent study the management consulting firm Vantage Partners also found that "relationship management skill development (training, coaching) for staff who have significant iterations with suppliers is a significantly small proportion of investment as compared to allocations for procurement and supply chain effectiveness and capabilities" (Hatcher & Hughes 2015:4). In these cases, companies that outsource spend more financial resources on developing outsourcing plans, finding vendors, and ensuring they comply with contract agreements than they do training their staff on how to interact with and coordinate the work with suppliers. Because customers' cost reduction reasons prompted most inO cases in this study, institutional support and systematic training for the change in social arrangements was sadly missing.

To fill this gap, managers quickly established the collective meaning of the new arrangement. At customers and vendors, they coached former colleagues on how to think about the working-out process. Most importantly, managers were there to help change employees' "mindsets" about their relationship with former colleagues. Like changing any established habit, this was a difficult task to accomplish, especially with limited guidance. So, managers were instrumental in setting the tone for an adversarial meaning to working relationships and the same corresponding posture, which meant either carrying an offensive stance (authoritarian) or defensive stance (procedural) in the working-out process.

At customers, managers were instrumental in helping fashion the new meaning that vendors were "not part of the corporation anymore." They were outsiders and they had a different role in the new organization. Using these new meanings, managers helped former colleagues change how they saw and interacted with the outsourced professional using an authoritative approach or stance.

> It wasn't so much the direct people that we worked with. They didn't think about it until their management told them. Technologies Inc. [the customer] went back to their managers and said, "Now they are vendors." So the relationships that you built, you figured they were the same until management said, "Oh no! They're not a part of our corporation anymore. They work for us. They're now our contractors." So, it did filter down. . . . In some cases, it

put a big rip in relationships, where they didn't know how to deal with you. Before they'd pick up the phone and you'd talk and stuff. Now they didn't know how to interact with you because now their manager's telling them, "It's different! So you have to act differently towards them."

(Fran, Executive Account Manager at Tech Leader)

Directors like Ross and Russell, who worked in governance roles at customer companies after their outsourcing deals began (the Bravado Hospital and Merchant Inc. cases respectively), discussed a psychological transition that occurred among their staff over how they began to view employees of the vendor. They viewed them not as a former colleague and collaborator, but dispassionately and "like a commodity." Both directors described the divisive language of "us and them" that clouded and changed previously cordial and friendly work relationships.

I felt that collectively we [Bravado Hospital management and staff] treated the people that went to the outsourcer differently, that they were more of a commodity, much like you would buy electric or gas. You know, I want to flip the switch, I want the lights to come on, and you send me a bill and I'll pay it. And I think that there was a divestiture on the Bravado Hospital side of the emotional connection to these people who, through no fault of their own, had been loyal employees up to a certain point. I think collectively there were two groups after outsourcing. It was not collectively, "We are information services." As much as we sold it to our constituents as, "We are information services. We're a family here and we'll get it done." But, I really feel behind the scenes there was an "us" and a "them" collective mentality. I hope I wasn't a part of that.

(Ross, Clinical Systems Director at Bravado Hospital)

From the perspective of newly outsourced professionals, customers' approach toward them strongly implied that – in the new market relationship – as vendors they were there to ensure that all the work in contracts was being addressed and completed. Because they represented the customer now, old colleagues needed to "manage" the work of vendors. When the work vendors were doing was not being completed according to the parameters or levels in outsourcing contracts (or their expectations for the work), customers needed to "escalate" the problem. Below, Tanya worked in an account management role for Tech Leader for three years after her business function was outsourced, and she described the amount of problems her former colleagues at Titan Inc. escalated in hopes of getting redress. It made her working life miserable, yet interestingly, Tanya also recognized that some part of the offensive posture her old colleagues were taking toward her and the work by the vendor had a lot to do with the greater job insecurity they now felt after multiple, large deals Titan Inc. had negotiated with outsourcing suppliers.

T: So I'm constantly putting out fires. That was my life for about three years after [the deal began]. Putting out fires. . . . And as they started to roll out a process and you had to learn the process, and then they would audit your projects. So it just kept getting harder and harder and harder over there. Around 2003, there was an announcement at one of the management meetings that they were going to flatten out the organization [Tech Leader]. And I went to my boss and I was, "take me out . . . I've had it!"

J: *You don't feel like they gave you enough education on their processes before you made that transition . . . ?*

T: It might have been in that binder but I didn't have, between that and everything else that was going on. There were a lot of people on the Titan Inc. side who made it adversarial. Remember I said there were two of us managers [back in the hierarchy] and I got outsourced? So he was my counterpart and he was on the phone with me and he started cursing me out and I said, "I'm sorry but you cannot talk to me that way! I will call you later." And I hung up on him. You don't put up with being cursed at but that's how it had gotten. . . . There were other people who were doing something wrong in production for ten years and now they're escalating to get it fixed. You know what I mean? "It's your problem you have to fix it!" So were constantly trying to sift the chafe from the wheat. What's the real problem? . . . So I have to say I wasn't a very good manager those three years because I could just barely function. I was trying to keep, it's like trying to change everything on the plane. You know? The wheels and the wings while you're flying. That's really what we were doing.

J: *Lots of people have talked about that adversarial relationship with a former very-close colleague.*

T: That was part of everybody losing or in fear of their jobs though! They were showing they were of value still to Titan Inc. So that A. they wouldn't lose their job, or B. god forbid get outsourced to Tech Leader! On the next wave. They were going to show that they were invaluable with managing Tech Leader. So I think that's partly driven by fear for most of them.

Through managerial rhetoric, outsourced professionals also learned that an essential meaning of the market relationship was adversarial. Like Don below, managers instructed outsourced professionals to use ticket processes instituted by vendor employers as defensive measures to document their work and avoid potential financial consequences. If service was not satisfactory to customers, explanations and costly financial penalties could be incurred by outsourcing companies because they failed to fulfill their contracted obligations. With the strong possibility of public reprimand (or, per Tanya, "heads being cut" at the largest outsourcing companies), as Hochschild (1983) and Leidner (1993) explained, outsourced professionals quickly learned they needed to convey the normative deference and defensive posturing expected in customer service work.

But, when I was with the Ballast Group [the vendor], we felt like we were playing defense and we had to do certain things to cover our butts. So, some conversation was always around how we can make sure that we're meeting our service level agreements and we are doing what we need to do, from a contractual perspective, to meet the needs of the customer.

(Don, former Senior Manager at Ballast Group)

Yet, because they too were participating in the market and had proprietary goals, employees of vendors needed to control their interactions with customers. Managers reinforced that their employees had to direct customers to use the new ticketing systems. These systems identified new work possibilities as well as designated what work, if approved by customers, would financially benefit the vendor. Thus, managers at vendors reinforced an assertive posture that outsourced professionals needed to take when old colleagues made work requests to them personally and outside of the purview of the formal ticketing processes. Because her manager instructed she take control in her interactions with old colleagues, Courtney, below, described how she internalized the mantra "I don't do anything now without a ticket." In the second quote, Morgan emphasized that outsourced professionals were forcefully trained to perceive their interactions with customers and the new relationship with the new market logic. Being instructed that "everything is billable now" and that any slip-up in procedure could result in loss of revenue, managers reinforced that the vendor accrue financial benefits whenever the customer requests work. Therefore, it was up to outsourced professionals to put their employer's financial interests first in their social interactions with customers.

Well internal at Cloud Inc. [the customer], before people would come up to my desk constantly and ask me questions. Now, they have to have a ticket. I don't do anything now without a ticket. So it's been a matter of retraining the Cloud Inc. population.

(Courtney, Desktop Support at Circuit)

From Bravado Hospital to Ballast Group it changed because now everything is billable on the outsource side. So we were getting our hands smacked for answering the phone . . . it needs to go to the help desk, because the help desk is getting $20 per call. By me answering the phone, they're missing out on money.

(Morgan, former IT Analyst at Ballast Group)

With an adversarial meaning of the relationship cultivated by their managers, both old colleagues and outsourced professionals were coached to use offensive and defensive approaches in their interactions with each other. For outsourced professionals, defense was necessary if delivery of the work to customers was in jeopardy. Offense was necessary if the customer approached you about changing the work in some way. Thus, adversarial meanings shaped the particular interactional approaches former colleagues took toward reworking a new arrangement and articulating work with inO.

"Chewed-up": reworking a new arrangement with inO

As the articulation of work theory (Corbin & Strauss 1993) predicts, reworking a new arrangement with outsourcing was political in nature because employees of customers and vendors struggled over the new ownership and control of the work. Struggle was especially apparent given an adversarial environment, where customers and vendors had different objectives in markets. And because workers were left to work out the new arrangements largely on their own, per all subjects and especially those intimate with the beginning years of a deal(s), as Tanya conveyed in the previous section, the process was difficult and "barely functional" in some cases.

In the process of reworking the market arrangement, employees of vendors described a more political nature to their interactions and the work with inO. The metaphor "chewed up" (or similar signifying language) was used by subjects, like Lynette below, to describe the now politically charged, emotionally taxing, undignified, and unsatisfying interactions they had with former colleagues after they were outsourced.

> I think what was so frustrating to me was, I wasn't satisfying anybody! Wireless Inc. was upset because they weren't getting services, yet they wanted to push back. "I hope you don't mind but we're pushing back on this." "Yes I know but on the other side I'm getting *chewed up* (my emphasis)! Up one side and down the other! Thank you very much!"
>
> (Lynette, former dual Account Manager and
> Strategic Business Unit HR Manager at Web Tech)

The greater politics of work with inO also resulted from customers' lack of understanding that, in contracts, outsourced resources always had finite terms for the scope of work that was now covered. In cases here, most inO deals involved a reduction in the number of human resources and the financial cost of doing the outsourced work – especially over time. Yet after signing the deal, few upper managers at customers "communicated" the reduced service levels in outsourcing contracts to their affected employees.

Fran had been an account manager at Tech Leader for nine years when we spoke. Every year to year and a half, she moved from one customer account to another. A few weeks prior to our interview, Fran had relocated to a troubled inO account at Insurance Inc. where she ran into what she called a familiar, recurring scenario of "customer expectations that are off the chart!" Yet, in her account manager role, they were expectations she must calmly handle. Over the course of this study, the regular problems and conflict that subjects faced from the customer's misguided "expectations" over service were one of the most common themes across the interviews. Unfortunately, with the customers' heightened expectations, vendors were required to engage politically in their interactions with them with the goal of changing or aligning their beliefs about their work with the levels described in the contract. This political work required taxing emotional labor by vendors as they attempted to overcome the conflict from differing expectations with customers.

To many outsourced professionals, the greater political nature of markets was largely invisible from the perspective of executive leadership and the strategic partnership rhetoric about markets, making the task of working-out potential conflicts even more challenging.

> So, and then sitting at the customer location with them sitting right next to you, I mean they're constantly beating you up going "Hey!" you know? I've all these explanations for these people because they're not getting the service that they expected. For one, you didn't sign up for the same services, but you didn't go back to your people and tell them. I mean the whole reason they came to us in the first place is to cut their costs. But there is no expectation back to the end users saying, "Look. We went to them to get a lower cost provider for the services that we're providing. So you're not going to get the same level of service that you expected before." Nobody does that. Nobody communicates on their end anything. So they'll still expect, if I put in a request to get my ID, a new ID, I'm gonna get it the next day. Even though the contracted schedule says I have 2 days to provide this to you. So I get 100 escalations because 100 people put in IDs, they didn't get 'em the next day. So I go to the customer and say "You have to share this stuff with your end users." And they're just like, "Well there's no way I can communicate to all of them, so just deal with it." So not only am I trying to deliver a service, their expectations are way off the chart, and I have all these escalations to take care of as well, so I've just compounded my problem. And, every area that you go into, it's not a simple solution. It's always compounded. And, you get to the point where you say, "How am I ever going to be able to do well in a position like this given these constraints?" And nobody's been able to give me an answer.
>
> (Fran, Executive Account Manager at Tech Leader)

Either procedural or authoritative stances (Corbin & Strauss 1993) give insight into the working-out process with inO. Most outsourced subjects recalled interactions in the working-out process where customers began with attempts to negotiate work directly from vendors, as they were accustomed to in hierarchies. Customers would regularly contact vendors directly, either face-to-face, they approached them from across the hall, or they called them on the telephone. Their strategy to continue in old collaborative work patterns repeatedly failed because vendors emphasized using the new ticket processes, which will be discussed in more detail below. Then, from their elevated customer position, old colleagues began engaging vendors using an authoritative stance. They demanded some desired work from vendors. According to outsourced subjects like Salma, these customers felt they had the power and control to receive the work they wanted when they wanted it, despite the new outsourcing arrangement.

> A comment that I heard from one of my colleagues was, "Well, it doesn't matter. St. Francis Hospital is paying you, so why can't you do what I ask you to do?!" Those types of comments were never spoken before the Sourcing

> Central outsourcing, you know? That feeling of ownership, that now you own the IT department, which really is not the case. We are outsourced IT staff.
>
> (Salma, Project Manager at Sourcing Central)

Other subjects said customers engaged authoritative stances very quickly at the onset of the outsourcing deal, within "days" or a "month." In this circumstance, customers embodied the governance or SME (subject matter expert) role that was part of their new job description in the market relationship. For outsourced professionals like Paul, the assumption taken from the demanding stances of his customers now was they were purposefully trying to undermine the financial goals of the vendor. To capture their heightened political nature, subjects used terms like "heat" to underscore the high emotional tone, demands, and increasing pressure they faced from their interactions with customers in markets.

> Some of them [Paul's former colleagues retained for governance] I promise, within two days of the contract being signed, within two days they were looking for ways to screw the vendor! You know, to make sure that the contractor felt the heat.
>
> (Paul, Workplace Services Manager at Circuit)

Over time and after repeatedly hearing "I can't give you what you want," too often outsourced subjects reported harassing interactions where former colleagues at customers became insistent that vendors do more work because of "the contract!" When customers bullied them and expressed a lack of "caring" toward subjects, in the sociologist Hodson's view, former colleagues reduced the dignity of outsourced professionals and devalued their work (2001). Customers' incessant demands over the work of outsourced laborers sought to deny their "freedom and self-actualization" and, similar to past ways of reorganizing work, reduced the dignity of the people put in this defensive position (Hodson 1996:734; Blauner 1964).

M: It's about demanding work now from these other people [outsourced professionals] that used to work with them.
J: *So these employees are taking an attitude of "You need to work harder?"*
M: Right, and "I don't care if you work through the night you're getting this done, because this is a contract type of thing!" Yeah, it's been a lot of that.

(Maria, Security Analyst at Master Technologies)

From the vendor side of the working-out process, outsourced subjects commonly said customers at all levels in firms in this sample were challenged to accept that ownership and power over important decisions about the work was now under the jurisdiction of vendors. Thus, not only were they designated to deliver outsourced work in contracts but now a central role professionals at vendors played was to leverage and educate customers on their legitimate position of ownership, power, and control over the work in markets. Thus, vendors usually approached their interactions in the working-out process using a procedural stance. Procedural stances and interactions of vendors had to accomplish three outcomes that increased the political nature and tone of their relationships with customers. They included: 1. break customers' expectations of ownership and control over the work; 2. get customers to use the vendors' ticket systems; and 3. limit the resources customers could expect from vendors through the duration of contracts. I call these unexpected and invisible political parts of the interactional work with inO as *market labor*.

Below Paul carefully explained the procedural approach that he took now in interactions with his customers, compared to the collaborative approach he took in the old hierarchy. Paul's explanation exposed how the market logic and its problem of goal incongruence established and shaped new processes and the vendors' interactional strategies. It changed the stances vendors took in relation to the work being requested by their customers. Paul showed just how different the social atmosphere was in an internal market organization compared to the old bureaucracy. The ethos went from "let's go do it!" to one of "but first identify the revenue, arrange to get paid for it from the customer," and then we will go do it.

In markets, outsourced professionals had to walk a fine line in any offensive approach they used with customers. This was because they were a vendor and any secure financial position was the direct result of having satisfied customers. But, they were also charged with "managing (or breaking) the customer's expectations." Many subjects referred to "managing the expectations" of ownership and control by customers as the predominant political work of outsourcing. But, it was imperative for outsourcing companies to upsell new services to existing customers and increase revenues on the account and within their larger business markets (described in Chapter 4). Paul, meticulous in explaining changed relational dynamics with inO, compared the different stances he used in his job in a hierarchy role versus the market role. He also gave examples of interactional strategies he used with customers to accomplish the three desired outcomes of the political work necessitated by the new market: managing the customers' expectations, limiting the resources to them, and getting them to use processes to help upsell services to them.

There's now a whole new process to get things approved, for identifying new revenue, right? Whereas in the past, we would have said, "Hey, here's something that needs to be done. Let's go do it." Well now what we say is "Hey here's something that might be a great revenue generator," because it's outside of the existing contract of the work we used to do. So is it work that needs to be done? Absolutely! Should Circuit get paid to deliver it? Sure! If Concerto Inc. would like us to do that work, we'd gladly bid for the work. See the difference? [*um huh*] And so that's been a big culture change that not everyone has yet embraced. [It is almost two years into the deal.] And it's very hard, it's been easier for me because I moved [from the Midwest to the East for a bigger role on the account]. 'Cause I broke and I went to a whole new job role with a new team. So I'm not sitting there down the hall from Nancy or Bob who used to call me and say, "Hey Paul could you just." Because the tendency is to say, "Yeah sure! I used to do that for Bob, I'll just go do it." Well the reality is I'd have to say, "Well Bob, not really because that's not in the contract. That's not work we deliver. We'd love to do it! And here's the process to make that request so then we can bid for that work." You're taking an already very political process and politicizing it.

(Paul, Workplace Services Manager at Circuit)

When customers began escalating the tone and tenor of their conversation about the changes in the control of work, outsourced professionals utilized a procedural stance to leverage the power of their ownership position in the market and negotiate the customer's compliance to new "ticketing and RFP (request for proposal)" processes that would ensure that the vendor got paid for any new work. Like their staff, account executives at outsourcing companies were also tasked with compelling department heads at customers to recognize the constraints on their financial resources in a market. At her senior management level, Lynette gave a sense of the continuing political saga that was the working-out process to rework the new arrangement in the Wireless Inc. and Web Tech case. She used a procedural stance in her politically charged yet emotionally controlled interactions with her customer Wireless Inc. to get them to: use tickets, manage their expectations of ownership and control of the work, and acknowledge the new limit on HR resources. The added political stress, along with the high expectations of working time in her dual role managing a large customer account and growing the HR business for Web Tech, caused Lynette to quit her job after only one year.

And so this is very difficult to sit there and say, "Ok Jacqueline [signifying me as her customer counterpart at Wireless Inc.], you can no longer look at it that way. You've got to look at it this way. You are a customer and every time you change your mind there's a process and we have to fill out this paperwork." . . . And so the first time when Wireless Inc. asked for something and we said, "Okay. Write down the requirements." They're looking at us saying, "We never had to do thaaat!!" "I understand, but now you do. And tell us what it is you want, and tell us the pieces that you need so that we can tell you how much it's going to cost you." "What do you mean it's going to cost me?!!" "Okay you have a bundle of money, and this is how you got it spread out. Now if you want us to take money away from these, then you need to tell us which projects we're not going to do anymore." And that was, a *real* (she stressed) education for both sides.

(Lynette, former dual Account Executive for Web Tech
and Strategic Business Unit Manager)

The added politics of their interactions in markets peppered interviews with subjects who had varying tenure in jobs with outsourcing. For example, professionals with one year of experience like Lynette and Maria to senior managers with a decade of experience like Fran and Tanya described the greater political nature to their work with outsourcing. The consistency across interviews underscored that the politics in markets was an added element to the work there, and it did not go away. It continued daily because, as Sheldon (a former CIO) implied below, two companies were negotiating around their enduring goal incongruence problem. In an example, the market changed for the customer and now they no longer needed a particular service. Or, perhaps a new technical capability would enhance the customer's operations, and so they want to negotiate the work with the vendor to adopt the new functionality in their business process. Their economic and technological environments necessitated operational changes for customers. And, not to forget, the strategic partnership relationship with vendors had been promoted and sold on its flexibility and the market's purported penchant for meeting the needs of both companies.

> It's exhausting. It wears you out because it's operational and it's grind. It's an everyday, you gotta fight the fight. And every day, when you're dealing with a scenario, the company, not the individual but the company and your contract you wrote with them, I often thought, "Man the supplier must have wrote this contract, it's so sweet." You can put those SLAs [service level agreements] in blind folded. . . . In the end, it's about trying to make things at the micro-level dysfunctional, actually work. What works, at the micro-level, may not work at the macro-level. So, it's not easy.
>
> (Sheldon, former CIO at Sourcing Central)

Additionally, the political haggling involved in reworking the arrangement – or, per Sheldon, the "everyday fight and grind" – endures because a contract renegotiation for the work is always on the horizon. For example, Sally, a Project Manager for Master Technologies, said the customer Mammoth Inc. began exploring the postulates for a new outsourcing deal among their managers in the seventh year of their ten-year IT deal. Whereas, Norm, the former President of a Global Region, foresaw that ChemRegional Inc. would be "bidding their logistics deals out every one to three years and periodically changing them." As described by industry analysts, the terms for outsourcing deals have generally shortened over the past two or more decades and have directly contributed to the growing precarity of work during the same time (Overby 2015; Weil 2014).

> I knew we would actually bid that business out, I mean, they didn't get it forever. But, we periodically changed them. You know, if we weren't happy with their service level, we would have maybe a one–three-year contract with that outsource company. And if they weren't meeting our requirements, we would bid it to other people in the area.
>
> (Norm, former President of a Global Region at ChemRegional Inc.)

The psychological demands of jobs in service occupations have been previously conceived as "emotional labor" (Hochschild 1983). Service jobs require occupants to contain their emotions and abide by the feeling rules of employers and norms of good service. Emotional labor captures some aspects of the political work required in reworking a new arrangement in markets. For example, customers sometimes became irate and pushed back on vendors to deliver new work in contracts at all human costs. As the vendor in the market, outsourced professionals could not react to customers in these exchanges in a similarly irate and offensive manner. Jobs that require more surface acting, emotive dissonance (expression of emotions not felt), and/or emotional labor (emotion management is a formal job requirement) are found to be more stressful for their human occupants. Important from employee and employer standpoints, high levels of emotive dissonance and emotional labor in service work contribute to lower organizational commitment and higher employee turnover rates (Conroy, Becker, & Menges 2017; Grandey 2003).

For vendors, the adversarial market dynamics produced emotive dissonance for them and led to their estrangement from old colleagues at customers. As a result of the political and emotional work, the social conflict, and (in some cases) undignified treatment they endured, most outsourced subjects said the collegiality and attachment they previously had with former colleagues at customers permanently eroded. Paul was especially poignant because his voice exuded resentment through the telephone line when he said he was alienated from former colleagues at Concerto Inc. in the process of reworking a new arrangement with outsourcing. Many others, when asked, simply stated relationships with former colleagues at customers were "strained" and/or just "over."

> (Notes from an un-taped interview.) Relationships with old team members at Merchant Inc. are strained. Front line workers at Merchant Inc. don't trust front line workers at Master Technologies. They treat them like they will steal something, they treat them like thieves. Questioned. They now expect Master Technologies workers to do the impossible; they know this because they did the work before. People that were the closest to Keith, are now the most strained relationships.
>
> (Keith, Senior Manager at Master Technologies)

> The Technologies Inc. folks, if you had any relationships on that side of that, well that's over. They're two different companies now.
>
> (JB, former Data Center Manager at Tech Leader)

In conversations about the persistent actions of former colleagues to cause and escalate problems for them, interestingly, some subjects acknowledged that the level of their cooperation in the working-out process had waned over time in their outsourcing jobs. From a social psychological standpoint, it is not hard to imagine that people chose courses of action to deflect the enduring abuse of others (Hodson, Roscigno, & Lopez 2006; Hodson 1995). For example at Ballast Group, subjects described resisting the ongoing badgering from staff at Bravado Hospital – a highly regarded institution with a culture to match – to satisfy their requests for work favors or work outside of the contracted services. Below Lisa described avoiding confrontation with certain situations until the issue was "escalated" to higher management and she was forced to address it.

> You always felt like you were safe behind the Ballast Group, if that makes sense. So you always want to please the users, which are hospital employees.

You want to make them happy. You want to make sure that they can get the patient care. But, at the same time, we don't report to the same people, so I get to hide behind a Ballast Group mask if I needed to. So, if users are getting irate that something wasn't getting done, you want them to be able to do whatever they need to do, but at the same time, it would be easy just to, "Well, whatever. I'll work on it when I can. I got X, Y, and Z thing going on over here," and then you waited until it got escalated up through somebody and then you're like, "OK, well now I'll work on it."

(Lisa, former Interface Analyst at Ballast Group)

From my conversations with subjects, I did not get the impression that subjects who restricted their cooperation in the working-out process were doing so in a shirking or malicious way. Rather, the ongoing high political nature of the work took an emotional toll and outsourced professionals became inclined to reduce their cooperation with customers to a perfunctory or reserved level. This compared to the consummate cooperation subjects commonly said filtered through the hierarchical social organization before inO. Very likely, perfunctory cooperation levels were not good for work relations, productivity, and the personal satisfaction of workers. It was probably a significant factor in the "hidden" "transaction costs" that have persisted in market organizations through time (Williamson 1975). Per subject testimony, reduced cooperation levels, in part, contributed to the termination or nonrenewal of several outsourcing deals in this sample (e.g., Merchant Inc. canceled their agreement with Master Technologies after only one year; there were several other nonrenewals of IT deals that included Accolade Hospital and Bravado Hospital).

Invisible political work in market relationships

In this chapter, I have argued that the changes to the social arrangement with inO fostered adversarial relations between the staff at customers and vendors. Outsourced professionals were expected to handle the added political and emotional work in the inO arrangement. This work was not acknowledged, planned for, and supported with material resources. And outsourced professionals were not compensated for the added work of its market labor. Thus the market organization with inO represents a more degraded social context and, overall, poorer employment conditions for professional workers.

Scholars in the labor process tradition argue that the way that work is organized in capitalism functions, in part, to estrange workers from one other. For example, studies of factory and contingent work find that the organization of work on the assembly line and different employment designations (e.g., temporary workers, unionized laborers) fostered alienation among people and between groups (Blauner 1964; Henson 1996; Rogers 1995; Smith 1994). As they were directed by their managers and they embraced the new market logic, customers and vendors in this study attempted to leverage work in favor of their employers. Alienation between outsourced professionals and former colleagues at customers resulted from the adversarial relations and interactions from the new organization of work in markets.

Feminist theory explains why scholarship on changed interactions and social relationships with inO has been limited. Scholarship in this academic field describes the invisible nature of interaction and the relational work that is done – especially by women – to produce important social institutions and social processes including the family, the economy, religious traditions, and unionization campaigns (Brodkin 1988; Daniels 1987; DeVault 1991; Fletcher 1999). Because this relational work is not recognized with significant cultural symbols, material, or ideological resources, it has the function of reproducing the historical inequality between social classes and genders. For example, studies of managers and executives describe the unpaid role that wives have played in the careers of husbands as they progress the company ladder (Kanter 1977).

More recently, economic sociologists have begun unpacking the previously invisible relational work that is done to support social and economic activities of all kinds. For example, Zelizer (2012) argues for a relational work approach and identifies several elements to it, including: "1. Distinctive social ties; 2. Set of economic transactions; 3. Media for those transactions; and 4. Negotiated meanings" (151). Findings from my study of the relational work with markets show how the distinctive roles of customer and vendor were adversarial, required interactional work specifically targeted toward negotiating the market organization, and had costly human and organizational consequences from the social conflict in their interactions. Because of these negative relational consequences, companies should openly acknowledge, better plan, and prepare for the more political nature of work in inO markets.

The political work and emotional labor that professionals were required to give to rework the arrangement with inO was unexpected and came with psychological and material costs. Front-line professionals at both firms were forced to negotiate the goal incongruence problem in markets. There were few or no economic, material, or cultural resources on which outsourced professionals could draw upon to feel supported or make their interactions and this work less challenging. This work was invisible, and it degraded the job quality in outsourced labor markets. By failing to recognize the interaction work and compensate people required to rework a new arrangement with inO (i.e., with supportive symbolism, education, and material resources), employing firms on both sides of the market relationship cheapened the value of people expected to do it and the importance of collaborative social relations in the workplace.

Notes

1 In hindsight, many of the directors attending the 2004 OI Roadshow may have had little idea of how work was actually articulated on the front line of their organization in the inO environment. Although the 2004 OI Roadshow allowed me to network and later interview an industry "insider," a Director of Outsourced Services from Industrial Solutions Inc. At another OI event in 2008, I networked and later interviewed another industry "insider," a lawyer with IT Offshore Advising Group. Both acknowledged the added challenges and recurring social conflicts from negotiating the ongoing work between two or more companies.

2 Over the time of this study, press releases, editorials, and news stories have all conveyed the high rates of dissatisfaction with outsourcing. For example, in 2005, I pulled the following report, dated April 19, from the PR newswire: "Outsourcing Falling from Favor with World's Largest Organizations, Deloitte Consulting Study Reveals; Study Shows Hidden Costs, Added Complexity Have Prompted 25 Percent of Participants to Reduce Outsourcing Activities." More recently, in 2013 to 2015, several articles about a decline in IT outsourcing appeared in various publicly accessible journals. This one was published online on October 14, 2015 at the *Wall Street Journal*: "Why Companies Have Stopped Outsourcing IT" (Davenport).

References

Blauner, Robert. 1964. *Alienation and Freedom: The Factory Worker and His Industry.* Chicago: University of Chicago Press.

Brodkin, Karen. 1988. *Caring By the Hour: Women, Work, and Organizing at Duke Medical Center.* Urbana, IL: University of Illinois Press.

Conroy, Samantha A., William J. Becker, and Jochen I. Menges. 2017. "The Meaning of My Feelings Depends on Who I Am: Work-Related Identifications Shape Emotion Effects in Organizations." *Academy of Management Journal* 60(3): 1071–1093.

Corbin, Juliet M. and Anselm L. Strauss. 1993. "The Articulation of Work Through Interaction." *The Sociological Quarterly* 34(1): 71–83.

Daniels, Arlene K. 1987. "Invisible Work." *Social Problems* 34(5): 403–415.

Davenport, Tom. 2015. "Why Companies Have Stopped Outsourcing IT." *Wall Street Journal*: October 14.

Davis-Blake, Alison and Joseph Broschak P. 2009. "Outsourcing and the Changing Nature of Work." *Annual Review of Sociology* 35: 321–340.

Deloitte Consulting. 2005. "Outsourcing Falling From Favor With World's Largest Organizations: Study Shows Hidden Costs, Added Complexity Have Prompted 25% of Participants to Reduce Outsourcing Activities." *PR Newswire*: April 19.

DeVault, Marjorie. 1991. *Feeding the Family: The Social Organization of Caring as Gendered Work.* Chicago: University of Chicago Press.

Fletcher, Joyce K. 1999. *Disappearing Acts: Gender, Power, and Relational Practice at Work.* Cambridge, MA: MIT Press.

Grandey, Alicia A. 2003. "When 'the Show Must Go On:' Surface Acting and Deep Acting as Determinants of Emotional Exhaustion and Peer Rated Service Delivery." *Academy of Management Journal* 46(1): 86–96.

Hampson, Ian and Anne Junor. 2005. "Invisible Work, Invisible Skills: Interactive Customer Service as Articulation Work." *New Technology, Work, and Employment* 20(2): 166–181.

Hatcher, Ashley and Jonathan Hughes. 2015. *Supplier Relationship Management Study: Preview of Select Findings.* Boston, MA: Vantage Partners.

Henson, Kevin. 1996. *Just a Temp.* Philadelphia: Temple University Press.

Hochschild, Arlie. 1983. *The Managed Heart: The Commercialization of Human Feeling.* Berkeley, CA: University of California Press.

Hodson, Randy. 1995. "Worker Resistance: An Underdeveloped Concept in the Sociology of Work." *Economic and Industrial Democracy* 16(1): 79–110.

Hodson, Randy. 1996. "Dignity in the Workplace Under Participative Management: Alienation and Freedom Revisited." *American Sociological Review* 61(5): 719–738.

Hodson, Randy. 2001. *Dignity at Work.* New York: Cambridge University Press.

Hodson, Randy, Vincent J. Roscigno, and Steven H. Lopez. 2006. "Chaos and the Abuse of Power: Workplace Bullying in Organizational and Interactional Context." *Work and Occupations* 33(4): 382–416.

Kanter, Rosabeth Moss. 1989. *When Giants Learn to Dance: Mastering the Challenge of Strategy, Management, and Careers in the 1990s*. New York: Simon and Schuster.

Kanter, Rosabeth Moss. 1977. Men and Women of the Corporation. New York: Basic Books.

Leidner, Robin. 1993. *Fast Food, Fast Talk: Service Work and the Routinization of Everyday Life*. Berkeley, CA: University of California Press.

Ouchi, William G. 2006. "Markets, Bureaucracies, and Clans." In *Sociology of Organizations: An Anthology of Contemporary Theory and Research*, edited by A. Wharton. Cambridge: Oxford University Press.

Overby, Stephanie. 2015. "IT Outsourcing Deal Values Hit 10-Year Low." *CIO*: May 1.

Rogers, Jackie Krasas. 1995. "Just a Temp: Experience and Structure of Alienation in Temporary Clerical Employment." *Work and Occupations* 22(2): 137–166.

Schieman, Scott and Sarah Reid. 2008. "Job Authority and Interpersonal Conflict in the Workplace." *Work and Occupations* 35(3): 296–326.

Smith, Vicki. 1994. "Institutionalizing Flexibility in a Service Firm: Multiple Contingencies and Hidden Hierarchies." *Work and Occupations* 21(3): 284–307.

Spinuzzi, Clay. 2015. *All Edge: Inside the New Workplace Networks*. Chicago: University of Chicago Press.

Thornton, Patricia H. and William Ocasio. 1999. "Institutional Logics and the Historical Contingency of Power in Organizations: Executive Succession in the Higher Education Publishing Industry, 1958–1990." *American Journal of Sociology* 105(3): 801–843.

Vallas, Steven P. 2003. "Why Teamwork Fails: Obstacles to Workplace Change in Four Manufacturing Plants." *American Sociological Review* 68(2): 223–250.

Weil, David. 2014. *The Fissured Workplace: Why Work Became So Bad For So Many and What Can Be Done to Improve It*. Cambridge, MA: Harvard University Press.

Williamson, Oliver E. 1975. *Markets and Hierarchies: Analysis and Antitrust Implications*. New York: The Free Press.

Wolff, Kurt H. (ed). 1950. *The Sociology of Georg Simmel*. New York: The Free Press.

Zalewski, Jacqueline M. 2007. "Discretion, Control, and Professional Careers With Outsourcing Companies." *Sociological Viewpoints* 23: 121–137.

Zelizer, Viviana A. 2012. "How I Became a Relational Economic Sociologist and What Does That Mean?" *Politics and Society* 40(2): 145–174.

4 "It all revolved around numbers"

Greater commodification of the work and culture with outsourcing

Salma (2008) and Tanya (2010)

Salma and I spoke in mid-fall 2008, days after getting an email introduction via my neighbor, a contractor whom she worked with. Salma surprised me. First, when we met in the lobby of St. Francis Hospital – local to the community – Salma was dressed and interacted with me in an expressively gendered way. She wore a youthful dress and knee-high shiny black boots that were eye-catching. Salma smiled warmly while she shook my hand and made me feel at home when we got to her office. She wasn't the typical IT manager type. For example, Salma differed from Dominic, her colleague, who I interviewed later. Dominic was male, older, more casually dressed, and very reserved with his emotions. Yet, like so many of the other male and female IT subjects I spoke with, Salma's greatest enthusiasm emerged when describing her diverse experience as a hands-on technical manager and her dignified treatment of, watchfulness over, and collaboration with her staff in technical systems' implementations and modifications. Primarily, her technical background came from working in IT at a small visiting nurses' office prior to the outsourcing. Also, like most other subjects Salma significantly saddened when she talked about the change in how others perceived and valued her work at a multinational company in the outsourcing industry. She said, "*It all revolved around numbers* (my emphasis)." Salma (and her close colleague Dominic) stood out because of this direct emphasis on the increased commodification of the work and culture at their outsourcing employer Sourcing Central. Furthermore, she described the personal effects of heightened commodification with outsourcing using an intriguing sports-related phrase explaining, "I am made to feel like I don't have 'skin in the game.'"

Meet Salma

Salma was a single mother. Like many subjects I interviewed for this study, her introduction into the field of IT was accidental; Salma came to IT by way of HR. Like most other accidental careers in IT, at the time when computers and software evolution were in their infancy, Salma outwardly expressed the desire to learn more about the evolving information technology systems in her medical workplace. Employers willingly let eager staff they trusted move into technology development and troubleshooting roles. Thus, before the outsourcing of her job, Salma had been the hands-on manager of a small IT department at Home Nurse Care Inc. She was cross-trained on both the "software applications development side and the network side of IT." Multiple times, Salma described herself as the "tinkerer" and the "techie" in our interview, underscoring the passion she felt for the technical, problem-solving qualities in her work. While at Home Nurse Care Inc., Salma stressed the mentorship she gave her staff of four when they collaborated on projects to upgrade their IT environment. Salma reported to the CIO at this organization.

After several years, she learned Home Nurse Care Inc. was merging with St. Francis Hospital. As they prepared for the merger, Salma said, St. Francis management welcomed her and her IT staff. Yet, just before the merger happened she learned that St. Francis was outsourcing all IT staff – including those from Home Nurse Care Inc. – to Sourcing Central. Sourcing Central was a major competitor in healthcare IT outsourcing. At first, Salma was demoted to a systems analyst position. But she was quickly reassigned by Sourcing Central managers to project management (PM), and she was mentored in the new role. Project managers bid for work, plan projects, and keep track of the progress and financial costs of the materials and the work on it. At that time, Salma was managing seven projects, which she said exceeded normative standards for the role. Salma commented during the interview that after three years working in PM for Sourcing Central, she felt stagnant. She was not going anywhere professionally (e.g., to a larger customer account or up a career ladder), and it was "not the role I had envisioned for myself." For Salma this meant that PM was not meaningful like the hands-on technical work and collaboration with others in her previous position.

After speaking with Salma, I met Tanya, another professional with a similar experience in her outsourced field.

By happenstance, I met Tanya in June 2010 at a personal development workshop that a good friend hosted. Two months later, I arranged and drove several hours to interview Tanya at her home. Reflecting her enthusiasm for and experience in strategic roles, Tanya was one of the two longest interviews I conducted for this research project. Like Salma, Tanya embodied a profound enthusiasm for the IT project management work she completed for Tech Leader – "the problem-solving, the consulting with smart people to put together stuff at a high level." Tanya talked non-stop about the many late-nights she had over ten years' time at Tech Leader. In outsourcing, pulling late night working marathons were necessary to bring a system into "production" or a webpage online for a customer. Tanya appeared to me as the self-described "go-to person," "the fire-jumper" that – along with her extended tenure at Tech Leader – had ensured her continuous employment at one of the largest outsourcing companies in a highly competitive industry. Yet, to my surprise, Tanya felt differently about her position. She expected that the "tap on the shoulder" could happen to her on any given day because of the great emphasis Tech Leader gave to "numbers" that got produced within jobs, on accounts, from projects, and in the value of their company stock.

Meet Tanya

Tanya was solidly experienced and a well-educated professional. She lived in an urban area, part of a large urban megalopolis in a 1950s style, cookie cutter, one-story home. Tanya talked about the three generations of her family who currently lived there. In her field of IT and project management, Tanya built an impressive portfolio of IT consulting and technical experiences at several of the largest companies in the financial and technology industries. For six years before the outsourcing, she worked at Titan Inc. Titan Inc. was a large telecommunications company with multiple offices located near Tanya's home. During her six years of employment, Tanya transferred from the billing department to the strategic planning department – or from a cost center to a profit center within the firm. In 2000, Titan Inc. outsourced 3,500 IT jobs to reduce their costs from operations and to focus on further development of their core business including web technology services. With ten years under her belt in the outsourcing industry, Tanya moved into the PM role at Tech Leader with a strategic location in the division of web-hosting. To underscore how core this function was to Tech Leader's revenues, Tanya emphasized the high visibility she had in this area and the "bazillion dollars" it could cost her employer if such web services went offline for even a few minutes.

Tanya gave the impression that she was a strong force of reckoning in her job area and level of work. She also spoke about esteemed colleagues and collaborators she worked with as well as her established reputation as reliable in delivering projects, especially those in dire contract circumstances (when the customer account "was in the red"). Yet to my surprise, this did not give her the benefit of job security from her perspective. The real possibility of having her job cut, according to Tanya, was "always hanging over my head" at Tech Leader. Tanya, in this respect, was like most other professionals employed in outsourcing. Most companies had regular employee layoffs called "resource actions." During our interview, referencing both internally to the company and on customer accounts, Tanya repeatedly described resource actions with the poignant metaphor "cutting heads." Similar to many others in this sample, Tanya identified that the increased commodification of work and the regularity of job cuts created fear among outsourced professionals. It manifested in a workplace culture of hyper-vigilance toward the amount of work assigned, competition among staff, and the undermining tactics used between employees to maintain tenuous jobs with outsourcing firms.

An important part of this research study was to develop an understanding of outsourcing's effects on professional work, workplace culture, the meaning of the work, and the self and identity of professionals. As they contemplated new positions with outsourcing companies, professionals always discussed what they were told about the benefits of working as technicians for a technology company. Foremost they were moving to a technology firm, a company whose core business represented the work that outsourced professionals would be employed to do. There, professionals would experience the most cutting-edge technologies in IT or HR work – i.e., aspects of work that technicians would find most appealing. With this mindset, professionals would employ these new technologies because the job they occupied at the IT or HR outsourcing company represented a profit center within the outsourcing firm. Profit centers are those departments that produce and sell the commodities that constitute the revenue-generating activities for the company and most directly impact the profitability of the firm.

By inference then, outsourcing companies would allocate more financial resources to profit centers and their staff to develop, market, and institute the technology processes and systems that defined the current "best practices" in the field. Professionals working for outsourcing companies therefore could learn and work with others on the most current technology and technical processes in a variety of business operations and industries. In the case of IT staff, these opportunities would especially support core professional identities as technicians and problem-solvers. Thus, subjects would find many more job opportunities and career paths in business services when technology work was situated at the profit center and became the valued commodity. Nevertheless, the stories and explanations of professionals in these situations refutes this idea and its logic.

For most of the subjects across 20 in-house cases in this sample, a reinvigoration of professional jobs and careers did not occur with outsourcing. This chapter seeks to explain why.

"It all revolved around numbers": greater rationalization and commodification of the work with outsourcing

The title to this chapter and section – "It all revolved around numbers" – refers to the greater rationalization and the commodification of work in an outsourcing environment. In sociology, formal rationality involves the "rational weighing of utilities to costs," and it is the dominant ideological approach institutions and people use to make decisions for social action in everyday life today (Parson 1947:32). In this study, formal rationality explains the great scrutiny outsourced work received in these cases, the continuous processes of attributing quantitative values to it, and the highly flexible and lean structure of the service organization at outsourcing companies. Commodification, from a Marxian perspective, involves the shift in the focus and meaning of work from its personal use value to the emphasis today on the exchange value of work in markets (Tucker 1978). A key question for most persons obtaining work today – and one that stresses work's significant commodification in modern society – is [Fred, my dad, asking me] "how much are you going to make at this job or writing and publishing this book?" With outsourcing, I show that companies have instituted the structural means for squeezing every bit of exchange value out of labor and the service requests of their customers in order to "make the outsourcing model work." As a result, its greater rationalization and commodification at outsourcing companies opposed its promise for work revitalization in the two professional fields of IT and HR.

Work became more rational and commodified with new codified and quantifiable measures, a more flexible social organization, and new roles that were required because of the internal market environment. Professional work that was previously invisible in hierarchical organization at customers was recognized, codified, and assigned explicit quantitative values in outsourcing contracts, "service level agreements," and other contract "metrics." Work and people were reorganized into "silos" of job functions at outsourcing companies (e.g., identity management, security). They were seemingly dispersed but simultaneously networked between and across clients and regions while enabling service delivery and the application of standard work procedures to customers in a "just-in-time" manner. Account managers were assigned to one (or more) customer(s) to monitor progress on projects, scrutinize costs on the customer account, and upsell services to them. Finally, the roles of governance and project managers supplemented the onsite social structure and correlated with the new market environment and its emphasis on rationalization and commodification of the work.

To start, most customer companies rationalized their decision to outsource publicly with numbers and quantitative values. For example, outsourcing lowered the cost of the work because outsourcing companies had expert knowledge and "best practices" that would enable the work to be completed more quickly and efficiently. Or, using similar logic, outsourcing changed labor from a variable cost to a fixed cost that was more easily planned for in the administration of the company's resources. Using numbers made for easy comparisons of the cost of outsourcing work compared to the cost of directly employing workers. Numbers were also an acceptable explanation in a society with strong basis in ideologies and norms of formal rationality (Parson 1947). To give an example, in 2004, a short news story reported that Merchant Inc. had recently signed an outsourcing deal with Master Technologies for a total contract value of 1.6 billion dollars. The public report stated Merchant Inc. would save $40 million a year over 10 years. This remark implied that outsourcing significantly lowered the cost of the work, and – for this reason – it made sense to most people for the company to make the decision to outsource.

At customers, rationalization and commodification with outsourcing the work meant all the business processes and systems that were migrated to and completed by the outsourcing company were identified, quantified in comparable ways (e.g., percentages and times), and assigned an exchange value. In deciding to outsource, customer companies spent significant time locating an appropriate vendor and identifying, considering, and rationalizing all of the parts of the IT or HR function that would be sold and migrated to the outsourcing company. The business management community called this investigative process "doing due diligence." The phrase "due diligence" carries great weight in managerial circles in a market environment.

Russell – the Director of IT Security at Merchant Inc. and involved from the inception of the company's idea to outsource – said that preparing for outsourcing took more than a year's time and required ample research and work. Russell gave a sense of the extensive preparation involved in deciding on outsourcing deals at customers and, in so doing, showed the great rationalization of the work with outsourcing. In order to know what work was being sold and purchased between the customer and vendor in the market relationship, ideally everything about the work involved or affected by outsourcing must be considered and documented. If not, there would be serious ramifications for the production of work, for its future cost, and for holding the vendor accountable for providing it.

J: *What was involved in preparing for the information technology outsourcing at Merchant Inc.?*

R: *A lot of preparation* (Russell stressed). I mean, initially, selecting the vendor out of the five finalists. We had to come up with our own set of questions for every specialty [in IT]. Ask them how they did, what they did, show us examples of how you do this to make sure that we were giving everybody equal weight. We had them on a matrix, what's the responsibility, here's the five finalists, how do they rate from one to five? You end up with a quantitative value of how you selected the vendor you selected. So, a lot of preparation in that. And then when they actually signed the contract with them, then came all the work of coming up with the SLAs [service level agreements], the operating plan, how it was gonna work. So it was an awful lot of preparation involved in the relationship. 'Cause you have to document everything you do. When you think about it, it just takes a lot of time to sit there and think of EVERY *process* (Russell stressed), in a certain department. How that works, what's the flow, what's the interfaces? Get that down on paper because that's what they're going to be telling you they're going to do for "X" number of dollars. And you have to determine, "Okay how are they going to prove that they're doing it?" And that's the SLAs. So, it's just a lot of prep work involved. I mean it's a hell of a lot of work for the year prior and the year, maybe the following year for outsourcing.

In summary, it is essential for customers to document and monitor the work being outsourced because they are purchasing it from a market. Market institutional logic is "focused on the accumulation, codification, and pricing of human activity" (Friedland & Alford 1991:249). In theory and practice, markets are governed by norms of self-interest (Thornton, Ocasio, & Lounsbury 2012). Historically, markets have had notable problems delivering the work outcomes both parties expect from the agreement (Williamson 1975). Companies and management understand this history when they spend considerable time doing "due diligence" preceding an outsourcing deal.

In scholarship on economic organization, compared to hierarchies, markets have been described as yielding problems, called "transaction costs" which are the unexpected and added costs of market organization. Because of this, markets have a higher susceptibility to fail. In two hypothetical examples, transaction costs can manifest from vendor behaviors like slacking on product or service delivery or from cost problems that arise from incomplete contracts. When I first began research in 2005, in an April 19 PR Newswire survey conducted by Deloitte Consulting LLP of 25 multinational corporations (half Fortune 500 companies) found that 70% of them had negative experiences with outsourcing and 25% of the sample had discontinued some outsourcing relationships because of its "hidden costs". Numerous business sources such as *Forbes* and the *Wall Street Journal* have continued reporting the persistence of problems in outsourcing (Davenport 2015; Sealock &

Stacy 2013). From the experiences of the subjects here, it is the norm for markets to foster self-interested behaviors among people and firms on both sides of the transaction who perceive they must protect the financial well-being of their employer companies. This idea was explained to me during most interviews; subjects almost always discussed the "conflict between customers and vendors over differing expectations" on the scope of the outsourced work to be delivered. Social conflict on the front line between the two firms reduced the general trust there and, in several cases, it led to (early) termination of the outsourcing deal. Merchant Inc. ended the deal after one year and other deals here were not renegotiated so the work and people were brought back under the direct control of customers.

To protect both parties in the outsourcing deal then, the market relationship was conceptualized, quantified, monetized, and controlled through a service contract and in tasks and roles that enabled clear understanding and measurement of the work being exchanged. Thus, in the overall theme of the chapter, the work and culture became more rationalized and commodified due to the new market organization. Unfortunately, the commodification had implications for the satisfaction and meaning of the work and the professional identity of many subjects employed in outsourcing.

In contracts, the work was most often conceived in terms of the "service levels" the customer expected the vendor to provide. Russell gave several examples of a service level agreement (SLA) in the Merchant Inc. deal including:

> With the exception of scheduled downtime, the network will be available 99.99% of the time. Moving or changing computers and network lines, or adding a new employee in a software application will occur within two business days.
>
> (Russell, former IT Security Director at Merchant Inc.)

SLAs were conceptual, descriptive, and quantifiable with numbers for easy comparison and control. Numbers made the commodification process transparent so that customers could easily hold vendors accountable for services, and laborers at all levels in outsourcing were better evaluated and controlled.

Contracts also itemized and quantified penalties outsourcing companies incurred when service levels were not met. For example at the beginning of the chapter, Tanya implied Tech Leader would incur a "bazillion dollars" in penalties if the web services the company provided their customer base failed for even a few minutes. Furthermore, in my interviews subjects often described other "metrics" or "benchmarks" found in contracts. When contracts included installing new technology systems, outsourcing companies guaranteed they would meet particular deadlines and quantifiable targets in the project implementations. The end goals of these projects, commonly, were planned job losses. As Fred explained in the Technologies Inc. agreement with Tech Leader,

> By such and such date, a system would be installed and running. It will have automated this many jobs, and this many people will be gone.
>
> (Fred former Data Center Manager at Tech Leader)

Another important way in which the work in outsourcing became more rationalized and commodified was through changes to the social organization. Especially the case at the largest outsourcing companies, the social organization included "functional silos" representing the different areas in IT or HR – e.g., identity management in IT and compensation in HR. Each area had hierarchical levels of experts that created flexible, "just-in-time" staffing structures to support the delivery of necessary services to multiple customer accounts in a region. For example in the Merchant Inc. case Brad joined an IT security silo, moved up one level to "expert," and joined a group of 15 colleagues who worked from home to resolve escalated problems for a group of clients in the nearby metropolitan region. Functional silos helped outsourcing companies negotiate the delivery of all of their contracted services despite continuous employee attrition and regular company-instituted layoffs. Not only did functional silos utilize flexible "just-in-time" labor methodologies to meet nonstandard work requirements, functional silos also ensured that employees expended only the necessary or most exact amount of human resource labor to do the contracted work. Therefore, the outsourcing company incurred only the necessary and minimal costs.

The social organization also changed to meet the administrative "governance" needs of the new market organization. Markets meant the delivery of contracted work and its cost had to be monitored and scrutinized. As I described in Chapter 3, employees' relations differ in markets. Because of the nature and norms of markets, relations across organizations were inherently proprietary, adversarial, and were often strained. Additionally, requested work by clients in markets – not currently being paid for – had to be sold to them. These services had to be rooted out, the work needed to be bid on by vendors, and approval with the promise of compensation by customers had to be obtained. For this capacity, customers were assigned an account executive or account manager who monitored the delivery of outsourcing services and acted as the primary contact at the outsourcing company for customers.

Because of added governance, work was vigilantly scrutinized under the microscope at outsourcing companies. Account managers ensured that applications and business systems were efficiently installed at clients and maintaining those new systems were kept to a minimum cost. Fran, an Account Manager with extensive experience at Tech Leader, suggested that her employer struggled to keep the cost of most contracts low because contracts were initially priced to be sold but not priced according to the actual cost of delivering the work. Meeting the numbers for profitability margins set on an outsourcing account was another primary concern of account executives and managers. Fran and Tanya – both Account and Project Managers at Tech Leader – stressed they continuously scrutinized the costs of delivering the work on an account or project to ensure that they were not exceeding a predetermined ratio of costs to necessary revenues, or "tolerances." As Tanya implied below, account managers who exceeded the permitted tolerances for too long did not last in their jobs at outsourcing companies. To emphasize the level of scrutiny accounts and account managers endured, for outsourcing companies like Tech Leader, "too long" could be as little as two weeks.

When we go in and price it, we price it so that it will be sold, not that we can deliver. And secondly is, there's so much pressure on the accounts to deliver, and when they don't, what do they do? They take more costs out. And costs come from people. . . . You know the contract was written incorrectly if the sales guy wanted the commission. So, they agree to a contract that we, no way we can deliver. But now, I'm at a point where I have to now look at India, and Czech Republic, and Hungary, and Latin America, to take over some of my services because the people cost is so much cheaper over there.

(Fran, Executive Account Manager at Tech Leader)

You would have these regular grain reports and if your finances were, they had these tolerances, so if your finances were like, "Wow! Within those ranges then you were great." But if you were in danger, like 2% on being near either end of the range, then you might be yellow. If you were outside the range then you would be red, and God forbid if you were red! Then you had to go in front of people explaining why you were red and what you were going to do about it. Then you would go back the next week and God forbid if, it was like two weeks later, you'd have to explain why you were still there.

(Tanya, Project Manager at Tech Leader)

To offset the costs of delivering the work in contracts, the goals of Account Managers always included increasing the profitability levels on each customer account. Primarily, this meant securing new revenues by upselling more business services to their existing customer companies. Per account managers here, outsourcing companies placed heavy emphasis on upselling services to customers; there were lucrative bonus structures in place at outsourcing companies to do just that. As Lynette explained below, the bonus structures helped keep employees accountable to the primary aim of outsourcing companies – selling more of their goods and services. In her words, outsourcing companies were "built to sell." Bonuses underscored the heavy market logic that drove the greater commodification of work and culture at outsourcing companies. Below, an Account Executive at Tech Leader (Fran) and a dual Account Manager and Strategic Business Unit Manager at Web Tech (Lynette) stressed the emphasis on upselling and increasing revenues for outsourcing companies by regularly rewarding those professional staff responsible for fulfilling this significant role.

How well the overall account does as far as GP [gross profit], revenue, customer satisfaction, and my individual ranking. My at-risk money, or what Tech Leader calls it at-risk money [her potential bonus], is anywhere from 10% to 33% of my salary. So if you're on an account that does really well in the finance and sales you can get 33% of your salary in a bonus.

(Fran, Executive Account Manager at Tech Leader)

At Web Tech, for me the bonus plan worked out beautifully because I was paid on a monthly basis. It was based on my P and L [profit and loss]. On a quarterly basis, I was given a bonus for my revenues. And then on a yearly basis, I was given a bonus on my overall performance. So it made me accountable.

(Lynette, former dual Account Manager and
Strategic Business Unit Manager at Web Tech)

To support this revenue-growth prerogative, outsourcing companies increased the presence of project managers either onsite at clients or in centralized regional locations. Project managers' (PM) role was to put together bids for any new work requested by existing customers. Bids consisted of an accounting for: labor costs for delivering the work, the cost of any new technologies, and the costs for maintaining the services and any other ongoing support. Bids included profit markups on these cost items. To ensure the cost of delivered work was within acceptable profit ranges, PMs also closely coordinated tasks and monitored the costs and progress of projects at customers. Signifying their importance, subjects like Salma found outsourcing companies like Sourcing Central had extensive training and provided significant mentorship to professionals occupying PM roles.

Finally, because of the risks historically associated with markets, outsourcing companies instituted new "ticketing (or work order) processes" and governance roles to scrutinize and squeeze every earned penny from their contracts with customers. New ticketing processes significantly changed interactions between outsourced professionals and their former comrades who were part of "stay back teams" at customers. Almost always, subjects mentioned "tickets" when I asked them how the work had changed. From the view of customers and the outsourced, tickets represented an "obstacle" to getting work done. As such, subjects said it was the source of social conflict between employees of the two companies (discussed extensively in Chapter 3). Ticketing systems symbolized the new proprietary nature of the outsourced work. First, they documented the work that outsourcing companies completed as part of the contractual services they provided to customers. Second, and more importantly, tickets helped find the work that was not accounted for in the outsourcing contract. Vendors then bid on the excluded work and, if accepted by customers, the revenues on the given account increased.

Various systems in outsourcing conceived and organized professional workers to sell their labor power to the exact parameters approved and paid for by customers. Labor power in outsourcing experienced greater rationalization and commodification with an applied market logic that codified and priced it for the purpose of growing markets, margins on accounts, and accumulating profits.

Next, I discuss how the application of rationalization and the commodification of labor power manifested in the work and the workplace culture with outsourcing.

"Just a number": work and culture with outsourcing

Outsourced professionals who worked onsite at customers were universally challenged to describe any unifying company culture at outsourcing companies. This was because of logistics and because outsourcing companies did not spend the resources to develop any sort of institutional knowledge of the company among professionals that were located onsite at customers. Subjects came up with creative ways to describe a "nonexistent culture" with outsourcing companies. Their descriptive metaphors included: they worked at "an outpost, a distant organization, or an island somewhere," the culture was "sterile," there was "nothing to put your arms around," they felt like "foster children or step children to the larger company," and they felt "forgotten." One analogy seemed lifted from the film *Wizard of Oz* when Lisa, formerly an Integration Analyst at Ballast Group, said that she and her colleagues felt that mandates from management came from some "man behind the curtain." These responses gave the strong idea that outsourcing companies cared very little about the people they employed onsite at customers, what the effects of heavy commodification and continuing job contingencies had on their well-being, or if the work they completed was perceived as meaningful to them. In this section I discuss how the new measures of commodification, lean and flexible social organization, the roles with outsourcing, and their underlying market logic helped redefine the work and shaped the barely there culture professionals experienced at onsite locations of customers.

As defined in Thornton, Ocasio, and Lounsbury (2012), the outsourcing of work was characterized with an institutional logic shaped exclusively by the market. This is especially so because of the context for outsourcing deals. Industry growth had occurred and continues because of the rationale of customers seeking outsourcing services. Customers outsourced jobs to cut the costs of their operations. They then focused more upon core areas of the firm with the goal of "innovating" (Norm) and growing their own product and service markets.[1] Because of that context, there were periodic targets to meet whereby the number of people and costs in most outsourcing deals were reduced. Additionally, many finalized contracts were priced "to sell," meaning that the contract value was too low to cover the actual costs of delivering the work. For these reasons, the market logic of rationalization, commodification, and profitability were particularly salient in the outsourcing environments in this sample. Cutting employee costs became imperative when the vendor promised to: 1. deliver best practices in fields, 2. reduce the costs of producing this work, and 3. start at a cost disadvantage on many outsourcing deals.

In addition to reducing costs by eliminating employees, production costs were lowered significantly through applying "remediation" processes. Business processes were remediated when outsourcing companies applied their expert technologies and methods to business processes at customers and both standardized and automated the work. To accomplish their remediation goals, outsourcing companies required strict observance to their related business process protocols, a lean and flexible labor force, and the as-needed leveraging of knowledge and business tools from across customer sectors to deliver work within time frames formalized in contracts and SLAs. This was the context for the work changes, and this context is what heavily shaped the culture and experiences in jobs at outsourcing companies.

At its very essence, outsourcing changed professional work. With outsourcing and related to the market context, subjects emphasized their employers' greater control over new work processes. Systems of market control may be a new evolutionary stage in managements' control systems over the labor process (Braverman 1972; Edwards 1979; Kunda 2006). In the outsourcing environment, the emphasis in work was on SLAs in contracts, ticket systems that registered requests to change work or to fix problems, and "change management" procedures that systematically remediated business processes. With outsourcing, these control processes corresponded with reduced professional discretion and autonomy over work and more control by employers (Zalewski 2007).

According to subjects, SLAs dominated the conversations and social action in the outsourcing environment. Account managers from outsourcing companies met regularly with governance staff from customers to discuss SLAs and the vendor's performance on each one of them. If the vendor's performance fell below the benchmark set in an SLA, penalties would (generally) be assessed. Subjects stressed that SLAs were "driving" what mattered for work goals with outsourcing. They impacted the approach professionals took to complete work and how it was evaluated by management. As Donald wryly noted below, when you create an SLA, you must report on it regularly. The incurred financial penalty of Ballast Group (the vendor) when it missed one SLA in its contract with Bravado Hospital was $17,000 per violation. The heavy emphasis on SLAs with outsourcing underscored the great commodification in conceiving the work and shaping the culture around it.

> There were weekly meetings between the account executive on the Ballast Group side and the leadership on the Bravado Hospital side. And, anytime SLAs weren't met, it was usually a $17,000 penalty for the month. At the end of the month, they produced an SLA report and if they missed something like their first call resolution, for example, at the help desk, then it should be a $17,000 penalty or that's $17,000 less that Bravado Hospital would have to pay that month. There would always be an SLA missed because there were a god-awful number of SLAs. It was way too many that should have ever been written into a contract because you've got to report on them and manage them and then make them every month. If an SLA was missed but there was some extenuating circumstance, then Bravado Hospital would let it go. So, there was some negotiating. And ultimately, that was driving how we worked and how we operated on the Ballast Group side. It was all about making the SLA and, if we didn't make the SLA, doing some CYA to cover why we didn't make it. It changed the work environment.
>
> (Donald, former Senior Manager at Ballast Group)

Another way in which subjects explained the greater commodification of work was through outsourcing's market logic embedded in new steps of initiating and completing work and change requests – AKA "help desk tickets." From a commodification perspective, tickets and resolution times for the problem documented the billable hours of outsourced professionals, and they were used to evaluate the vendor's actual performance on SLAs. Does the vendor have adequate dedicated personnel that handle this work? How much time per week or month was involved in meeting this need? Was the vendor responding to a ticket on a particular system in the time contractually agreed upon? Tickets also helped identify new work that fell outside of the work parameters in contracts which were already being paid for by customers. Vendors therefore could bid on that work and, if customers approved, they increased the vendor's revenues on the account. Most important for the greater commodification of the work with outsourcing argument was: the work was getting done, the vendor had proof of it, and any work that was not being paid for was not being doled out to customers for free. The decision to comply with work requests was not under the discretion of IT or HR professionals in outsourcing (Zalewski 2007).

Doing work that was not paid for by the customer had serious ramifications for vendors, and this was especially true in large outsourcing deals like the one between Concerto Inc. and Circuit. As Paul so clearly described in our interview (see below), laws existed that protected vendors and customers in a market relationship. While companies did their due diligence to plan for services they would be outsourcing, it was also assumed that not everything would be accounted for and that presumptions about what the work entails would be made (on both sides of the transaction or for both buyers and sellers). Employees of outsourcing companies could incur significant financial obligations for their employers through their onsite work actions. If the outsourcing vendor completed a task not covered in the contract from the beginning of the agreement at one customer location, they became obligated to provide this work at the other customer locations too. Because of this, professionals employed by outsourcing companies were always being warned by managers about "the risk of giving away business." As discussed in Chapter 3, especially in the initial years, managers on both sides of markets and former colleagues at customers helped to create an intensely political atmosphere for the newly outsourced.

What rolls down to us from our mid-level management is, "You can't do anything without permission!" Because, you, YOU (Paul stressed) don't want to be the manager that took the risk of giving away the business! Here's the classic, and I hear this all the time. The moment you say "Yes" at your site, that'll mean you obligated your local resources to deliver that work. Now, you've obligated the whole company to deliver that work. Because Concerto's going to come back and, there's a phrase they use all the time called "Whereas, as is," meaning, if you did it before, you gotta keep doing it. So, so even if it's not quote "in the contract," it's a service you were always delivering therefore you must deliver it. At no additional cost. So now the problem is, if Circuit has obligated itself at one facility, Concerto Inc. can come back and say, "Well now wait a minute. They're doing it at [Midwestern town.] You gotta do it here!" You don't want to be the manager that puts all the other managers in that position. Right? That's the added complexity now, of having to walk this fine line. You *never* (he stressed) want to say "Not in the contract." But you oftentimes have to say, "We'd love to do that if you put in the request." Because it could be additional revenue.

(Paul, Workplace Services Manager at Circuit)

Outsourcing companies were highly process-oriented, according to subjects, and especially focused on labor processes and systems known as "change management" among IT professionals. Change management was an approach outlined by the Information Technology Infrastructure Library (ITIL), a go-to resource for knowledge, frameworks, and "best practice" methodologies (i.e., the most systematic, efficient, and effective) for IT departments to utilize when they implemented new systems and processes in the company. For outsourcing companies, systematically and quickly rolling out their expert business processes and systems was to their financial advantage. These systems (eventually) standardized and automated the work, making it cheaper to produce for customers. Per former industry executives like Jay, "automation is why an outsourcing company can do the job." Accordingly then, any work related to change management was the strategic work outsourced professionals were doing for their employers.

It's a big leverage thing. So, like in the data center here, there are 20 people that will run an operation for over a thousand hospitals. Well that's a thousandth of what the hospitals would have to spend doing it themselves. And that's done with automation and a lot of backroom people who generate software and tools to allow those 20 people to run that operation. So, it's all business and leverage, leverage, leverage. That's why an outsourcing company can usually do the job is leverage. . . . [In comparison to consulting services, with] [o]utsourcing . . . the leverage is incredible.

(Jay, former Executive VP of a division at Sourcing Central)

Because of its strategic nature, as Davetta described below, outsourcing companies mandated strict adherence to their change management systems.

They had very intensive training on their culture and how they do business. And some of the things that were just non-negotiable, as far as practices within Master Technologies. They did in-depth training on, "these are the systems that we use. These are the processes that we follow. They are non-negotiable. If you don't follow them they can be reasons for termination." So you learned.

(Davetta, Team Leader Identity Services at Master Technologies)

Another important way that outsourcing companies applied market logic with outsourcing was by way of instituting the lean and flexible social organization of their labor resources. This included the use of lean production staffing and flexible job silos representing work area specializations (e.g., clinical systems or integration services in healthcare IT). Professionals in silos came together to quickly tackle a problem that front-line workers on a customer account escalated to a higher-level group of experts in the region. Lean staffing was both the result of employee attrition, and it was purposefully induced by outsourcing companies. Almost every professional I interviewed talked about the high attrition levels of employees at outsourcing companies. They used common phrases for contingent workforces like "here today, gone tomorrow" or metaphors like "moving ship" to convey the high mobility of labor at outsourcing companies.

> On Accolade Hospital's part, I don't think there was a lot of desire to get close or to mingle with us because we were just always a moving ship, people coming on and off you know?
> (Hope, former Telecommunications Manager at Accessible Hardware)

Within the first months of a contract, typically the labor landscape was littered with people who left their jobs. Per subjects' descriptions, outsourcing employers did not care much about losing employees nor did they perceive high attrition levels as a problem for the company in satisfying the requirements in their contracted obligations. Attrition helped outsourcing companies meet their urgent and greatest goal of reducing costs as soon as possible on any new customer account. To make up for the work gaps from employees who quit at customer sites, employers required professionals who remained on the account to do more work.

Outsourcing companies also reduced the number of employees on a customer account or across a job function in a region rationally, purposefully, and regularly. This was a continuous theme across my interviews. For a customer account, outsourcing companies developed exact target ratios for revenues in relation to costs. To meet the various compartmentalized targets, regular employee layoffs were executed to reduce costs on a customer account, across accounts, and internal to job functions within the home office locations of the outsourcing company.

> You're putting that work up for bid and having people compete. Those companies are going to try to do whatever they can to try to cut back costs so that they can win the bid. . . . So, from that standpoint, you realize that you're a pawn in that vendor's desire to get the contract and in Bravado Hospital's desire to get the most bang out of their buck. So, that's never going to work in your favor. It's always going to mean either you lose your job or you lose part of your team or you lose budget or something, just because everything is drawn towards scaling back costs.
> (Steve, former IT Analyst at Ballast Group)

Tech Leader (one of the biggest firms in outsourcing) was represented in three cases in this sample (e.g., Technologies Inc., Titan Inc., and Trading Inc.). *All* subjects employed by Tech Leader described regular or planned "resource actions" (i.e., employee cuts) on their account. Resource actions occurred as a consequence of excessive costs on an account, recessions and poor "Wall Street quarters" (Tanya), or the vendor's declining markets in selling services. Other layoffs resulted from not achieving the metrics and timetables listed in contracts.

Outsourcing companies were constantly reassessing and resetting the profit ratios on customer accounts and in their internal departments. By constantly evaluating staffing and reducing their levels through layoffs, outsourcing companies leveraged numerical flexibility. Outsourcing companies were effective stewards of "numerical flexibility" or methods that brought financial benefits through reduced labor costs (Smith 1994; Peck & Theodore 1998). Subjects reported that the "numbers" on an account or on a new project were often scrutinized (weekly, monthly, quarterly, and so on) to help ensure the profit and cost margins were within the acceptable range. If not, Project Managers like Tanya in one of the introductory features, could be pulled and replaced with "fire jumpers" (i.e., people experienced and proven able to salvage projects that were losing money).

Eliminating staff also helped outsourcing companies achieve their overarching goal. Upper-management subjects referred to the "prize" in outsourcing as obtaining "economies of scale" or "leverage" (subjects Gerri, Russell, and Jay all discussed this goal of outsourcing companies). Essentially, outsourcing delivered standard services with a minimum number of staff to a considerable or growing market base. In accordance with the strategic management plan, periodic employee job cuts occurred through the term of contracts. When projects to standardize work were accomplished, the number of workers could be reduced and the level of profitability would increase.

In addition to regular layoffs, outsourcing companies utilized job silos to obtain the financial benefits from a lean and flexible workforce. In job silos, professionals in a job function (e.g., data centers in IT) were located across a region but networked, on-call, and able to report into designated digital spaces to provide knowledge, technical support, and solve problems as needed within the company or at customers. In this way, outsourcing companies capitalized financially on the numerical flexibility of lean labor resources and the "functional flexibility" of job silos (Peck & Theodore 1998; Smith 1994).

> At Master Technologies it's a big network of people, tools, and experience. You can tap resources within the company on other accounts to help you with a certain task or a certain product, or that type of thing. And they call them LERMS, you can contact LERMS from different accounts and they come to your aid to give you education about this tool or this process or this task. . . . And that's a really good thing with outsourcing overall that they tap knowledge from the whole company not just in an immediate work group.
> (Maria, IT Security Analyst at Master Technologies)

Using social networks, information on how one company performed a business process was shared with employees working at other customer sites. For IT professionals, the processes of learning and sharing one's expertise in digital meeting spaces like "LERMs" was the biggest benefit they valued with work and jobs at outsourcing companies. I would argue these collegial networks and meeting spaces represented the promise of work revitalization with technical outsourcing. However, such practices also demanded work speedup. Significantly, this flexible labor structure and strong pattern of information sharing in digital forums quickened the processes whereby standard tools and patches were instituted across more and more of the vendor's customers. In sum, outsourcing companies capitalized financially on the knowledge transfer and quick fixes to problems that occurred from flexible social networks in functional job silos.

Because of the ways that outsourcing companies incorporated flexibility in their lean social organization, many subjects said a culture of overwork character-ized the workplace. For example, at the higher tiered job rankings in outsourcing, Lynette (below) described weekends and late nighters where her counterparts and executive managers were scrutinizing "budgets" on HR outsourcing agreements or developing and negotiating bids with customers to increase the sale of their business services. The expectation of meeting profit and sales targets shaped the amount of hours that Lynette's counterparts gave her employer Web Tech. Firm expectations produced a culture where high performance became the standard benchmark for everyone's work. Lynette's colleagues reinforced expectations for high performance in their interactions with her and others. When high time-givers encountered others who were not willing to work as long – Lynette gives a poign-ant example below – they were quick in expressing disapproval of what were perceived as substandard performers in an outsourcing environment.

> At some point in time you have to figure out, "Do I have a life or not?" And that was a lot of mine. Okay, I don't mind working hard, I've always worked hard, I've always put in 200% effort. But when you call me and I'm sitting in the church parking lot, and you're asking me to go over budgets. And you're upset because I don't have the information in front of me, it's like "Okay!" At that point, I sat there going, "Okay this is really ridiculous!" To them, when they were making deals and working till 4, 5 o'clock in the morning, get a couple hours sleep, and then come back and continue to do the negotiations, I mean a lot of people thrived on it. I can tell you a lot of people looked at it and said, "You know, I got a family. I can't do this!"
> (Lynette, former dual Account Manager and HR Strategic Business Unit Manager at Web Tech)

At other levels, areas of the job spectrum, and companies in outsourcing, the expectations for overwork were similar. In the conversation I had with Hillary – a Senior Manager at Dynasty Co-Affiliate Inc., she described the long hours man-agers and employees there were expected to expend to meet and exceed require-ments. Subjects conveyed varying levels of "loyalty" to outsourcing companies and the services they guaranteed to customers. In Hillary's case and others, loy-alty to outsourcing companies meant enthusiastically accepting the extra time requirements to be able to utilize lean and flexible organization and sustain the service levels promised and required by customers.

> And as the manager, when something broke, you could be on a conference call at 9 o'clock, 10 o'clock, or midnight. I was on conference calls all night

because something was wrong or we were moving the data centers. So very much the time increased, but I felt it was okay to do that because my loyalties shifted to the vendor, to Dynasty Co-Affiliate Inc., and my loyalty meant I needed to service the customer. The way to service the customer was to spend the night on the phone because I had to get it done. The patients were coming in the next morning or whatever the reasons were. The business needed the application the next morning and by golly we're going to do the best damn job we can. And if that means I'm on the phone all night, I'm on the phone all night.

(Hillary, former IT Senior Manager at Dynasty Co-Affiliate Inc.)

In contrast to accepting the heightened requirements, other subjects reported that many IT and HR colleagues were "frustrated" by the expectations for doing more work and putting in more hours at outsourcing companies without a commensurate increase in employee pay.

The work definitely increased. Now everything needed to be done that we did before, the full-time job that we did, but now we had all this transitional work to do too. Moving stuff from Merchant Inc. to Master Technologies as far as papers, stock, stuff like that on top of what already filled our eight, nine-hour day. Then they wanted new metrics, they wanted new status reports, they wanted processes documented, everything like that. The work tremendously increased! That was frustrating for a lot of people because, the pay never increased but our work load was non-stop.

(Brad, IT Security Expert at Master Technologies)

As one might expect, constantly overworked professionals would want to shorten their work hours. Reductions of work hours typically occurred in inO cases after the transition of the work to the outsourcing company was complete, new systems were in place at the customer, and all processes were documented. But, because of the increased commodification of work, its ongoing scrutiny, and the routine cutting of costs, reduced work levels on an account did not bode well for continuing in jobs at outsourcing companies. Because the intention in most outsourcing deals was the automation of work and reduction of costs, the amount of available work over the term of contracts decreased. And the outsourcing company, as Sally implied above, took regular action to purposefully cut staff that did not have enough work to keep them busy. So instead of feeling relief at declining work expectations, employees of outsourcing companies quickly realized that it meant that the customer account and your employer probably "no longer needed you." Solidifying this commodification of work was the deal between Master Technologies and Mammoth Inc. According to Sally with nine years of experience on the account, in periodic layoffs, the outsourcing company let go of scores of employees who were not keeping a steady and ambitious workload.

If it went down, you should be concerned, because you either weren't going to get that work back, and therefore they didn't need you. It was good to be getting it, because you had to have billable hours, right? So if you weren't doing anything, you were considered on the bench, and that's not good. You weren't on the bench too long there. Master Technologies, well they said they couldn't afford it – so you really weren't non-billable for long.

(Sally, former IT Project Manager at Master Technologies)

The fear of job loss due to a reduction in the workload was emotionally taxing for professionals in an environment acutely focused on commodification. Fears were continuously stoked by the routine planned and unplanned resource actions on accounts. Subjects' fear of job loss, in part, were push factors for making decisions to move from one outsourcing account to another one. Yet, new opportunities at another customer with outsourcing companies were significantly hampered by the social bridging challenges of employee logistics and the constricted flows of important information on job openings within the firm in social networks.

According to the professionals like Fran, with nine years' experience at Tech Leader, building important "social networks" with colleagues was essential to any type of employment longevity at her company. As work declined and job cuts became imminent, information about opportunities on another account, any possibilities that might exist on a new account, or another type of mobility opportunity mostly circulated by way of social networks in the firm. In her example, Fran moved "almost every year, year and a half" in nine years at Tech Leader. Like some professionals Fran got bored with work in the same role. But, having steady work with the same employer by avoiding job loss also prompted some of her moves. She acknowledged the very unsteady nature of work in outsourcing and challenges to one's tenure when she stressed to me below, "having a network is key there, or you're dead and gone!"

FRAN: There's never any job postings or anything so it's whoever you knew who told you where the next position would be. If you don't, if you're stuck in a place where you don't have that access to other Tech Leaders, you're dead! If that account goes away, you're gone! Because you will not find another job, because even the ones that are posted, they already have candidates for. They have somebody that they know who they're going to fill that position with. So you're dead if you don't have a network. Every job I've had, and like I said, I move almost every year, year and a half, I've got

J: *To a different account?*

F: To a different account, or a different position same account. *Everything* (she stressed) I've gotten is though networking! It's key.

Therefore culturally, routine job cuts prompted outsourced workers to perform at very high standards. The professionals I spoke with often commented on the "high achievement," "smart," and "uber" colleagues they had at outsourcing companies and about their common focus on change management processes and accomplishing remediation and other projects by putting in long hours for their employers. Certainly some of the high performance was due to traditional American culture and its proscription for working hard and displaying this to others as a "badge of honor" (Sennett & Cobb 1972). Americans have been at the top of the leader board in average weekly and annual time on the job (see e.g., Addady 2016), and they are renowned in the industrial world for leaving paid vacation time on the table (see e.g., Vasel 2016). But as the precarity of work has notably increased and particularly so at outsourcing companies, like studies of the culture in companies that were downsizing, it is impossible to discount how important the threat of job loss was to increasing employees' focus and improving their productivity and hours on the job in the cases here (Heckscher 1995). In the next chapter I will discuss the despotic methods outsourcing companies used to obtain professionals' consent to the degraded working and employment conditions in outsourced positions.

Professionals who understood that staff eliminations were part of outsourcing contracts and/or witnessed the steady reduction in staff on the account over time described the competitive attitude that occurred between professionals to maintain steady work as one result. After significant staff reductions began five years into the Master Technologies deal at Mammoth Inc., Sally described one instance when she had taken responsibility for an undesirable project. She had prepared the foundation plan for the project, and progress was being made on its goals. Once the project was "starting to get legs," another team member within the project management group – in "fear of losing their job" – underhandedly took control of it from Sally with the hope of better ensuring his ongoing job tenure at the firm.

> There was more competition at Master Technologies because there was that fear of losing your job. Everybody was trying to out-do everybody else to get that next job or to shine or to find that next opportunity. I was actually in a situation where nobody wanted this project so I took it and I was running the project. . . . So then this guy actually told me I was no longer on the project. . . . Now that I was running the project, it was starting to get legs, and starting to take off. Everybody wanted it then. It's like, "Where were you people three months ago?!"
>
> (Sally, former IT Project Manager at Master Technologies)

After hearing about the occurrence, Sally's director "listened and didn't blow it off." She offered to intervene on her behalf, and reestablish her position leading the project. (Sally declined her offer.) The director's behavior was not typical of management in outsourcing at most of the large firms. It contrasted with what most subjects said about the lack of management's recognition of individual's work at outsourcing companies.

From the perspective of the majority of front-line workers in outsourcing, managers did not know the "granular" nature of the tasks they performed nor did they show much interest in the people who worked for them. Rather, a favorite saying of subjects was managers knew their subordinates as "just a number." Typically, account or executive managers only had regular contact with key managers responsible for the network and applications systems at the customer. Conversations centered on: monitoring the costs and profit margins in project development, bidding for new projects at existing customers, and meeting the various service levels in contracts. Most front-line professionals and lead technicians had limited contact with account managers at outsourcing companies. Subjects sorrowfully said they missed any meaningful recognition or appreciation of their work from account managers or the management at corporate offices. Similar to Lisa and Dominic below, they attributed it to rigid top-down management and being in a bigger, more disconnected organization.

> The only real high-up Ballast Group was our account manager, who I barely knew. He came to meetings every once in a while and would ask a question like, "What do you think?" But, it wasn't a serious, "Let's figure out how we can resolve this." Being lower on the totem pole, maybe that came through my managers, but I didn't really have interaction with the change-makers at the Ballast Group to say, "I really think we should do it this way."
>
> (Lisa, former IT Interface Analyst at Ballast Group)

> I don't know what they think. I don't have an understanding of their appreciation of my work because it's a large, more distant organization. They seem to just assume that the work's going well and that I'm doing a good job. I think management thinks, "Well, if you have a good employee and he's doing a good job then he should know it," and, subsequently, that should be enough. For somebody who's self-motivated, it can be. But every once in a while you'd like to know that they appreciate what you're doing. Sourcing Central doesn't get that, the funneling back down to let people know. People like Salma [in the chapter feature] need to understand that she's doing a good job from them more than they do.
>
> (Dominic, IT Manager at Sourcing Central)

Across all outsourcing companies, there were strong tendencies for management to "forget" about their employees onsite at customer companies. This was the case even in the one or two deals where subjects were most happy with the work and job circumstances in outsourcing. Out of 20 cases, Rapture Hospital and Right Technology Solutions was the best example of high job satisfaction and a more collegial social blending of the two organizations in an outsourced deal. Still, subjects there were critical of the lack of thought and care their outsourcing employer gave them at their onsite location at the customer. Doris, a Systems Support Manager for Right Technology Solutions, was especially clear about the many knowledge gaps about the employment relationship and other job opportunities in the larger company for her onsite technicians. Below Doris, similar to many subjects with experience working for outsourcing companies, was very critical of the lack of an onsite HR presence that left them doing their own research on nonuser-friendly employer websites.

> D: I think they could have more presence at our location. We don't even have an HR rep. Sometimes you feel like the red-headed step-child, being at an

outsourced site, because there's a lot of things that get done at corporate head-quarters that we don't get to do, like social Friday or whatever. So socially yes, I think that piece we miss out. But then you also have the HR piece that, as a manager, I find really frustrating because I don't have someone there that I can talk to or that I consider an employee. You always either have to go online, look up something, or go try to find your HR person. It's all phone conversations or email and, when we used to have an HR representative come in and visit twice a week. And they cut that out. I think that there needs to be more of a personal representative who comes out and my employees can talk to and say, "Hey this is our Right Technology Solutions representative and he's talking about the company and this is where the company is going and these are what your options are." And I think we should be able to get an HR representative. Because employees always have concerns, you know there's workman's comp, there's my benefits, I need to know if there's other opportunities, there's always questions that people have. And now they come to me. I try to track down a question. But sometimes they may have an HR issue that they don't want their manager to know.

J: *And that certainly is a theme in interviews. It's common.*

D: Right. It's a leg, it's out there, it's yours, it's just forgotten a lot. It really is. It's like an auto-pilot thing. That's how I feel.

Outsourcing company's business logic, management, and the culture divested any displays showing emotional commitments to employees. Employees were conceived and treated as a commodity in the culture onsite at customers and by managers at outsourcing companies. This was by continuously emphasizing responsiveness in service delivery, meeting numbers, and billable hours. Foundationally, the great commodification of employees was sustained by the market context and the business needs and requests of customer companies. Customers needed some service, made the appropriate request, and expected action because of the market relationship and outsourcing contract. Below, Ross, who worked for the customer in the Bravado Hospital/Ballast Group case, was especially cognizant of the erosion in human connection and empathy to people who were former colleagues and to the customer's more commodified view of labor in the market relationship.

I felt that collectively we treated the people that went to the outsourcer differently, that they were more of a commodity, much like you would buy electric or gas. You know? I want to flip the switch, I want the lights to come on, you send me a bill, and I'll pay it. And there was a divestiture on the Bravado Hospital side of the emotional connection to these people that, through no fault of their own, had been loyal employees up to a certain point [in time].

(Ross, Clinical Systems Director at Bravado Hospital)

From the outsourcing company's side, numbers and billable hours were used to constitute, evaluate, and (only) reward *exceptional* work that was being done by front-line professionals and managers. Management recognized and rewarded "fire jumpers" like Tanya, "SMEs" who could run the operation for a thousand hospitals, and account executives like Fran who consistently upsold services to customers. Yet, from the perspective of the exceptional employee, this did not guarantee job security for anyone at outsourcing companies. Tanya and Fran below – both exceptional managers at Tech Leader – weighed in on the job insecurity they felt at their employer after nine and ten years' worth of excellent records bringing in unique projects under budget and troubled accounts back in the black.

JACKIE: *Job security?*
FRAN: There's no such thing.
J: *But for an outsourcer is it particularly so?*
F: I think so. Um, we just went through a RA [resource action]. I have been a manager and had to initiate it. It seems like every year we have a resource action.

JACKIE: *Any drawbacks?*
TANYA: To working here?
J: *Yeah.*
T: I think that RA thing hanging over your head is tough.

I had the opportunity to interview several (former) upper-management executives who either facilitated deals at outsourcing companies or made the big decisions at customers that gave their directors the consent to outsource. From these conversations it was clear that senior management at outsourcing companies and C-suite "change-makers" usually conceived labor in outsourcing as a "commodity." Former executives like Sheldon and Norm, below, espoused the market institutional logic where the basis of strategy is to "increase the efficiency profit" (Thornton, Ocasio, & Lounsbury 2012:108). Through this reification process at the executive and organizational cultural level, a qualitative relationship between workers, their colleagues, and their products and services was transformed into a purely quantitative one.

If it's a function that's viewed as a so-called commodity, the pressure will be on to move the whole smear. Move all your help desks, move all of your network desks. These are things that I would have readily acknowledged are commodity-like.

(Sheldon, former CIO at Sourcing Central)

I know you're sociology. I know that's what you're looking at. But the reality is that almost anything we did was cost related. And yes, we were cognizant of the impact on employees, and so you're saying, "Is the morale impact gonna be so deleterious? If the cost value is minimal, is it really worth it?" Then we wouldn't do it. We weren't just looking for every little penny. We wanted to make sure the tradeoff was worthwhile, but generally it was almost always cost related. How can we make more money?

(Norm, former President of a Global Region at ChemRegional Inc.)

Numbers and billable hours were instrumental to completing projects, but they did not recognize individual contributions and relationships that made accomplishments in a team environment possible. It was a terrible way to work for most professionals, and most often they claimed, the lack of management recognition by outsourcing companies was one of the most significant drawbacks to work there. Because of this and other reasons, most professionals didn't stay in jobs at outsourcing companies (discussed, in depth, in the next chapter).

"No skin in the game"

An important reason for completing qualitative research on professional work in outsourcing was to understand how the meaning of work and jobs compared in markets versus hierarchies and how jobs in markets affected notions of identity and self. To better understand these issues, I asked outsourced subjects about 1. the general benefits and drawbacks to work in hierarchies and markets, 2. perceptions about their future careers with outsourcing companies, and 3. subjects' personal values about their work. Collectively, their responses illuminated outsourcing's effects on the meaning of this work, personal identity, and the perceptions of selves.

Meaning is a central focus in research and analysis in the sociology of work. In the past, sociological research found the meaning for workers most affected by social organization (or social structure), social interaction, and identity (Adler & Adler 1999; Dudley 1994; Garson 1975; Gowan 1998; Terkel 1974). Guevara and Ord (1996) argue that meaning in the workplace has traditionally derived from questions addressing: where do I belong, who am I, and what is my value? They caution that these bases could presently be changing because of continuing organizational changes and job contingencies across industries (716). In this section, I establish that, in general, professionals with experience in outsourcing found the work and work relationships less meaningful there. Features of hierarchical workplaces traditionally perceived as meaningful were absent in outsourcing because of the hyper-focus on commodification and reducing costs of producing the work.

Issues of identity and self are historical foci in sociological theory too. Social interaction is central to processes in identity and self-development. In theory, the self is conceived as a "social experience" and involves our ongoing relationships to others (Hewitt 1997:80). Identity derives from important social categories and the roles we satisfy in the various aspects of social life (90). The positions and roles we occupy in the social structure "produce functional communities of beliefs, values, and shared purposes with others" (91). These communities represent important sources of identity. Recently, for example, Gideon Kunda (2006) showed how new cultural controls by one high-tech employer shaped the ideologies, behaviors, sense of identity, and selves of professional workers there. The employer had carefully crafted a "member role" that defined and mandated ways for professionals to view the company and oneself in relation to it as well as sanctioned the ways for members to participate in social interaction and organizational life there.

Unlike work in hierarchies, like Simmel's "stranger" in social theory (Wolff 1950) the market organization pushes outsourced professionals to an outsider position of "vendor." At outsourcing companies, usually professionals occupy one of three generalized service roles. As discussed earlier, the three roles in IT – frontline technician, account manager/executive, and project manager – were heavily controlled. Most important to subjects, jobs at outsourcing companies undercut important bases of their past professional selves. They used to be recognized as the "go-to" source for technical problem-solving. They used to think pridefully about themselves as "tinkerers" that did "cool" work and were respected by other "stakeholders" for their particular strategic knowledge and skills that produced direct benefits for the organization. Some subjects, like Tanya in the feature, seemed to flourish in a culture emphasizing the hyper logic of "numbers" and a tight, lean, service machine at outsourcing companies. Yet, even in individual examples of success – meaning job longevity at outsourcing companies and the embodiment of a market-oriented self – at some point in the interview most of these subjects explicitly said that the experiences doing the technical, human resources, or management work they did in hierarchies was more satisfying than the hyper-commodified service role they occupied in inO.

Directly addressing meaning, I begin with Salma – the project manager featured at the beginning of the chapter and the source for this section title. In our conversation, Salma had been wistfully responding to questions about the effects of outsourcing on her work. When I pressed her about the differences in work and working relationships between hierarchies and markets, she noted how different the experience was and the way it made her feel.

> [When directly employed by Home Nurse Inc.] we all had skin in the game. Whereas now that we're Sourcing Central, we're made to feel like we don't have that skin in the game.
>
> (Salma, IT Project Manager at Sourcing Central)

I was intrigued by her reference to a well-known sports metaphor, and I asked her what she meant by it in relation to outsourcing. For Salma, "skin" referred to the personal investments employees made in the work. "The game" referred to the embodied work process, its roles, rules, and outcomes at employers. Salma used the sports metaphor to compare work and her personal investment at two different organizations: hierarchies versus markets. With six years of experience in a hierarchy and four years of experience in outsourcing, Salma said that the social organization and interactions in hierarchies fostered greater purpose, a sense of belonging, and personal investment in the work, its rules, and work outcomes. In contrast, with outsourcing, the same level of personal investment was not realized, even after a progression of time.

Lack of personal investment was present because outsourced professionals moved outside of the core decision-making structure at customers and into the service organization at vendor companies. At customers, outsourced professionals occupied the position of "strangers" or outsiders (Wolff 1950). In interactions within this social organization, they were referred to by employees of customers as "vendors." At vendors, their authority in the labor process as a decider and one who exercised discretion was significantly reduced (Zalewski 2007). Instead, their value was strictly conceived by customers and outsourcing employers in terms of the labor power they were expected to provide. Subjects were visibly marked as a vendor with employee badges that conveyed difference and tied them directly to outsourcing companies. Finally, because of their outsider status to customer companies, access to parts of the physical space there were restricted to them.

Subjects did not have a strong understanding of where they fit in the larger organization at vendors nor did they have a sense of belonging. After rebadging to her new employer Circuit, for example, Courtney felt like an outsider to the new and larger organization. As one of three newly outsourced employees in desktop support from Cloud Inc., Courtney was cut off from the "team" there that used to make her feel a part of the family and foster feelings of belonging somewhere. Circuit's absence of any social overtures toward employees working off-site showed a lack of "mindfulness" for their personal well-being. In her example, when Courtney asked her manager for some information, her request was brushed off. Such an abrupt response did very little to foster a sense of belonging to the company – an important source of meaning – or that the firm valued or "cared at all about the employees." The latter was a common gripe of outsourced subjects, like Carson's summation of his experience with Tech Leader below.

J: *Drawbacks?*
C: It's the family feel. I like to be on a team, I don't feel like I'm on a team. I feel like I'm on my own team on an island somewhere, getting ready to be sunk by a tidal wave. It's a "you're out of sight, out of mind" kind of mentality. If you have a question, they'll be, "Oh, that's a good question! Why don't you try to figure that out on your own."

(Courtney, Desktop Support at Circuit)

I was thankful by the time they laid me off [after 18 months]. I didn't want to be out of work, but it was the most frustrating job I've ever had! I got no sense that they cared at all about the employees. It was about money, money, money, money. The benefits I thought we would get, like being part of the Tech Leader culture, none of that ever surfaced. It was draining. It really was draining work because it very quickly became the place you showed up, you did your work, and went home. There was no incentive to be there.

(Carson, former Desktop Support Supervisor at Tech Leader)

Professionals also found work less meaningful with outsourcing because of the changed nature of market interactions about the work. In Chapter 3, I described how interactions in the articulation of work were often adversarial between outsourced professionals and their former colleagues at customers. In this chapter, I have described the ways in which work became more rationalized and commodified in SLAs and billable hours with outsourcing. Because of this Paul felt that his "work was more complex" and his interactions with colleagues were more political and resulted in anxiety and emotional unease. Paul said he and his rebadged peers felt outsourcing jobs lacked benefits to keep professionals happy and secure. In fact, his managers at the vendor Circuit encouraged him to leave the company in search of "better jobs." For subjects like Paul and his colleagues (about 18 months into their outsourcing deal), the raised emotionality in their interactions with colleagues and customers in markets significantly loosened their personal investment to the work, jobs, and work relationships and it reduced their meaning for them. As Paul implied below, he and many of his colleagues thought about quitting jobs at outsourcing companies to obtain work elsewhere.

> The benefit to me was I got this job which brings me closer to my family. [Paul was promoted, which involved relocation from the Midwest to the East Coast, within a year of rebadging.] That's my only benefit. From the way it has made my work more complex, my relationships more political, and my network of coworkers – and by coworkers I mean both Concerto Inc. and Circuit – more tense, no I see no benefit to rebadging. I see a benefit to the corporation. . . . For the overall amount of emotional turmoil it puts people through, it's not been worth it for me. And the unfortunate truth is many of my peers that I speak with in the same work areas are all saying the same thing. I even hear my own upper management saying, "Look you oughta be putting together your resume, you could go get a better job." That's unheard of! At Concerto Inc. my managers were always saying, "Man, you could be with Concerto Inc. for the rest of your life, you could retire from here! You've got great opportunities!" Now my management is saying, "Man, you're too smart to stay here." It's a big difference.
>
> (Paul, Workplace Services manager at Circuit)

Below Rob insightfully used two family relationships – a sibling versus a cousin relationship – to compare interactions in hierarchies versus market organizations. His interactions as a direct employee now at Accolade Hospital – a hierarchy – were infused with honesty, transparency, and symbolic markings of being a core member or sibling within a family. Families have a shared value and commitment to core members and toward their larger familial whole. This allows members to "challenge each other more directly" without the fear of jeopardizing the relationship and being expunged from "the family fold." These family qualities were lost for subjects who worked insecure outsourcing jobs at onsite locations of customers. In contrast, subjects in outsourcing satisfied an "outside" service role. They were "working for the family" (Steve), or the customer institution. As peripheral "cousins," their perspectives did not matter that much to customers because they were "not even real employees [or family members]." Rob's family institution reference, particularly, was easily transferable to an in-house outsourcing organization and to the different professional identity that is supported there. In a hierarchy, "stakeholders" in the broad organization get "aggressively challenged" on an emotional level and this implies expectations for transparency, and overtures of commitment while – at the same time – attaching "feelings" and value between people. In markets, outsourcing professionals were positioned "outside" the inner workings of the nuclear organizational family. As a result, they were not privy to the social spaces and "honest" interactions where different perspectives were shared, recognized, and respected. And part of the family, social value, and meaning were conveyed and developed.

J: *What's the social environment like now, the culture, after moving to Accolade Hospital [as a Network Manager]?*

R: It's good! I think people are more honest with us now. When we worked for Accessible Hardware – I don't think honest is the right word but – you always felt you were outside. You know, someone had made the comment, "You're not even real employees." Okay. I heard that before. When we become employees, now everyone treats you very good but people are more likely to say, "That's bullshit!" They'll challenge you more aggressively than they would before. It's like you'll tell your brother or your sister, "Screw you you're wrong!" But your cousin Ryan won't think that's correct. So, I got that feeling. It's good. You feel more! Sometimes it's more frustrating because now you're being challenged more directly, but you definitely feel like you're in the fold. You're part of the family and the dirty laundry you air between each other is there.

Many subjects said the physical and mental work was less meaningful in outsourcing compared to work in hierarchies. When asked about what they valued about their work, many technicians gave responses similar to Salma and Tanya below. They were "tinkerers" with expertise. They were passionate about working with other intelligent people to repair and rebuild technical things. In general, I found managers enthusiastically spoke about the business process reengineering happening in the workplace and said they valued making work easier, more efficient, and reliable. Human resource professionals especially valued the social side of their roles. Subjects said these features were the most meaningful for them because they corresponded with primary values in the profession and, conversely, supported strong work identities that tied them to professional communities. These valued features of work corresponded with higher levels of personal attachment and satisfaction.

I want to be the tinkerer. I want to be the, "Oh my god, Salma! It's two o'clock in the morning and the server's down! I need you to come right away!" And . . . I want to have the knowledge to fix that. Those are the types of things I was prepared for as a manager when I was doing Home Nurse Inc. work. And we all did it! We did both sides – network and applications. I like making things work.

(Salma, IT Project Manager at Sourcing Central)

I like consulting with people and problem-solving, and it was part of why I became a fire jumper eventually, because I was good at problem-solving. Colleagues were like, "Oh, you have a problem? Let's go talk to Tanya about it." So that is what I really liked. I have a lot of discretion. And I get to work with a lot of really smart people, and I learn a lot, too. . . . I'm good at putting stuff together at a high level, and I do that here.

(Tanya, IT Project Manager at Tech Leader)

In general, professionals in the sample had progressed in jobs and careers with companies as direct employees either before or after outsourcing jobs. Many subjects learned the scope of jobs and roles in hierarchies, central knowledge and tools of the profession, and they participated in functional communities there. Subjects found these social and embodied experiences with colleagues important for sustaining a professional identity and a professional self. They enthusiastically recalled collective narratives of face-to-face opportunities to engage in "interface specific talk," for example, conversations about detailed, technical aspects of the work. The professional work and community shop-talk were "fun," respected by others in firms, and technicians "loved them." Below, Rob and Lisa described the passion they had for discussions with their professional colleagues and the enjoyment they felt when others perceived them as fulfilling difficult and important work.

And that's the attractive part, it's a cool feeling like no one really understands what you do but you're very important to the organization.

(Rob, Network Manager at Accolade Hospital)

I love it! I love having common conversation topics with [other interface technicians] – to the point where we make jokes about it, especially with interfaces because interfaces are not as technical as everybody likes to think they are. It's more of like putting a puzzle together is kind of how I equate it. So, there's very interface-specific talk, that you can have a conversation with someone and be throwing out segments and fields and they'll know exactly what you're talking about and everybody else will just be puzzled. It's fun watching the other people around you think that you're some masterminds and it's really, it's not that difficult! If you're not involved in it every day, it sounds more technical than it really is. . . . But having people that work in a common field is awesome. I think it's great. It's fun!

(Lisa, IT Interface Manager at Bravado Hospital)

With outsourcing, in contrast, the nature of articulating the work was about fulfilling service levels in contracts, accruing billable hours, and negotiating the work in controlled environments and from adversarial positions. Subjects were exempt from big decision-making at vendors, which usually occurred in upper management levels. Professionals in outsourcing often said they were not doing the collaborative, autonomous technical work to achieve important goals – which they loved – and they perceived the work as less meaningful. Below, I include quotes from Lisa and Tanya. Lisa suggests that, as a direct employee of Bravado Hospital, she was more attached to a professional community and found her work more connected to the organization goal to "perform better healthcare." Subjects like Lisa and Tanya felt that roles that directly link to helping others made their technical work "more humanly meaningful" and gave them feelings that they had a professional identity with a moral purpose.

> I'm attached to the people that I work with, specifically. I'd have to say it wasn't necessarily a question of the cause with the Ballast Group [the vendor], whereas here I feel like it's more of I'm attached to wanting to perform better healthcare. I still like the people – that's still there, I'm still attached to that – but now it's more the meaning behind the job whereas I did not feel that before.
>
> (Lisa, IT Interface Manager at Bravado Hospital)

> My sister-in-law became a nurse after a divorce. My sister is an assistant physical therapist. Not that I want to go into their side of life. But at the end of their day, they've done something very humanly meaningful. At the end of my day, I may have had nice interactions. That's the way I've been looking at it from a Catholic perspective. I try to be as much of a light in the workplace as possible, and I do feel like it's a vocation. I've always loved the problem-solving, maybe I'm called to problem-solve. And then I thought maybe I could problem-solve in areas that have more deep human meaning and IT projects.
>
> (Tanya, Project Manager at Tech Leader)

Franca, a former HR Relationship Manager with People Solutions, captured the change to her work and work relationships made by its commodification with outsourcing. Mainly she suggests the replacement of human elements in the work with constant references only to legal contracts was the most negative. Franca said her work in outsourcing became more "transactional." By this, she meant that the emphasis in her role as recruitment and relationship manager in outsourcing became solely about meeting service levels in contracts and no longer performing the tasks to her learned professional methods and standards. From an institutional logics perspective (Thornton, Ocasio, & Lounsbury 2012), Franca described the shift in legitimacy from a professional logic to a market logic (73). As an example, she cited that a new hire at People's Banking Inc. needed to occur within 45 days of an initial job posting to "meet an SLA." The emphasis in her role was not on creating community with others within the company anymore but rather meeting a quantitative measure that represented the work. The changes to her work and its reduced meaning caused Franca to leave her job in HR outsourcing after only a few months.

When we spoke four months after leaving the job, Franca – self-proscribed as a master builder of "social networks" that she nurtured and leveraged as needed – was a "Senior Excellence Consultant" employed by a metropolitan hospital. She was passionate about the HR programs she was helping design to increase "employee engagement" at the metropolitan hospital. The first topic of her conversation with me, as we walked down a hallway at the hospital and she greeted several others, was her ability to have comfortable, small talk or "hallway conversations" once again. To put this point in a nutshell, Salma identified the feature of work and work relations in hierarchies that casts a professional identity and fosters greater meaning – feeling like she belongs and is making a tangible difference. Unfortunately, this aim becomes overshadowed in markets by their internal logic and culture of commodification.

> The only thing that kept me here once we found out we were being outsourced was the staff that reported to me that I was very close to. The staff that we have here now is a tight-knit group, so I feel a part of that family too. So, that's why I continue to stay and manage the multiple projects and mentor and provide support. I feel like I'm making a difference for St. Francis Hospital. I don't feel I'm making that difference for Sourcing Central.
>
> (Salma, IT Project Manager at Sourcing Central)

Conclusion

I investigated in-house outsourcing to develop information about its effects on professional work, relations in the workplace, and important aspects of the workplace culture in markets. Subjects also gave a sense of what they found most meaningful in their work, how this strengthened professional identities and selves, and how these features were generally absent in outsourcing markets.

Propaganda in support of the outsourcing of jobs has proclaimed that professionals will experience a revitalization of work. Specifically, they argue this is because work becomes the commodity in outsourcing markets and employers are competing to develop and sell the latest innovations in technologies and business practices to customers across industries. Therefore, professionals will benefit from being exposed to cutting-edge knowledge of best practices and tools in their fields and be able to practice their craft in the various work environments of customers.

However, despite these claims, subjects overwhelmingly relayed that these claims were invalid. The work was codified in SLAs, other metrics, and billable hours. Work processes were rigid because outsourcing companies applied change management systems to transition custom business processes into the standard ones at outsourcing companies. And the work and labor on customer accounts and on major projects were scrutinized regularly with a primary goal of reducing costs and improving revenues for outsourcing companies. Subjects' workplace interactions and the culture onsite at customers primarily reflected the quantification of the commodified work.

The effects of this commodification on the subjects in the sample were reduced meaning of both the work and of professionals' future commitment to outsourcing jobs. With outsourcing, subjects also found they were no longer a valued member of professional communities. They were vendors, perceived as outsiders by customers, and valued by both customers and vendors solely for their labor power.

In the vast majority of cases, subjects found outsourcing employers did not demonstrate care toward them, especially outsourced professionals working onsite at customers. Onsite, they lacked feelings of belonging in a larger social organization. They were strangers to customers, and their direct employer was a "distant organization." A lack of an emotional connection to the work, to colleagues, and to employers in market organization did little to sustain a positive professional identity and strong sense of self for many subjects in this sample.

The "way the outsourcing model works" did not translate well for the financial livelihood or psychological well-being of most people with direct experience in outsourcing in this sample. Professionals employed in outsourcing always feared the "tap on the shoulder" and rolling away of "heads." And, if they did not quit prior to this, job loss became an actuality of many of the subjects I interviewed and their colleagues. People were unhappy with the circumstances of the culture at outsourcing companies including its greater commodification of the work, the constant fear of job loss, and overwhelming competition that arose over billable hours. Outsourcing cast monetization, politicization, and negativity upon the interactions, feelings, identities, and meanings that support professional work and its market outcomes. It was a "draining" way of working and, as discussed in the next chapter, many professionals did not maintain a steady prosperous career in outsourcing.

Note

1 See two examples of public business support for outsourcing because it allows companies to focus on their core competencies. "Companies Look Beyond Cost Reduction When Choosing an Outsourcing Partner, According to Capgemini/IDC Bi-Annual Survey; Companies More Concerned with Focusing on Core Competencies, and Want a Collaborative Partner to Share Risk and Reward" appeared on the *Business Wire* April 25, 2005. More recently, Dan O'Shea wrote for www.retaildive.com/news on August 25, 2016: "Why more and more retailers are outsourcing their IT; In turning to third parties, retailers can more easily experiment with a multitude of technologies to reinvent their businesses for the omnichannel era."

References

Addady, Michael. 2016. "US Workers Put in Staggeringly More Hours Than Europeans Do." *Fortune*: October 18, 2016.

Adler, Patricia A. and Peter Adler. 1999. "Transience and the Postmodern Self: The Geographic Mobility of Resort Workers." *The Sociological Quarterly* 40(1): 31–58.

Braverman, Harry. 1972. *Labor and Monopoly Capital: The Degradation of Work in the 20th Century*. New York: Monthly Review Press.

Capgemini. 2005. "Companies Look Beyond Cost Reduction When Choosing an Outsourcing Partner, According to Capgemini/IDC Bi-Annual Survey." *Business Wire*: April 25.

Davenport, Tom. 2015. "Why Companies Have Stopped Outsourcing IT." *The Wall Street Journal*: October 14, 2015.

Dudley, Kathryn M. 1994. *The End of the Line: Lost Jobs, New Lives in Postindustrial America*. Chicago: University of Chicago Press.

Edwards, Richard. 1979. *Contested Terrain: The Transformation of the Workplace in the 20th Century*. New York: Basic Books.

Friedland, Roger and Robert Alford. 1991. "Bringing Society Back In: Symbols, Practices and Institutional Contradictions." In *The New Institutionalism in Organizational Analysis*, edited by Walter W. Powell and Paul J. DiMaggio, 232–263. Chicago: University of Chicago Press.

Garson, Barbara. 1975 [1994]. *All the Livelong Day: The Meaning and Demeaning of Routine Work*. New York: Penguin Books.

Gowan, Teresa. 1998. "American Untouchables: Homeless Scavengers in San Francisco's Underground Economy." In *Working in America: Continuity, Conflict, and Change*, edited by Amy S. Wharton, 432–443. Mountain View, CA: Mayfield Publishing.

Guevara, Karmen and Jacqueline Ord. 1996. "The Search for Meaning in a Changing Work Context." *Futures* 28(8): 709–722.

Heckscher, Charles. 1995. *White-Collar Blues: Management Loyalties in an Age of Corporate Restructuring*. New York: Basic Books.

Hewitt, John P. 1997. *Self and Society: A Symbolic Interactionist Social Psychology*, 7th ed. Boston: Allyn and Bacon.

Kunda, Gideon. 2006. *Engineering Culture: Control and Commitment in a High-Tech Organization*. Philadelphia: Temple University Press.

O'Shea, Dan. 2016. "Why More and More Retailers are Outsourcing Their IT." *Retaildive. com*: August 25.

Parson, Talcott (ed). 1947. *Max Weber: The Theory of Social and Economic Organization*. New York: The Free Press.

Peck, Jamie and Nikolas Theodore. 1998. "The Business of Contingent Work: Growth and Restructuring in Chicago's Temporary Employment Industry." *Work, Employment, and Society* 12(4): 655–674.

PR Newswire. April 19, 2005. "Outsourcing Falling From Favor With World's Largest Organizations, Deloitte Consulting Study Reveals; Study Shows Hidden Costs, Added Complexity Have Prompted 25 Percent of Participants to Reduce Outsourcing Activities." Deloitte Consulting.

Sealock, Andy and Christopher Stacy. 2013. "Why Some U.S. Companies Are Giving Up On Outsourcing." *Forbes*: January 16, 2013.

Sennett, Richard and Jonathan Cobb. 1972. *The Hidden Injuries of Class*. New York: Alfred A. Knopf.

Smith, Vicki. 1994. "Institutionalizing Flexibility in a Service Firm: Multiple Contingencies and Hidden Hierarchies." *Work and Occupations* 21(3): 284–307.

Terkel, Studs. 1972. *Working: People Talk About What They Do All Day and How They Feel About What They Do*. New York: New Press.

Thornton, Patricia H., William Ocasio, and Michael Lounsbury. 2012. *The Institutional Logics Perspective: A New Approach to Culture, Structure, and Process*. Oxford: Oxford University Press.

Tucker, Robert C. (ed). 1978. *The Marx-Engels Reader*. New York: WW Norton and Company.

Vasel, Kathryn. 2016. "Half of American Workers Aren't Using All of Their Vacation Days." *CNN Money*: December 19, 2016.

Williamson, Oliver E. 1975. *Markets and Hierarchies: Analysis and Antitrust Implications*. New York: The Free Press.

Wolff, Kurt H. 1950. *The Sociology of Georg Simmel*. New York: The Free Press.

Zalewski, Jacqueline M. 2007. "Discretion, Control, and Professional Careers With Outsourcing Companies." *Sociological Viewpoints* 23: 121–137.

5 "(Only) better for some"

Consent, resistance, and professional careers with outsourcing companies

Brad (2005) and Dwayne (2010)

Brad sat with me in 2005 for an interview, my 16th. This was near the end of the data collection stage for my dissertation research. Brad and I were meeting an hour away from my home in a suburban chain restaurant for lunch. By that time, I knew the added challenges for recording and transcribing interviews because of the noise in public venues. But, I did not know of an alternative. Brad had been promoted a level up in the service organization at Master Technologies (the vendor) shortly after his job was outsourced. Now, he was an IT security "expert" and provided virtual support to 15 customers. Because he had no office at the physical location of a company, Brad worked predominantly from his home in the suburbs. He suggested that we meet at the restaurant.

Meet Brad

Brad was raised in the suburbs, and he was college educated in computer science. At 26, he was the youngest professional that I interviewed. By 2005, in his short work life, he was showing clear signs of a professional career that was going places. After three months at Master Technologies, he had been identified as an "A-player" by superiors and moved into a position of IT Security Expert. Brad was responsible for resolving issues escalated to his level by the technicians located onsite at one of the 15 different customers he served. The expert position gave Brad greater authority, the opportunity to work from home, and it offered some of the perks of consulting. For example he flew for free across the country to attend team meetings, meet with clients, and experience new entertainment. I was struck by the confidence and passion in which Brad enthusiastically spoke about his challenging new work as a security expert, the opportunities he had to learn from others and share his expertise in the technical field because of outsourcing, and the career possibilities he felt he had at Master Technologies.

As compared to the possibilities back at old employers before the outsourcing, many professionals in my sample perceived that there were better career opportunities at outsourcing companies. Based on the outcomes at the time of my interviews and since then, a few subjects did experience upward mobility in professional careers at outsourcing companies that might not have happened at customer companies. I will discuss the common characteristics among this select group of subjects whose professional careers benefited from outsourcing. I expected some of these qualities. Traditional social, economic, and organizational theory (e.g., Granovetter and Weber) has shown, for example, the importance of charisma, a penchant for strategic networking, exhibiting passion for your work and expertise, and a high motivation to share knowledge and mentor others (i.e., demonstrating leadership). Other qualities exhibited by those with careers benefited by outsourcing supported a more pop science (e.g., Malcolm Gladwell) or common sense perspective on success. For example it helped being in the right place at the right time and having the appropriate skill set to resolve high value tasks for the company. For Brad, this meant being present when the problem with IT security in the new era of Internet hacking and electronic communication noticeably arose. It also helped being "very vocal" or extroverted. Being charismatic, confidently vocal, and outwardly passionate about work characterized each of the mobile professionals in my outsourced sample, including my impression of Brad during the interview.

In contrast to Brad and several others with promising careers in outsourcing, jobs at outsourcing companies did not hold these benefits for the majority of professionals in this sample. Most were either:

1   struggling with the new labor and working conditions at outsourcing companies,
2   they were already laid off from their jobs when we spoke,
3   they had chosen to quit jobs with outsourcing companies of their own volition, or
4   the outsourcing deal had been terminated and subjects (many, most happily) had been offered positions back at the original company.

Compared to subjects' widely held belief that being employed in outsourcing yields greater career possibilities, the actual career outcomes for most professionals I spoke with – including Dwayne who I discuss next – fell below this mark.

Meet Dwayne

We spoke five years later, in 2010, when Dwayne agreed to meet me at a quiet coffee house close to my home to talk about the recent outsourcing of his data center management job. It had happened only four months earlier. I remember thinking that Dwayne's willingness to meet me at a place that was convenient for me was unusual. During our conversation, Dwayne further struck me as someone who always went the extra mile for others and who was uncompromising when it came to giving his best effort (the epitome of "consummate cooperation"; see Williamson 1975:69) to produce work of a very high quality. At 53, he had worked his way up over the past ten years to the position of a First Shift Manager in the data center at one of the largest employers in his region, the customer, Digital Services

Inc. Because of outsourcing, however, Dwayne was now employed by the vendor, or the global outsourcing company Default Technologies.

Dwayne described his demotion from manager to supervisor because of the outsourcing. He also told me that Digital Services Inc. was collaborating with Default Technologies to develop a complex but highly automated billing system. Future job losses in the data center were expected, and there were severance package clauses written into the outsourcing contract. Dwayne expected that his job at Default Technologies would end one day very soon. His interview, my 39th, encapsulated the meaning of outsourcing for the majority of my subjects. To them, outsourcing meant greater job insecurity. Dwayne described outsourcing's effects on him personally and on the way he approached his work now. From his perspective, Dwayne was working in his job more out of "desperation" as compared to "the pride" he used to feel when he worked directly for the customer company. On this human scale of feelings, emotional attachment, and material needs, most professionals fell closer to Dwayne – they were desperate – as compared to Brad who remained prideful about his work at the outsourcing company. In contrast to the positive nature of scholarship on portfolio work, careers, and "itinerant experts" (Barley & Kunda 2004; Griffin 2008; Meiksins & Whalley 2002; Platman 2004), most professionals here embarked on contingent paths with outsourcing because they had little choice or power in the matter.

Dwayne's comparison of the different way that he approached and felt about his work is very insightful. It is especially useful for discussing how outsourcing companies obtain the consent of their employees to jobs with working conditions that offer fewer professional benefits than their previously held jobs at customers. Sociological studies (e.g., Burawoy 1979) in industrial settings have shown how employers "manufacture consent" to jobs and working conditions in mutually beneficial ways (e.g., through the game of "making out," where the employee gives more effort to the task at hand because they gain incentive pay). Essentially both parties perceive that they are negotiating freely and obtaining something of value from the relationship. Dwayne had been paid and treated reasonably at Digital Services Inc. and, as a result, he consented to and felt pride toward his work and commitment to his employer.

In contrast, with in-house outsourcing (inO) Dwayne's consent to his job and employer were obtained in a "despotic" way (Burawoy 1979). Dwayne maintained the hardware and managed the batch processes of customer billing in a data center. Compared to a decade earlier, there were already far fewer people employed in these operations' jobs because many of these business processes had already become standardized and automated or sent to the cloud. Consequently, there was little special or institutional knowledge that helped data center workers at Digital Services Inc. leverage good jobs in these roles at the outsourcing company. Additionally, former employment practices that underscored the value the companies had for their employees and their commitment to the work – e.g., job ladders for mobility, good pay and benefits, and job security – had been steadily disappearing (DiTomaso 2001). The result was that the compliance of people like Dwayne to take jobs in inO was attained because of their limited choices. There simply was not a better position for them to apply for and to obtain given the United States' tenuous job market during this time.

The playing field for jobs that were heavily outsourced, not just data centers, have become a lot "meaner" to committed working people. Similar to Digital Services Inc., most customer and outsourcing companies in this sample demonstrated to workers they were inconsequential to their operations and expendable. As a result, subjects across this sample described a general resistance to jobs at outsourcing companies. According to their accounts, it was common for professionals to quit jobs. Many subjects I spoke with had already quit outsourcing jobs at the time we met. Often, if they stayed at outsourcing companies, professionals eventually lost their job. On the basis of outcomes in this sample, outsourcing was *"(only) better for some"* (Russell) – or a limited number of professionals and their careers. For most, it represented an increasingly despotic type of employment relationship that left subjects with heavy feelings of high job insecurity and often jobless. Lucky for Dwayne, he dodged a job loss for several years even while Default Technologies executed them regularly. Eventually, as Dwayne described it, "my number came up." Default Technologies released Dwayne from his job in May 2014. When we last spoke in December 2014, he had been unemployed for seven months and he had no strong job prospects.

Introduction

When I began this research project in 2005, organizations built to promote outsourcing heralded it as a "new opportunity" for technical workers. At an Outsourcing Institute (OI) Roadshow I attended in Chicago in 2004, a spokesman for the organization enthusiastically remarked: "Outsourcing revitalizes careers!" He explained, technical professionals left a cost center at firms with few mobility opportunities sans employee retirements from the company or new technologies that corresponded with the creation of new jobs. At outsourcing companies, the spokesperson continued, they became part of a profit center with much more complex job matrices. In the case of IT, professionals would also engage with the latest technologies and best practices in their specialty field (e.g., IT security). According to his theory, professionals would have many more jobs, mobility, and career prospects at outsourcing companies. The OI is an organization that pitches positive claims and research on outsourcing to expand business support and use for it. I sat feeling very conspicuous among the mostly male audience of business professionals who appeared completely drawn in by the spokesperson's glowing rhetoric on outsourcing and the outsourcing of jobs. As a trained sociologist of work, in contrast, I was highly skeptical of the OI's claim of positive job and career outcomes with outsourcing.

In fact, at the same time, stories and advertisements in their own trade publication *Outsourcing Essentials* contradicted the rosy claims of this spokesperson. For example, a fall 2003 article said that professionals who took jobs with outsourcing companies early in this evolution in business organization would benefit (i.e., obtain or maintain jobs) because of their "first mover" status.[1] At that time, companies had been expanding their workforces to accommodate the demand of growing markets for outsourcing. For example, professionals in all six of the IT inO deals I learned about in the 2005 set of interviews were offered jobs. But, the OI article forewarned that this growth phase would come to a close, and it would become far more difficult for customer companies to negotiate any transfer in the ownership of their employees in conjunction with the outsourcing of their work. In other words, with the exception perhaps of the very best, inO would mean job losses for professionals at customer companies in the near future. With the possibility that these were the best years for professionals who took jobs with outsourcing companies, it was important to observe outsourcing's effects in more cases and over time. In 2017, strengthened by sociological data from 20 cases spread over two and a half decades, my conclusions differ significantly from the business community's promising rhetoric about inO's positive effects on professionals, their work, and careers.

In the first half of this chapter, I discuss outsourcing and how employers produced the consent of professionals who were forced to rebadge to new employers. In the early cases of IT outsourcing especially, employers manufactured consent using a hegemonic approach. Pre-Y2K, outsourcing was relatively new, and the information technology outsourcing industry (ITO) continued to appear primed for major growth. The largest outsourcing companies (e.g., Tech Leader, Circuit, and Master Technologies) were signing mega deals with Fortune 100 companies. In some deals – for example the 1997 Mammoth Inc. case – the entire IT department at the company's global headquarters was split into two outsourcing agreements with Master Technologies and Digitize. The deal included 2,600 jobs and the rebadging of most of the IT professionals at Mammoth Inc. affected by the outsourcing. Benefits for outsourced professionals at Master Technologies, like Sally, were equivalent to compensation and paid time off that they previously earned at Mammoth Inc.

In many of the early IT cases and early inO deals, compliance to the job and the outsourcing company was generally created through new learning opportunities in the IT field and perceptions of mobility, career opportunities, and overall professional growth. Subjects like Davetta below frequently commented favorably on the breadth of new learning opportunities on cutting-edge technical systems, actually instituting needed changes to work systems, completing new projects, and the possibility of greater career choices. All these aspects functioned to generate the consent of IT professionals to take jobs with more intense working conditions at outsourcing companies.

> The benefit is, there is so much more out there to know about what you do! Because this is what they do! You're working for an IT company. So the advantage is that you learn so much more. Now you're not only moving from left to right. "Oh you mean I can move from right to left and back to? I can do more than that and still get the same thing? Okay!" Yeah, it's just alarming, the exposure to other things.
>
> (Davetta, Team Leader in Identity Management at Master Technologies)

Very quickly, however, companies began using a more despotic approach to obtain the compliance of employees to take and/or keep jobs in outsourcing. Just as the article in the OI publication *Outsourcing Essentials* had forewarned, job losses and lower job quality were more often the case in deals post-Y2K (Zalewski 2015). This was, in part, because outsourcing companies had already assembled their core workforces. If jobs were offered in the post-Y2K cases, they had fewer material benefits. For example, Courtney had worked various IT jobs at Cloud Inc. over a 12-year employment period. In 2012 she was working in Desktop Support, making a living salary, and had accrued five weeks of vacation a year. When Cloud Inc. outsourced Desktop Support, Courtney took a $12,000 pay cut and lost three weeks of vacation when she rebadged to Circuit.

> [In December 2012] Circuit finally got their paperwork in order and they called me and I'm like, "Alright. . . ." Because in my head I'm like, "You know what? Job prospects are pretty bad out there, see what the salary is, if it's not too bad I'll take it and see what happens." So that's what I did. They docked me about 12 grand, which is not that bad, considering what I heard other people got docked – because Circuit is really low-balling people right now, and I lost my [three weeks of] vacation.
>
> (Courtney, Desktop Support at Circuit)

Outsourcing companies benefited when people affected by the deal decided not to accept inferior job offers. Voluntary attrition at the onset and through the term of an outsourcing deal only helped outsourcing companies to more expediently institute their cost reduction priorities. On the labor side, the attrition of colleagues who had previously helped to produce the work was not beneficial for outsourced professionals. Already expected to accomplish much more in their jobs, which I will discuss later, work demands at outsourcing companies quickly soared to a "breaking point," and many chose to leave their positions shortly after deals began. However, companies did not care much when people quit. No subject ever discussed management at outsourcing companies making an effort to keep an employee who had given their resignation. Furthermore, companies did not care whether the level of staffing they retained was enough to do the work outlined in outsourcing contracts. They simply mandated the remaining outsourced professionals on the account work more hours to meet service levels agreements (SLAs) and get other tasks accomplished.

The main goal at outsourcing companies was always about "reducing headcount," so unsatisfied employees deciding to quit came at no real cost to outsourcing companies. At the midpoint in a contract, it was common for the outsourcing company to start conducting regular "resource actions" or broad layoffs in order to achieve the progressively larger profit margins targeted for each customer account. The desired outcome for the outsourcing company, according to former senior managers at Sourcing Central, was to reduce each job function to a small number of strategic employees referred to as "subject matter experts" (SMEs). In the example of data centers, SMEs design and maintain systems of highly automated batch processes. In the end, after remediating the business processes of many customers (i.e., automating them), SMEs were the only professionals that outsourcing companies cared to retain.

In the middle of this chapter, I will describe the ways in which outsourced professionals resisted their work conditions. Subjects said quitting their job was a primary form of resisting the demands of the work and deteriorated conditions of jobs at outsourcing companies. With forced and voluntary attrition and poor working conditions, professionals quickly recognized when they were not steadily making headway on a successful career path at outsourcing companies.

As the discussion on generating consent and resistance to jobs makes clear, professional careers seemed promising at the beginning of this research period (pre and immediate post Y2K). In fact, several of the professionals who were outsourced around that time have since experienced varied modicums of success at outsourcing companies. I describe significant commonalities among these professionals and how they achieved longevity in their careers at outsourcing companies. Yet, for most other subjects in my sample, the outsourcing of their work did not revitalize their careers and led to worsened job conditions. In addition to greater work demands, work speedup, and job contingencies, subjects (even SMEs) experienced constrained professional career tracks. They did not progress as far with outsourcing companies as they originally expected. I argue this lack of progression is the direct effect of the new market organization and its emphasis on the market logic of hyper-commodification. In addition, the outsourcing company's strategies of lean and flexible production methods and their emphasis on standardizing and automating work systems at customers were additional obstacles to professional careers at outsourcing companies.

In fact, I found that the promise of greater progression in professional career tracks was a misnomer because outsourcing companies' strategic planning always involved the future elimination of jobs. A discussion on the outsourcing company's focus on standardization of work will come later in the chapter. In short, outsourcing companies focus on changing the customary business processes and systems at customer companies to their standard packages of services. Through this process, the costs from "human resources" are reduced on each account and the profitability from the account grows. Standardizing business processes and systems make them ripe for automation when they become embodied within technical "software and tools." As Jay, a former Vice President of a Business Division at Sourcing Central, described, it is in the outsourcing company's best interest to reduce the amount of employees doing the work in order to cut costs.

> I mean it's a big leverage thing. So, like in the data center here, there are 20 people there that will run an operation for over a thousand hospitals. Well that's a thousandth of what the hospitals would have to spend doing it themselves. And that's done with automation and a lot of backroom people who generate software and tools to allow those 20 people to run that operation. So, it's all leverage, leverage, leverage! . . . We [companies that supply

outsourced services] love the highly leveraged, small number of people supporting large revenue flows, kind of business.

(Jay, former Executive Vice President of a
Division at Sourcing Central)

From this perspective, standardization and automation have significant implications for deskilling work and forcing job losses on outsourced professions in the future. The flexible social organization at outsourcing companies almost certainly increased the rate of standardization and automation of business systems at customers. As a result, outsourcing's effects on rates of deskilling and job losses in professions like IT and HR were compounded.

Approaches to consent

Despite the deteriorated conditions at the outset of deals, many professionals expressed positive feelings about their work at outsourcing companies. And, to this end, some stayed at their jobs for several years. Subjects consented to the working conditions at outsourcing companies, despite the harder work. But, I had to ask, why? Theory about how worker consent is generated on the shop floor is a useful starting point to show the varied ways that compliance was obtained in the inO cases in this sample. Because of the power outsourcing companies wield in increasingly constrained labor markets, outsourcing employers increasingly resorted to despotic approaches to generate forced consent from professional workers and initiate them into jobs with deteriorated employment conditions.

Michael Burawoy explains worker consent in his book *Manufacturing Consent: Changes in the Labor Process under Monopoly Capitalism* (1979). According to Burawoy, industrial workers gave their consent to coercive working conditions in monopolies when they felt they had a choice in whether to participate in the employment relationship. In tandem, industrial workers saw the direct financial value of participating in games on the shop floor, such as the game of "making out." With making out, workers process more parts than required, and, as a result, earned extra money. Therefore, organizations secured compliance when, in Burawoy's terms, workers made the choice to participate in the labor process at the point of production. Burawoy called this a hegemonic organization of work under monopoly capitalism, and described the labor process as using a combination of consent and coercion. He compared this to a despotic organization of work. Coercion – i.e., leveraging power to influence the personal choices of others – is the primary component in this type of work organization; consequently, the notion of balanced and voluntary compliance rings hollow. Appropriate analogies for despotic consent would be indentured servitude in the Middle Ages and forced slavery in early United States history.

Hegemonic and despotic approaches to the manufacturing of consent make a useful distinction for analyzing this process within inO. First, they enable an examination of how employer's approaches to the construction of compliance with inO have shifted over time. Second, these frameworks also effectively show that the manufacturing of consent was leveraged differently depending upon the level of standardization in the work being outsourced and the corresponding conditions within labor markets. Third, and perhaps most importantly, the framework is useful for describing how a hegemonic approach to organizing the work shifted to a more despotic approach as the outsourcing deal progressed. In this section, I will discuss the different approaches outsourcing companies used depending upon 1. the timing of the deal, 2. the type of work that was involved and its level of standardization, and 3. the point in time in the outsourcing contract (and especially near the end of its term).

The 20 outsourcing cases in this study began at varied times, mostly between the mid-1990s and year 2012. I determined some uniformity in the approaches outsourcing companies used to obtain compliance through three successive time periods. The successive outsourcing periods began with pre-Y2K or the mid-1990s to 2000 (six cases); then 2001 to 2005 (ten cases); and finally 2006 to 2012 (four cases). In the pre-Y2K period, customer companies in the sample included: hospitals (N = 2), chemical companies (N = 2), and telecommunications providers (N = 2). In their disclosures to media, the customer companies stated that they were using IT outsourcing to remediate outdated technologies and business processes. Subjects in these and other early cases, like Maria below, emphasized the breadth of remediation processes they helped to institute at customers after rebadging.

> There's a lot because Master Technologies takes up the support of all of this now. So we use Master Technologies tools for everything, Master Technologies processes, and we're tasked with the remediation transformation of the network servers. So we're involved with all that, and how to do it was up to Master Technologies.
>
> (Maria, IT Security Analyst at Master Technologies)

Outsourcing would also enable greater management focus on the company's core business, the primary source of its revenue. Outsourcing for cost reduction purposes was mentioned or implied as secondary. In his 1996 telecommunications case, for example, Fred said, "outsourcing was done to modernize and consolidate data centers" within the regional operations of Technologies Inc. With few exceptions, all professionals in the six cases in the pre-Y2K period were offered comparable jobs and benefits at outsourcing companies.

Because it was a relatively new staffing strategy among employers, subjects in these cases were skeptical of jobs with an outsourcing company. The majority of subjects would not have independently chosen to rebadge to outsourcing companies. They were forced by the outsourcing decision of customers to make the job change. Yet, it is important to note, many factors helped to persuade consent from the subjects to choose the outsourced job option. At the beginning of the six cases, there were no intended job losses. As subjects across these cases commented, "You were pretty much guaranteed a job." In addition, deals and financial benefits like wages and paid time off transferred unchanged to outsourcing companies.

Also, at this point, subjects resented old employers because they felt deceived by their decision to outsource their jobs, break up their work families and social contract, and jeopardize their stake in the American Dream. This resentment helped coerce their compliance to take jobs with outsourcing companies despite their initial aversion to the outsourcing. Employers also promised more career advancement opportunities with outsourcing. In four cases, ownership of the work, jobs, and people was transferred to a multinational company with leadership status in an industry and an iconic public image. From an employee identification standpoint, subjects lost "good jobs" with old companies, but they were moving to a job the general public would perceive as comparable or, perhaps, even better.

For a myriad of reasons then, most professionals in the early cases I studied consented to employers and took jobs at outsourcing companies. Fred and Sally discussed their leap of faith and the positive feelings they felt when they made their decision to rebadge in two different, pre-Y2K outsourcing cases.

> I figured, I would be happy doing what I was doing for the next 10 years. And I could do that for Tech Leader, which was a bigger company. I also thought that I could grow more, and being with the company that develops a lot of things, even robotics, I might get involved in other areas. So I thought that that was a good move for me as a 40-year-old man, thinking ten years out.
>
> (Fred, former Data Center Manager at Tech Leader)

> You were in it with a thousand other people, so it wasn't scary for me. I mean it was, "Ok, got it. I know this is coming. Let's go through the process, don't know what it's going to be like on the other side."
>
> (Sally, former Project Manager at Master Technologies)

In these early cases of outsourcing, coercion definitely shaped employees' decisions to accept jobs. Yet, the cases in the pre-Y2K period also show the hegemonic approaches that customer and outsourcing companies initially took.

After the job change, most professionals reported the speedup of their work. The immediate decline in work quality was a change in conditions that had the strong potential to raise criticism about job and employment conditions at the outsourcing company. Instead, however, the majority of IT subjects described the exciting opportunities they had to work on cutting-edge technologies and learn at other companies and from other skilled professionals. In expert fields such as IT security and IT healthcare, learning opportunities were the number one benefit that subjects reported after rebadging. Exciting learning opportunities also helped shift subjects' perceptions of the outsourcing from a coercive turn of events into a perceived opportunity through the lens of personal choice and optimism. Compared to the "scope creep, missed deadlines, and scrapped projects" that had been common in IT projects back in jobs at customers, many subjects like Davetta below described the satisfaction and accomplishment they felt from learning new things about their work at outsourcing companies.

The benefit is, there is so much more out there to know about what you do! Because here you're in a company, this is what they do! Especially in the case of IT, you're working for an IT company! This is what they do so, the advantage is that you learn so much more! You could bring so much more to the table now because you're not only, moving from left to right. "Oh you mean I can move from right to left and back to? I can do more than that and still get the same thing, okay!" Yeah, so it's just alarming, the exposure to other things. When we first became Master Technologies a lot of the people that came over from Master Technologies., that came over to the account, were from Wireless Inc. And we would hear all the time, "Well when we were at Wireless Inc.". . . . It was the exposure to the way that other businesses do what they do.

(Davetta, Team Leader in Identity Management at Master Technologies)

In contrast, in the outsourcing cases in the middle period of research from 2001 to 2005, the customer companies in my sample began utilizing outsourcing specifically for purposes of reducing the costs in the noncore parts of their business. For example the board of Diagnosis Hospital chose to outsource all of the positions in IT to reduce the costs of this work. Because of dire needs to lower costs for the county government, many people affected in this outsourcing deal at a public hospital lost their jobs. For example, Hillary reported that half of the radiology systems analysts at Diagnosis Hospital ("the B and C players") were let go. The work was outsourced to Dynasty Co. Affiliate, who had their national headquarters and plenty of their own staff located only 50 miles away.

The radiology director for example, she had eight systems analysts. Four of them were let go or reabsorbed into radiology and other capacities. Four were transferred to IT to Dynasty Co. Affiliate. Two of them quit then because they didn't want to work for [names the male founder of IT Dynasty Co.].

(Hillary, former Senior Manager at Dynasty Co. Affiliate)

Cutting costs had implications for the approaches that outsourcing companies used to generate the consent of professionals, and especially "the A-players," to accept jobs with them. In the ten middle cases, outsourcing companies were more despotic with prospective new employees from the start. In half of the cases, job occupants were not offered a new job with the outsourcing company. Outsourcing companies had already assembled their own workforces of professionals from earlier deals. Professionals who rebadged in the middle cases were thankful, but they also witnessed the troubling effects of impending job losses on colleagues who were not so lucky. Many survivors of these outsourcing cases, like Christina in the Drug Developer Inc. case featured in Chapter 2, developed deep resentment toward customer companies from this time forward. They felt these companies lacked concern for the emotional and financial toll that outsourcing and job loss took on their colleagues and friends. In addition, they resented how the company despotically handled the outsourcing announcement and job offers to only select colleagues.

> After it sunk in, I was just so upset because a lot of us were my friends! Then I was grieving that we're losing the family that we have. Very scary, I was so angry, just so so angry! I was like, "I can't believe they're doing this!" The thing that really pissed me off the most was, "You've got two weeks to make a decision. Either you're with us, or you're gone!" That rubbed me the wrong way. I don't like, it made it sound like an ultimatum. The ultimatum was that "We know you're going to take the job." That's not the way they said it, but its perception right? That's the way I heard it because it was happening to me. I waited till the last day to give them my paperwork. I knew I was going to take the job, I needed the damn job!
>
> (Christina, IT Developer at Digitize)

These negative feelings toward old employers also manifested from the lack of control that subjects felt in their decision to take new but degraded jobs with outsourcing companies.

Post-Y2K labor markets constricted because of the effects of large-scale business process reengineering, standardization, and automation happening in various functions in these professional fields (Burris 1998; Kalleberg 2011; Van Horn 2013). Wireless Inc.'s 2003 HR outsourcing agreement had immediately cut 14% of jobs in the HR call center, employee testing, and benefits offices. These had become highly standard and batch business processes – i.e., "commodity level" tasks according to Sheldon, former CIO for Sourcing Central – that were predisposed to automation. Before the outsourcing, Lynette had played a major role in standardizing and centralizing all of Wireless Inc.'s employment and employee records from multiple locations in the US into a single corporate location. Prior business strategies to "share services" – the term Lynette used to describe this project – constricted labor markets in the various lines of work affected by the centralization and standardization taking place in many professional fields. It meant a more competitive, deskilled labor market for professionals in them.

In addition to the lack of job offers, employee incentives were increasingly absent from outsourcing cases following Y2K. In the 2003 Trading Inc. case, for example, IT managers were demoted – "no one could be higher than a supervisor" at Tech Leader – and they lost yearly bonuses. Carson went from an Operations Manager at Trading Inc. to the role of Team Leader of Desktop Support.

> Tech Leader changed my job from day one. When they came in they said, "One of the things we're gonna do is we're gonna take this operations team, and we're going to move it to our operations center (in another physical location)." So my team was gonna go away. So they said, "Ok, you are now the team leader for desktop support."
>
> (Carson, former Team Leader for Desktop Support at Tech Leader)

In the 2004 St. Francis Hospital IT outsourcing case, Salma "got demoted, took a pay cut, and lost all [her] employees." Previously a "hands-on" manager, at Sourcing Central, Salma was pushed in the direction of project management by her supervisors, which "wasn't really the direction [she] thought [she] was going to go in [her] career." Instead of hands-on problem-solving with technology hardware and software, Salma now helped to manage timelines and resources for special projects that the outsourcing company Sourcing Central contracted and completed for St. Francis Hospital. Thus, in the post-Y2K period a more despotic approach coercively generated the consent of the professionals who felt lucky to be offered jobs by outsourcing companies.

In two of the four cases in the second post-Y2K period (2006 to 2012), as companies continued to consolidate and trim their costs to produce the work, jobs were only offered to professionals for a defined period of time. This was vividly described in the feature on the 2010 Digital Services Inc. case when Dwayne recalled the approach that his employer and Default Technologies took to negotiate the compliance of employees scheduled to rebadge. Professionals that took offers were only guaranteed a job for one year and, for managers, taking the job meant a demotion. In this case, a significant number of IT professionals (18%) declined positions. But the 82% who accepted jobs did so because of the terrible labor market for data center work or networking jobs at the time. In both this case and the 2012 Cloud Inc. case, subjects felt there was no *real* consent in the outsourcing matter. Instead, desperate professionals, like Courtney below, were coerced into consenting to jobs because of few comparable jobs elsewhere in the region.

> The week before Thanksgiving, they [managers at Cloud Inc.] were coercing me, "Oh, please go with Circuit, we don't really want to let you go!" I got them a little nervous . . . but in my head I'm like, "You know what? Job prospects are pretty bad out there. See what the salary is, if it's not too bad I'll take it." So that's what I did.
>
> (Courtney, Desktop Support at Circuit)

As the analysis of outsourcing cases in this sample – spanning 20 plus years – shows, manufacturing the consent of professionals to take and maintain jobs with outsourcing companies shifted in approach from hegemonic to increasingly despotic.

Patterns in findings also determine that the type of work being outsourced matters. For positions highly susceptible to automation (referred to as "commodity level" by former insider executives in this sample), the approach to rebadging was despotic, but in other cases involving more unique types of work, the approach was hegemonic. This trend was most obvious when comparing the despotic approaches used in the outsourcing of heavily routinized work with slack labor markets to the hegemonic approaches used in the outsourcing of expert work with workers in short supply.

In four cases involving the outsourcing of work in HR recruiting, training and development, and benefits administration – work that was highly regulated and standardized (Zalewski 2015) – companies were outsourcing to obtain an immediate cost savings. There were significant job losses in two cases: 14% in the Wireless Inc. case and 75% in the Peoples' Banking Inc. case. After rebadging, HR professionals also expressed high dissatisfaction in a work environment that combined more routinized work and immediate work speedup because of high commodification in outsourcing. For example, HR recruiters like Franca not only went through highly standard procedures to find and hire qualified candidates for her former employer Peoples' Banking Inc., but Franca was also expected to recruit qualified candidates for several other clients in the region in a standard time frame of 45 days. She said the work "became way too transactional for [her]," and she quit quickly after rebadging to People Solutions, the leading company in HR outsourcing at the time. Maintaining data centers and desktop support were other illustrative examples of the despotic approaches that outsourcing companies used to construct the consent of professionals who worked in more routinized IT fields. In three cases with subjects already discussed – Dwayne (2010), Carson (2003), and Courtney (2012) – all involved either demotions, the loss of material benefits, and/or a planned future job loss.

This contrasted with the more hegemonic approach outsourcing companies took to secure the consent of professional workers in expert fields with a labor shortage. The case of Merchant Inc. involved the outsourcing of professionals in IT security. Jobs were outsourced, in part, to obtain the expertise that Master Technologies had in the IT security area. Most subjects explained the need to update and protect security processes at Merchant Inc. in an age of online shopping. In 2004, when the deal began, IT security was an emerging professional field and business. It was headed by the concern of companies who processed large amounts of personal electronic data from their customers and needed to keep it secure from hackers. They could not afford to risk the trust and patronage of their customers with a significant security breach of their personal data. Labor markets in IT security were robust and companies like Master Technologies offered retention bonuses to encourage employees at customers to take the job. Brad, Davetta, and Keith, three of the four outsourced professionals I spoke with in this case, moved up a level in their "IT security silos" within months of transferring to jobs with Master Technologies. Keith described the tuition reimbursement he received on day one with his new job at Master Technologies. He received $30,000 dollars towards his MBA, and despite having one class conclude after only one day after rebadging to Master Technologies, they reimbursed Keith $7,000 dollars for the class.

There were other cases where hegemonic approaches to manufacturing consent corresponded with the new and widely adopted technologies in professional fields and the strong labor markets that were then associated with the lack of qualified candidates. This was the case for professionals who took jobs with the outsourcing company Ballast Group in 2001, which was contracted to implement an electronic medical records (EMR) system for Bravado Hospital. Around that time, most hospitals, including Accolade below, were installing the EMR system to better leverage the informating and automating capabilities of information systems (Zuboff 1988) and deliver better patient care.

EPIC to healthcare would be like SAP or PeopleSoft is to the Human Resources or the business side. So it's a single, huge application that, for your medical records, your radiology images, your pharmacy, your lab results, your census information, all that stuff is in a single application that's, all the caregivers have access to. It's huge, it's a big deal! Eight-year project, $52 million dollars, biggest non-construction project that the hospital has ever invested in.

(Rob, Network Manager at Accolade Hospital)

The financial windfall from this industry-wide investment in new technologies resulted in the growth of IT jobs in healthcare. Because of the presence of options, choice, and incentives in cases involving scarce human capital, consent was achieved through hegemonic approaches. In sum, companies used different approaches to leverage compliance depending on whether the work was considered routine or expert and whether workers were in short supply.

The approach to the manufacturing of consent was also tied to the phase in the outsourcing contract. Over the term of the outsourcing contract, there were strong tendencies, in the process of generating consent, to move from a hegemonic to more despotic approach. Outsourcing deals began with a transitional phase, where work was physically transferred from customers to vendor companies. During that time especially, outsourcing companies had to rely on the institutional knowledge of the professionals who rebadged to negotiate a smooth transition of people, data, and business processes. Consequently, they more often employed hegemonic approaches to obtain professional compliance to jobs and the initial working conditions. Professionals like Sally, who rebadged to Master Technologies in the Mammoth Inc. case, were enticed to take jobs at outsourcing companies. Wages and paid time off in this case and others were comparable to what subjects left behind at customers. In the Mammoth Inc. case jobs were also guaranteed for five years. As a result of the hegemonic approach the companies took in this case, most of the 2,600 IT professionals consented to jobs with Master Technologies.

But Mammoth Inc. actually made them put in stipulations that they would keep these people for five years, they would also take their pension and pay into it. They will get their vacation that they already have, because Master Technologies does not give more than four weeks. If someone already had five or six weeks they got to keep it, so they were grandfathered in. So there were a lot of things like that that made you feel comfortable. They could not just get rid of you as soon as they hired you on.

(Sally, former IT Project Manager at Master Technologies)

The remediation involved in incorporating the outsourcing company's standard processes and systems at customers created a lot of work that needed to be done at the beginning of the contract. Thus, added measures were applied by outsourcing companies to maintain the consent of employees during the remediation phase. Over the first few years subjects, like Ken below, often described various financial and social incentives outsourcing companies provided employees for meeting important benchmarks and deadlines in the contract. Incentives usually included monetary bonuses and after-work parties.

> Ballast Group seemed to be more, I don't want to say loose with the money. I mean if we worked an implementation and did something really well, or everybody did something well that we could expect a bonus.
>
> (Ken, former Implementation Analyst at Ballast Group)

Also, because of the added breadth and depth of work that needed to be completed to satisfy contracts during the remediation phase, some professionals advanced their position in the employment hierarchy at outsourcing companies. For example, Sally, the IT Project Manager in the Mammoth Inc. case, changed positions five times over nine years. She said, "Each job change was financially better for me." During remediation, outsourcing companies continued using hegemonic approaches to construct the consent of professionals like Sally commonly known as SMEs, "the A-group," or "fire jumpers."

Eventually, the remediation stage led to the standardization and automation of the work and the strategic goal of outsourcing: the hardline application of cost reductions across budgeted line items that included specific job cuts in contracts. In the Mammoth Inc. case, the remediation phase began waning in year five of the ten-year contract. It was memorable to Sally because Master Technologies began aggressively "releasing people."

> We were getting less work from Mammoth Inc., you know the contract every year was going down, we had a ten-year agreement. And once that was coming due, it just started dwindling, because Mammoth Inc. was like, "No we're not going to do that, we're not going to do this," and then the contract was up and they renewed it for a couple more years but for much less that they would have, so it just started getting tighter and tighter, and they would just release [handfuls of] people. For a while it was almost a weekly event.
>
> (Sally, former IT Project Manager at Master Technologies)

After midpoint in the contract, according to subjects, it was also common for customer companies to think about renegotiation and inviting other outsourcing companies to bid on the next round of work. (Some subjects described significant cost overruns in the first term of outsourcing contracts.) Because there was a possibility that the contract would not be renewed with them, vendors usually continued reducing their costs. Nearing the end of contracts also resulted in the loss of new and exciting projects and traveling regionally for meetings with peers. Benefits such as these had kept professionals like Sally and JB challenged and satisfied with management careers at outsourcing companies. The work was far less exciting as the end of contracts, and their renegotiation, neared.

In the despotic conditions of outsourcing, professionals like Dwayne reported feeling desperate in their roles at outsourcing companies. Employers did not care how subjects experienced the declining quality and rewards associated with the work. They did not care if subjects made the choice to quit their jobs and withdraw their consent. I discuss this dominant form of professional resistance to inO next.

Resistance is common

To better understand the common causes and forms of resistance, I first discuss the tradition of analyzing resistance in labor process theory in sociology (e.g., Clawson 1980). I will also describe scholarship about important work conditions that produce resistance (Hodson 1999) and provide an understanding of workers' different agendas when they resist jobs and work (Hodson 1995). These traditions help frame my findings on the two predominant ways that professionals resist inO jobs: quitting and withdrawing consent and cooperation to work conditions. Resistance forms such as these, along with high levels of attrition at outsourcing companies, have implications to market failure theory and its emphasis on structural causes as compared to micro-level sociological or interactional causes for this outcome (Williamson 1975).

Labor process theory, a predominant theoretical paradigm in the sociology of work, has captured the contested dynamics of the employer and employee relationship in capitalism over time. Scholarship shows a history of employers increasing the surplus value (profits) they obtain from exploiting their employees (Braverman 1972; Edwards 1979; Tucker 1978). These studies also account for the history of workers' struggles against exploitation by management. For example, Clawson (1980) describes the simple, technical, and bureaucratic control measures that industrialist employers developed through time to increase productivity and manage the recurring resistance of workers to each of these measures. Similar to dominant theses in labor process theory, my findings show that outsourcing companies have organized work in ways that significantly increased productivity while degrading work and working conditions for a majority of professionals in my sample. In this theory, the greater commodification and new lean and flexible labor measures outsourcing companies took to increase productivity and their profitability can be considered new market control mechanisms.

Ethnographic studies of the workplace describe the usual conditions preceding the resistance of workers and conceive the common reasons for employee resistance. Hodson (1999) analyzed 108 ethnographic studies of workplaces to better understand the causes for worker resistance. His work argues that job insecurity and undignified treatment by employers produces organizational anomie and resistance to the work. Because of the lean, flexible, and despotic conditions manifested in inO over time, job insecurity and undignified treatment appropriately explained the resistance across cases in my study as well. Hodson (1995) also offers explanations for what workers hope to achieve through resistance. He identified four agendas: "1. Deflect abuse; 2. Regulate the amount and intensity of work; 3. Defend autonomy; 4. Expand control through participatory schemes" (80). The first two agendas – deflecting abuse and regulating work – especially captured the rationale of professionals in this sample who resisted the increased demands of and undignified treatment in their jobs with outsourcing companies.

Because of generally negative assessments of jobs with outsourcing companies, subjects commonly said that job offers at the outset of deals were rejected by some of their colleagues. The lucky ones were able to bargain and find another job in customer companies, although in some cases this was not possible because of strict "moratoriums" against the internal reassignment of professionals affected by the outsourcing. Other former colleagues took the outsourcing of their jobs as an opportunity to leave customers and find something comparable with another company.

> A few people didn't take the offer. It started out by being 106, 108. And I think 89 took the deal and they are still here.
>   (Dwayne, Data Center Supervisor at Default Technologies)

Subjects across cases also said colleagues began leaving jobs with outsourcing companies, or "jumping ship," shortly after the beginning of contracts. Maria, an IT Security Specialist in the Merchant Inc. case, described the quick and ongoing exits of colleagues who had rebadged with her to Master Technologies. When we spoke in May 2005, Maria had just completed one year in the outsourcing job. She had also handed in her job resignation notice, and I was speaking with her on her second to last day at Master Technologies.

> Since being at Master Technologies, we've lost three people. But with the first person that we lost, to me it was like, "Well obviously we're going to replace that person" because we had tons of work. And they were like, "Well we're not going to replace that person" and I was like, "What?!" Because it seems to me that when we lose someone they're focused on the work that needs to be done, but not caring so much about the resources that they have to do it. It's like "Well okay there's more work, everyone's gonna have to just do more stuff" when you're already maxed out. It's not good news. But it seems to be the very budget-minded in outsourcing companies, where they don't want to replace people who leave. They're always trying to save a buck, because they're trying to reduce their costs. I've seen that now, more since I've been at Master Technologies Inc. than anyplace. And then we lost our manager, and they didn't replace him, then we lost our Director and they didn't replace him.
>   (Maria, IT Security Specialist at Master Technologies)

Outsourcing companies exemplify the idea of an "amorphous-like" (friend Melissa who introduced me to the 2002 Concerto Inc. case) social organization that contorts in one direction and then another. Contracts end, work gets standardized and people on the outsourcing account are no longer needed. Someone leaves an outsourcing account or goes to an open, higher role at a different customer and makes room for an internal candidate from somewhere else in the organization to take the open position. Or, equally likely, the position is simply eliminated. Management appeared comfortable with the fluid conditions of labor at outsourcing companies. A number of successful outsourced professionals described conversations they had with their managers where they were encouraged to change jobs, either by moving to a different account or quitting to find a "better job" outside of outsourcing. Several high-level managers – for example Lynette below, described their surprise at the high attrition levels, mobility between customer accounts, and the noncommittal culture that existed at their new employer and among senior management there.

> I'd say from a job security perspective, [I] never felt secure. I mean you were here today, gone tomorrow. And you'd meet someone or talk to someone on the phone and go "where's so and so?" "Oh they're gone." And people jump from account to account and no one thinks anything of it. Oh my gosh, this is crazy!
>
> (Lynette, former Dual Account Manager and Strategic Business Unit Manager at Web Tech)

Especially in low-end routinized work with outsourcing companies here, similar to business reports (Overby 2013), quitting was common. The conditions and incentives of low-end outsourcing jobs in IT – for example, help desk work – were perceived of as especially poor quality by job occupants. As testament, several subjects in this sample had used help desk roles to advance to more respected jobs in IT that yielded more authority and better benefits. For example, Rob had started in IT doing work at the help desk, but moved to technical work that he loved because of its "cool factor." As a consequence of their low value, subjects left these positions at high rates.

> I also have an interest in the help desk situation. I really would be interested in finding a way to develop the help desk so that it didn't have such high turnover. I'd like to find a way to somehow have a help desk where that position is valued and the person feels valued in doing it and, subsequently, it would become super effective. It would be hard to do that, but I would probably think I could do that with an older generation of people. Right now, IT people, somebody will say, "Gee, I'll work the help desk because that puts my foot in the door," but they're looking to move on. So, subsequently, as soon as they're really good, they're gone. And they should. If it's a young kid, that's what he should be doing, but it so destroys the effectiveness of the operation.
>
> (Dominic, IT Manager at Sourcing Central)

Hope discussed the high rate of attrition in an outsourced call center, another highly undervalued organizational role, when she was employed as its manager by Accessible Hardware. "Ship," either with the signifier "moving" or "people jumping," was a poignant metaphor that Hope and several other subjects in the sample used to describe the high rates of employee attrition at outsourcing companies.

On the hospital's part, I don't think there was a lot of desire to get close or to mingle with us because we were just always a moving ship, people coming on and off, you know.

(Hope, former Telecommunications Manager at Accessible Hardware)

While resigning or moving positions was a common form of resistance among outsourced professionals, another common form was to limit cooperation to meet added job requirements. This was similar to the resistance that sociologists reported in ethnographic studies of factory work in the 1960s (e.g., Halle 1984). Management called this behavior "soldiering" or "slacking" (Braverman 1972). Hodson (1995), more recently, described it as workers restricting their output in their attempt to control the intensity of the work. Below, Lisa defined the times when she reserved herself from completing the contracted work that was expected by Bravado Hospital and its staff.

I get to hide behind a Ballast Group (the vendor) mask if I needed to. So, if users are getting irate that something wasn't getting done, you want them to be able to do whatever they need to do. But at the same time, it would be easy just to [say] like, "Well, whatever. I'll work on it when I can. I got X, Y, and Z thing going on over here," and then you waited until it got escalated up through somebody and then you're like, "OK, well . . . now I'll work on it." So, yeah, I think I definitely felt less connected to the employees, with Bravado Hospital too, because I'm behind the scenes, I'm hardly out talking to you.

(Lisa, former IT Interface Analyst at Ballast Group)

Over time, economic organization scholars have conceived various theories of worker cooperation in the labor process. In a classic example, Blau (1962) distinguishes between consummate and perfunctory cooperation. A person shows consummate cooperation when they give their full cooperation to the task at hand. In other words, "they hold back nothing." Blau argues that organizations run more efficiently when consummate cooperation characterizes the company culture. On the other hand, a person demonstrates perfunctory cooperation when they exert only the minimum effort. Organizations run less efficiently in company cultures dominated by perfunctory cooperation. Employees shirk responding to some duties or the quality of the work is lacking. Picking up on this theory, Williamson (1975:69) implied that this difference may have salience in explaining some factors involved in the failure of market organizations. Applying this theory here, in the course of their work, outsourced professionals could collectively restrict their full cooperation and eventually bring about the failure of an outsourcing deal because the customer did not receive the level of service they wanted.

Williamson's theory played out in the Merchant Inc. and Master Technologies outsourcing deal. The outsourcing contract only lasted one year before Merchant Inc. canceled it despite the real possibility of facing financial penalties. I interviewed four subjects the week after Merchant Inc. publicly announced their decision to cancel the contract. I was shocked to learn that my subjects heard about the contract termination from local news sources rather than directly from their employer. I asked them why they believed the deal failed so rapidly. Russell – an IT Director who formerly occupied a governance role on the Merchant Inc. side of the outsourcing relationship – implied that reduced customer control, the failure to align "expectations" between the two companies, and the perfunctory cooperation levels from the vendor were likely important factors in the abrupt cancelation of this deal.

> After we outsourced it seemed like everything we needed, or needed quickly, was an additional charge. "[The Vendor] Well that wasn't part of the contract." "[Russell] We need this by tomorrow," but "[the vendor] It's gonna cost you 'X' number of dollars more." When it's your own staff, you tell somebody, "I need it tomorrow," you get it tomorrow! So you lose that kind of control. . . . I think the hardest part of when you're outsourcing a relationship is getting expectations set correctly. And I think Merchant Inc. was disappointed in the result and maybe 'cause Merchant Inc. didn't do, I mean they were supposed to do, clarifying or, making sure they understood the services that were going to be provided. There were frequent conflicts with what we thought we were going to get and what Circuit Inc. thought they were to deliver. And that stayed true throughout the whole relationship.
>
> (Russell, former IT Security Director at Merchant Inc.)

Although very few of my subjects went on the record in the interview and reported their personal shirking of their tasks, I presume restriction of output was more common than reported. Outsourcing companies expected and staffed their client accounts based on the work output of outstanding people who would get what was necessary done within a context of constrained resources. Even outstanding performers such as Lynette, who I quote below, quickly perceived that the work expectations in outsourcing were too much. These types of professionals saw themselves as people who always gave more to their work and employers than expected. They gave consummately. Yet, in circumstances where their best effort was only "just good enough" or it was criticized, outstanding professionals withdrew consent and looked for opportunities outside of outsourced labor markets.

> Also some of the attrition was from the fact that you were working a 12-, 15-hour day as norm. And so, at some point in time you have to figure out, "Do I have a life or not?" And I think that was a lot of mine. Okay, I don't mind working hard, I've always worked hard, I've always put in 200% effort but when you call me and I'm sitting in the church parking lot, and you're asking me to go over budgets. And you're upset because I don't have the information in front of me, it's like "Okay!" At that point, you sit there going, "Okay this is really ridiculous!" To them, when they were making deals to be working till 4, 5 o'clock in the morning, get a couple hours sleep, and then

come back and continue to do the negotiations. I mean a lot of people thrived on it. I can tell you a lot of people looked at it and said, "You know, I got a family. I can't do this!"

(Lynette, former Dual Account Manager and
Strategic Business Unit Manager for Web Tech)

Similarly to Hodson (1999:80), the subjects in my study reported one of their only means of control in regulating the intensity of work in an outsourcing environment was restricting the time and effort they gave to the work. Furthermore, they explained that the rate in which professionals quit jobs at outsourcing companies was higher than at customer companies. This was the most common way that professionals resisted despotic working conditions at outsourcing companies. People were often encouraged to switch positions or leave, and outsourcing companies did little to stop it. In this way, outsourcing companies instituted lean and flexible properties into their organization.

Professional careers with outsourcing companies

I opened this chapter with a vignette contrasting two of my subjects, Brad and Dwayne. Brad and other mobile professionals in my sample represent the successful career stories with inO. Outsourcing delivered on its promise of upward mobility in professional careers for the following subjects, including several who emphasized to me directly this probably would not have been the case at customer companies: Brad, Fran, Tanya, Christina, Sally, Paul, and Doris. Five of these subjects were still working at outsourcing companies at the time I was writing the bulk of this book in 2017, and two had carved out "careers of achievement" there (Zabusky & Barley 1996). It is an interesting question, and I have pondered what qualities help leverage success in more contingent or peripheral labor markets.[2]

In this section, I examine the careers of subjects in outsourcing, and I begin by discussing the professionals who succeeded in this sample. What factors explain why a few professionals survived and succeeded in an industry that "chews-up" most of the people who experience it intimately? I draw on classic social theory, economic sociology, popular social science, and academic advising to explain why a few particular professionals experienced upward mobility and success in careers at outsourcing companies. I then switch my focus to the professionals who walked away (both voluntarily and forcefully) from jobs at outsourcing companies. Rather than being a source of pride for these professionals, outsourcing for the majority of subjects was an experience that manifested in "desperation" for some of them and personal costs for many others. To finish, I describe what the group of professionals collectively identified as the costs of outsourcing to professional lives and careers. I also discuss structural causes for the manifestation of "portfolio careers" (Handy 1991; Hicks 2017).

Max Weber, the sociologist who first conceived of the social bases of authority, argued that outwardly demonstrating passion and charisma will evoke positive reactions and commitment from others (Weber 1947:359). Passion and charisma was precisely what I experienced in my interactions with two subjects in 2005, both Brad (featured in the opening to the chapter) and Fran. To give a sense of the level of passion Weber means and that these subjects exuded, below is an excerpt taken about two minutes into my conversation with Brad. The positivity and enthusiasm in which Brad explained his work in IT security, at this early stage in the interview, continued to its end. Just as passionately, he discussed various aspects of IT work, the outsourcing transition, and his work experiences in this job function at two corporations:

> As far as expectations, I just wanted to get into the organization (Merchant Inc.) and grow, share my knowledge of IT with them. My skill set. So it was a great opportunity when I first started, I had a great manager. Everyone I worked with loved their job. They weren't there to do the job, they loved doing IT! And it was great to work with people like that. And at first I was a little intimidated because I was younger going into this big corporation. I'm one of the youngest people working in the security industry, but I loved it! I shared a lot of my ideas and skills and it worked out great!
>
> (Brad, IT Security Expert at Master Technologies)

Brad was an example of a young professional who had leveraged his youthful enthusiasm, passion for technology, impulse to share technical knowledge, confidence in interpersonal interactions, and personal charisma to his professional advantage. Twelve years after this conversation, in 2017, Brad was in an elite Security Development Manager role at Master Technologies. His case is a great example of how passion, enthusiasm, and charisma around others have led to mobility and roles of greater authority with outsourcing. Brad's tone-elevated rhetoric of "great opportunity[ies], great manager[s], love of IT and security!" helped him obtain the desired features of a professional career. That career included challenges in the work, autonomy, and advancement in the design and development side of a company that specializes in providing IT security solutions for large firms.

Another example of the passion and charisma necessary in the social environment and to lead at outsourcing leaders was Tanya, a mid-range Project Manager at Tech Leader I interviewed in 2010. Flexible and lean production arrangements have a high tendency to produce regular situations of work chaos. At several points in our interview, Tanya called herself a "fire-jumper." She described assignments where she had to manage ad hoc teams to correct a project that was in crisis mode. Below Tanya describes one of these exciting yet "painful" project assignments where she, providing leadership, was able to finish jobs on a tight deadline. Over time through all of my interviews, I learned that leadership experiences like these get the attention and gain the confidence of higher-level management. They also lend themselves to job tenure and the possibility of advancement. Tanya had survived and prospered at Tech Leader for ten years, by 2010 moving into challenging new core areas like web development because of the passion and charismatic leadership she demonstrated in her project management work at times of both stability and crisis.

> They (Tech Leader) pulled me off all my other projects and it was in the red (Tech Leader's code for a failing project). I had some insane timeline. I think I got the project in November and it was red, and it was supposed to go live in April with brand-new hardware and everything. Fortunately I got a guide from mainstream Tech Leader who is the uber architect, he was unbelievable! I got this great systems engineering guide and I had one of the guys who had worked for me formally. I had a team of three project managers helping me and we just pushed this thing through and got it into production. And it worked! It was good! It was just a really painful experience. The good news was I was viewed by management as a go-to person.
>
> (Tanya, Project Manager at Tech Leader)

In 2005 Brad was working in the growing IT security sector, which was a clear advantage in terms of his mobility. This industry continues to help him today. Because of Brad's youthful age, he also benefited because he had tinkered with information technologies most to all of his life. In other examples of mobile professionals, "being in the right place at the right time" and being well prepared because of ample practice also appeared as significant factors in biographies. The right place and time and lots of practical experience support the popular "Gladwellian" (2008) perspective on success as well as the value of an old adage in American culture.

JB, on the older side of the age range in the sample, compiled one of the longest records for being in the right place and time. He capitalized on a hiring period in the 1970s at a good telecommunications employer in his region (Telephony Inc., later purchased by Technologies Inc. that later was acquired by Apex Inc.). Because of the growth and changes in digital technologies in the workplace beginning at that time, JB continued to benefit from regular mobility and promotions over the next 33 years of his professional career in the telecommunications field.

> I started when I was 20. I needed a job, and my uncle's neighbor worked for Telephony Inc. and said, "Well there's a couple of openings at the phone company why don't you go and apply." So I did, and the rest is history. I mean, I don't know if you could do that anymore. It's been a 33-year service. Started as a janitor and then I worked frames. . . . And then I had worked number 5 crossbar. . . . And then I went to the mini computer center they first opened downtown . . . and then. . . .
>
> (JB, former Data Center Manager at Tech Leader)

Finally, two closely tied personality traits that helped the successful professionals in the outsourcing sample leverage ongoing opportunities are the qualities of extraversion and networking. Below Christina described the opportunities she gained from different work experiences in the development of data analytics. She also commented favorably about the financial rewards she had received at the outsourcing company Digitize. In her personal case, Christina linked her mobility to being outspoken. In other parts of the conversation, Christina gave examples of how she vigorously pursued and asked for new roles at Digitize. By demonstrating extraversion, Christina and the other "A-Group" professionals placed themselves opportunistically in situations where they could learn, shine, and benefit from accomplishments they made in their work.

> For me personally, I may not be the norm, but this [outsourcing] was the best thing that has ever happened to me! As angry and frustrated as I was about the whole thing, I doubled my salary in like two years! I would have never, ever, doubled my salary with Drug Developer Inc. by now. I mean Digitize just gave us so much more opportunity! And again, because I was such a vocal person, they began to give me projects and other things to do. And I would run with it!

> (Christina, IT Developer at Digitize)

Economic sociology has historically included studies that emphasize the value of social ties for job mobility and economic well-being. Granovetter's analysis (1974) of the factors that lead to getting a job is often cited as a classic. Social ties, he said, have economic value because they are the source of information about available jobs; this information may not be publicly known (11). The old workplace adage, "it's not what you know but who you know" captures one of the implications for accessing jobs and experiencing upward mobility because of social ties. For some, accessing jobs and experiencing career mobility were less a matter of earning them as compared to having an inside track and a culture of cronyism that promoted insiders and the status quo. According to subjects like Fran, with 20 years of job advancement and including paramount success at Tech Leader, economic sociology does a good job characterizing "getting (and keeping) a job" in the outsourcing industry. In her personal case, Fran demonstrated initiative, skill, and extraversion combined with high levels of networking to obtain new positions with greater authority and financial compensation. Ten years after the interview below took place – i.e., by 2015, Fran had moved from an executive account manager position to a global leadership role at Tech Leader. Exemplifying Granovetter's thesis verbatim, Fran's meteoric ascent in the outsourcing industry over 20 years was due to passion for her work and her ability to obtain greater roles through mindful networking.

> You know I was too stupid back then [Fran is referencing the early 1980s and laughs]! I didn't think of it as IT, because back then IT really wasn't IT that we know it now. So it was just a job for me. It was an opportunity, and through that opportunity came other opportunities. I found that networking is key, more than anything else on the planet when it comes to *getting a job* (my emphasis). But back then, I didn't think about a career. After I'd been

there awhile then it's like, "Well what do I want to do next?" I started talking to people and they said, "Well there's an opening over here." You know there are never any job postings! So it's whoever you knew who told you where the next position would be. And that's how it was back then, it's a little bit different now, but not a whole lot [Fran laughs] . . . if you're stuck in a place where you don't have that access to other Tech Leaders, you're dead! If that account goes away, you're gone! Because you will not find another job, because even the ones that are posted, they already have candidates for. They have somebody that they know, that they're going to fill that position with. So you're dead if you don't have a network. Every job I've had since actually through, every job I've had and like I said, I move almost every year, year and a half, everything I've gotten is though networking. It's key.

(Fran, Executive Account Manager at Tech Leader)

In the interviews some professionals, like Fran and Christina, said the opportunities for new work experiences and upward career progression were possible only because of the context at outsourcing companies. If someone demonstrated the extra-ordinary work ethic and other qualities that helped to leverage success, there were other rewarding places and positions to advance towards within an outsourcing company. But, as I have demonstrated and argue, outsourcing was "(only) better for some" professionals and their careers. Most professionals (even the successful ones) acknowledged that there were aspects to the work that negatively impacted discretion and working time on the job, and there were major obstacles to an upwardly mobile career (Zalewski 2007).

In this chapter, I have spoken extensively about the speedup of work as it related to outsourcing. Ultimately, outsourcing companies needed to produce contracted work at a reduced cost, and they accomplish this primarily with lean and flexible production methodologies, standardizing, and eventually automating the work. After rebadging, work speedup resulted in most cases, and most subjects discussed the challenges of maintaining a work and life balance in professional careers at outsourcing companies. It was difficult to accommodate life when working 60-, 70-, and 80-hour work weeks.

Other negative outcomes typical of peripheral labor markets characterized outsourcing and professional careers in this sample too (Edwards 1979). For example socio-economic benefits including salary and job titles tended to be poorer with outsourcing. Professional jobs with outsourcing companies were more contingent than jobs with customer companies. And subjects expressed concerns over whether they wanted a continuing, long-term career working in outsourcing with its oft frenetic and "pressure"-cooker conditions. Ironically because of her success with Tech Leader then and since, in 2005 Fran candidly confided there was a forthcoming day of reckoning for her when she would decide whether to stay with outsourcing or pursue another entrepreneurial career course in IT work.

F: It gets to the point where I'm like, and the fact that they put so much pressure on certain positions, and they don't give you a chance to succeed. Um, I'm getting disillusioned I guess, and now I'm thinking that maybe this is not what I want to do in the future.

J: *What do you see with regard to your future career?*

F: I don't know right now. Like I said, I see myself fulfilling this position for at least a year. . . . As far as my future goes, I don't know. It all depends on how good, how I come out, either scathed or unscathed at the end of this year. I have opportunities to move into the project executive areas after this, if I want to. And the question is what I want to do, or do I want to run my own business the way I see fit. And just get out of the corporate world altogether. So there's big fork in the road coming [laughing], I just don't know which way I'm gonna go yet. I mean part of it is, I have two kids that I gotta get through college. So that's gonna be the biggest question is, do I have enough and is this the right time for me to go off on my own? Or do I look for just a smaller corporation where I can make a big difference, within a smaller environment with less bureaucracy. So maybe there's three roads, I don't know yet. I'm just taking it a day at a time at this point.

As I described in the two preceding chapters, cultures of hyper-commodification, lean production, and the typical social conflict that manifests in an outsourcing environment have the effect of chewing-up the human psyche.

Other structural constraints on careers and mobility

I will briefly discuss two more considerations (and obstacles) to obtaining a successful professional career at outsourcing companies. The first consideration is the direct detrimental effect of the market organization of work on labor markets and professional careers with inO. The second consideration is the ongoing negative effects of standardizing work on careers affected by it. Because of the negative realities of outsourcing that I have described, I argue that the broad outcome of inO and outsourcing will not generally live up to the positive outcomes that advocates described. Structurally, the greater job contingencies in outsourcing helped sustain the labor pattern of "portfolio careers" today (Handy 1991; Hicks 2017; Shaffer & Zalewski 2011). Findings here on the growing practice of the inO of jobs in the recent past reinforce the idea that employers have had great power and influence in affecting the high attrition patterns in professional careers today.

The ideology of advocates, like the Outsourcing Institute, said that professional careers will be "revitalized" in the broader job structures at outsourcing companies. Indeed, many subjects explicitly described the mobility possibilities at outsourcing companies as a primary benefit to working there. As my caveat, only a few professionals in my convenience sample actually had career growth at outsourcing companies that they believed would not have happened at old employers. And only one, Fran, appears to have reaped the rewards of her drive and commitment (and ability to network) at Tech Leader for the past 20 years to achieve a decidedly elite position – Global Program Manager – in the company in 2017.

It is important to acknowledge the workers employed at jobs with outsourcing companies for several years, they did what was asked, but they did not experience job mobility. As observed by subjects with tenure in inO, mobility mostly consisted of lateral moves from one customer account to another. Lateral moves, as Salma astutely noted below, were not about advancing up a career ladder.

> And I don't think it's necessarily Sourcing Central as a whole, I just think the larger the outsourcing company, the more the employees, I feel like I'm just a number, I'm just. . . . And I guess for some people that's fine, but for those of us who are trying to advance their IT career, who are trying to mesh my two worlds – there's applications and network – there's, no opportunity in there. I know that, I can go on the Sourcing Central site and go apply for all these other Sourcing Central jobs, but, at the same time, to what end? To do the same thing for the next four years just for someone else now or another Managed Services site? You know, that's not really what I want.
>
> (Salma, Project Manager at Sourcing Central)

In some of the deals that ended because contracts got terminated, outsourced professionals were rehired by the customer firm. In the former circumstance, though, how is it possible that most people that I spoke with who gave the job in outsourcing a shot did not experience the "revitalization" that advocates promised? In large part, limited revitalization of professional careers was because of the cost reduction reasons for the outsourcing of the work in the first place. Customers obtained the remediation services of outsourcing companies, who applied their new technologies and "best practice" methodologies to produce more standard, deskilled, and automated work that required minimal human support.

Most importantly, the work became far less costly to deliver back to customers. In this way, outsourcing companies achieved the original cost reduction goals of customers captured in the contract. However, the labor effect was that professionals who stuck with outsourced jobs eventually worked themselves into a "steady state" or maintenance phase in the work. This outcome seemed very similar to the routinized state of work for machine operators in Zuboff's iconic study (1988) of labor outcomes when employers adopted the new industrial and digital technologies in early computerization. Work was no longer putting in exciting new technologies, processes, and expert systems. Instead and in most cases, it was about maintaining system availability and occasionally addressing the needs of users with an application problem. Corresponding with the steady state phase, fewer professionals were needed to do the work and jobs eventually ended. If it was possible to move to another account, like Salma said above, new work for professionals at outsourcing companies consisted of doing the same remediation tasks yet again for a different customer. There was little growth opportunities in specialty fields of expertise, as in more traditional ideas of the "career ladder" (Mirvis & Hall 1994; Sullivan 1999).

Through these continuous processes of standardizing the work at more customers, outsourced professionals were not only helping their employers become more profitable from accounts, but they also constricted the labor markets in their own professional fields in the process. Human resources were limited on accounts because of highly regimented systems of lean production at outsourcing companies, which forced work speedup and subtracted the time available to complete the work. By their profitability standards, accounts then shifted into crisis and further intensified speedup because of the financial penalties outsourcing companies could face for missing contractual deadlines. According to subjects, crisis modes such as these and assessed penalties in outsourcing were common.

Lean production methods, compounded by an account in crisis mode, made it essential for outsourced professionals to quickly find and install standardized processes already developed at other customer accounts. Fran, an Executive Account Manager recently assigned to save an account "in crisis" at Insurance Inc. when we spoke in 2005, indicated how she pushed her subordinates to save time by copying similar processes as they move from one customer account to another. The excerpt below gives a sense of the important role managers play in shepherding the remediation of customers' business processes by ensuring that their subordinates institute only standard processes in their work. Fran's disparagement of her colleague for trying to do her work in a creative manner solidifies that, by 2005, work with outsourcing jobs was already becoming routinized. Professionals in outsourced jobs were paid to *do* but not to *think* outside of the already preconceived box of standardized systems of business processes. As I have argued previously, discretion is significantly reduced in jobs in outsourcing (Zalewski 2007).

> One of the women that reports to me now, she's responsible for making sure that all the processes and procedures for our desk-side support and our help desk are set up 'cause we're not in steady state [the maintenance phase of systems development] yet. . . . Well she's creating brand new processes and procedures! I'm like, "Why are you doing that?!" She goes "Well I can't find any of the same processes." I go, "How many other damn SL accounts do we have out there? What you've learned on other accounts, you know which ones are good, you know which ones are bad, go and get em!" . . . [Fran whispered while miming her subordinate.] "Well I've never thought of thaaat." And I'm like, "You've all been at other locations and done other accounts, why aren't you building off of that experience?! Why don't you go back and look for help where you know you can get it, quick and dirty?!" Some people walk around with, what's just frustrating as hell, is that they'll walk around with blinders and "Oh this is a new account so everything's gonna be new." Okay. The wheel was invented a long time ago, okay? The spokes on the hubcap may be different but, the wheel is still the wheel, and you have base stuff that you still have to do. You can update it with any nuances from your contract, but why reinvent it all over again?
>
> (Fran, Executive Account Manager at Tech Leader)

I will return to a discussion of standardizing work at outsourcing companies and how it constricts labor markets in my concluding remarks below.

There are some structural features of market organization in the inO cases in this sample that stifled the "revitalization" of ongoing professional careers at outsourcing companies. The professionals in this sample discussed limited levels of organizational positions and corresponding careers in outsourcing. Subjects most often stayed in the same position after moving to outsourcing companies or, less often, they moved up one job level. After rebadging, professionals also became part of a job "silo" (an area of specialization) at outsourcing companies. For example, the four subjects I spoke with in the Merchant Inc. case moved into job silos at Master Technologies in each of their areas of expertise in IT security (e.g., identity management, disaster recovery, etc.). In silos, professionals supported a larger set of customers in the immediate region when a problem escalated and quickly required the collective expertise within the level of that group. Across cases, silos also represented the only path for career advancement and this represented a significant drawback for career-minded professionals in the sample.

Professionals like Paul, who experienced quick mobility at outsourcing companies, surprised me when they were critical of their growth possibilities in the structured job silos. In Paul's case, in a year he went from Workplace Services Manager at one location to fulfilling the same role over three locations of Concerto Inc. In the excerpt below Paul explained the negative aspect of highly structured job silos and career paths at his outsourcing employer Circuit. From Paul's prior advancement experience in two companies, he felt that being pigeon-holed in a job silo cut him off from other opportunities to explore different facets of his employer's "business" or any of his own growing career proclivities. The only possibility for career growth at outsourcing companies was continuing the same job tasks but in a larger, more comprehensive role in a silo. To me Paul convincingly argued below, although highly successful in his current role, he would never be tapped for a larger role in another job function at Circuit.[3]

I came in managing only one facility. I apparently did a very good job because this past year they've given me two more. And within the next year or so I'm actually hoping to take on five more new facilities and manage them. So, I do think that my career will continue to grow as I continue to prove myself. My concern is the limitations on my career growth are [that] I will continue to grow in an IT field. Whereas in a larger company, and I'm going to go back to my experience at the bank, I started at that bank as a teller at a drive-thru window. . . . And, in a ten-year span, I was able to go from handing out money at the window, to managing their customer service department, to developing their LAN computer technology. [These were] completely unrelated fields, all within the same company, based on my ability to build that network of people and knowledge and grow in the business. Because I am not working for Circuit at the Circuit headquarters in [technology city], will I continue to grow across other areas of influence at Circuit? I don't think so. I don't know that I would have the opportunity to move into managing a Circuit sales team, or move into managing a Circuit acquisition, or a Circuit product launch. Where [in contrast] I would have had that at Concerto Inc.

(Paul, Manager of Workplace Services for Circuit)

Reiterating Paul's claim of the structural constraints to professional careers with inO, other subjects also said that movement up job silos was significantly hindered because jobs were located at the physical sites of their customer. They were separated from corporate home offices and from the managers assigned to oversee other customer accounts. As a result, subjects who were onsite at customers had difficulties networking with colleagues and managers who would tell them about other opportunities in the company. As Fran emphatically said earlier, "If that account goes away and you don't have a network, you're gone!" The physical obstacle to networking combined with the outsourcing company's central goal of leveraging larger revenue meshes well with leaner human resources on accounts and projects and constrained careers there per Kalleberg and Marsden (2005) and as others (Overby 2013) have noted. Partly because of the physical location of jobs and the constraint this had on the development of their social networks, jobs were more contingent and shorter termed with inO. This pattern lends itself to the "portfolio career" patterns that often are attributed to the desire of people who want more from their lives than the traditional outcomes from rigid professional roles and greedy institutions (Eyre, Mitchell, Milford, Vaswani, & Moylan 2014; Griffin 2008; Platman 2004). My findings underscore the structural causes of portfolio career patterns.

By late 2017, only five professionals in my sample were continuing in jobs with outsourcing companies (Fran and Tanya at Tech Leader, Brad at a now merged outsourcing company/division of Master Technologies and Circuit, Christina at Digitize, and Doris at Right Technology Solutions). In a way, these professionals support the industry claim in the 2003 edition of *Outsourcing Essentials*, which I described in the introduction to the chapter. Professionals who became employed in the first stages of growth in outsourcing fields benefited from long-term careers because of their "first mover status." The professionals in my sample who experienced long-term success at outsourcing companies all obtained their jobs early: in 1990 (Doris at Right Technology Solutions), in 1996 (Fran at Tech Leader), 2000 (Tanya at Tech Leader), 2002 (Christina at Digitize), and 2004 (Brad at Master Technologies). However, over time, rebadging and long-term careers with outsourcing happened infrequently. Employee ranks at outsourcing companies swelled to reach saturation, and the material returns – meaning roles and salaries – were not nearly as good. Furthermore, outsourcing companies also stifled professional careers by applying standardized and automated technology processes and systems of lean and flexible organization. This emphasizes how outsourcing companies quickly assembled their core workforces of the "A-players" or "SMEs." Professionals involved in the early stages of IT outsourcing were the only ones in my sample who successfully constructed long-term employment at outsourcing companies.

In my study, I would define success with outsourcing as long-term job tenure, with some signs of upward mobility. Fran, Tanya, and Christina – in particular – indicate that two career tracks were common to success at outsourcing companies: Account Management (AM) and Project Management (PM). AM and PM are highly important because of the goals of outsourcing companies including effective and efficient project development, implementation, management involving standardization and automation, reducing costs, and adding to the revenue flows and profitability of the company. The primary purpose of both these managers are shepherding new projects through a five-stage cycle that benefits the goals of the outsourcing company. Project managers initiate, plan, execute, monitor and control, and close.[4] Both provided strong direction to front-line subordinates to install the outsourcing company's standard and automated processes and systems at their customers as quickly as possible. The sooner these processes and systems were put in place, the sooner professionals would roll off of the customer account and onto a new one, or they would face job termination at the outsourcing company. Importantly, AM and PM work helped outsourcing companies achieve their primary ambition described above. Logically then, the AM and PM roles, directly supportive of this strategic goal, were two of the only roles with potentially handsome or long-term (i.e., job tenure) rewards associated with them.

Conclusion

In this chapter, I have explained how companies shifted their approach over two and a half decades to obtain the consent of professionals in outsourced jobs. Pre-Y2K years were the boon years for professionals affected by outsourcing deals. Professionals were offered jobs with outsourcing companies and kept their jobs indefinitely because of their first mover status. Typically and especially in the cases of IT workers, material benefits transferred unchanged in these deals. IT workers also found exciting new professional challenges and obtained expertise from new technologies and best practices in various areas of IT work. All the positive aspects about the work and its material benefits helped to offset the immediate drawbacks of outsourced jobs.

One of the biggest disadvantages was significant work speedup due to the new work in contracts and the new processes and work resulting from the market structure and the lean human resource methodologies at most outsourcing companies. Maria, a front-line IT security specialist, most poignantly talked about the increase in work she faced when former team members "left and weren't replaced." Maria very bluntly stated, "When you are already maxed out, it's not good news."

Incentives to come on board and stay with the company existed for professional workers in the pre-Y2K cases because outsourcing companies were assembling their own core set of SMEs. These were professionals who developed the automating technologies that threw "a thousand people" out of work, or they were the Project Managers who helped install the standard processes and automating technologies at customers. Because they were in the first wave of professionals to move, a few of the subjects who rebadged prior to or around Y2K found continuing success at outsourcing companies and were still employed in outsourcing as of 2017.

Outcomes related to professional careers with outsourcing companies deteriorated very quickly following Y2K, and outsourcing companies used despotic methods to obtain compliance from employees to jobs and deteriorated work conditions. After 2000, outsourcing deals typically involved job losses or a decrease in material benefits. Degraded job conditions in post-Y2K outsourcing deals included work speedup, demotions, less pay and vacation, more routinized work, and greater job contingencies. These circumstances were the effect of ongoing cost reduction strategies that outsourcing companies, and companies across other industries, applied to keep lowering the costs of their noncore business functions. For two decades, outsourcing companies have relied on lean and flexible organization and automating technologies to reduce their need for and cost from human labor. Because of constricting labor markets for work in their field, many professionals affected by post-Y2K outsourcing deals felt lucky at the prospect of being offered another position. Despite the deteriorated conditions, they accepted jobs in outsourcing because of more limited job opportunities elsewhere.

Some professionals did resist outsourcing companies' demands by quitting their jobs. Compared to levels as direct employees at customers, the vast majority of subjects said rates of abandoning jobs were high in outsourcing. Outsourcing companies did not mind potential staffing problems because high rates of attrition actually helped them achieve the leaner and more flexible social organization they needed to be profitable. While quitting was one way to resist, at times several subjects also reported restricting their full cooperation in the course of the work day. For example, to offset heavy work demands, a few outsourced professionals described the way they ignored customers' urgent requests for support by not answering the telephone. However, like the physical affordances from the periodic breakdown of Fordist assembly lines, these were only temporary reprieves for outsourced professionals. Ultimately, they were forced to respond to customers because they escalated requests to an emergency level. Both forms of resistance, quitting jobs and constraining cooperation and output in the work process, were results of the acute application of lean organization and work speedup and declining job satisfaction with social conditions of jobs in markets.

Several subjects I discussed experienced success in their professional careers with an outsourcing company. There were both structural and personal reasons for this prosperity. Structural factors that supported their achievement included the early timing of the deal, recent technology advancements in professional fields, which guarantee a limited labor supply, and the level of standardization in the work already. The ability to develop and leverage social networks was also an essential part to success in jobs in outsourcing. When the work and people were dispersed across great physical distances, the job was inherently more insecure because contracts were tenuous and the work would eventually be automated. Individualized factors that helped leverage success in careers in outsourcing included passion for the work, personal charisma, and an extroverted personality. With the exception of a few people who were in jobs with outsourcing companies in 2017, however, the outcome for most other subjects in this sample was not close to the 2005 promise of a "revitalization of careers."

Contradicting this early positive claim, I found that professional jobs and career tracks were in fact constrained for most professionals rather than revitalized because of the new market organization of the work. Constrained job silos represented the one predominant path for professional career progression at outsourcing companies. Subjects like Paul quit successful jobs at outsourcing companies specifically because they felt cut off from career opportunities in "unrelated fields in the company." Two predominant career paths were common to the few successful professionals still working for outsourcing companies in early 2018. These career tracks were in the account management and project management roles. It makes sense that the professional roles designed to upsell and institute standardization and automation changes and the roles meant to eliminate the need and reduce the costs of human labor on customer accounts were the roles with job and career longevity at outsourcing companies. In sum, after analyzing professional jobs and careers with inO over a span of two and a half decades, it is clear that outsourcing was not the pioneer of job revitalization and growth that the industry portrayed to the business community or to the public.

Instead, outsourcing companies, especially the large global players, homogenize, deskill, and mechanize the work they are contracted to deliver to their customers. Their eventual goal, according to industry insiders in the sample, is to "leverage" large revenue flows through automation and with the minimum amount of human staff to support the technology infrastructure. Outsourcing companies in this sample achieved this objective with some business processes and technology systems. One of the obvious examples is the case of outsourced data center work that Jay discussed earlier in this chapter, where only a few people managed technology operations that served thousands of their customers. Outsourcing companies achieved their leveraging goals in a relatively short amount of time because of their concentrated focus on standardization. They employ SMEs to develop the tools necessary to quickly institute automated technologies. In this respect, outsourcing companies delivered on their promise to customers. They automated the work and made it less costly to produce. But, in this process, the industry created a leaner and more prohibitive employment landscape that was and continues to be "a lot meaner" and more competitive for people whose professional work has come under the purview of outsourcing.

Notes

1 The fall 2003 *Outsourcing Essentials* article is subtitled "How Recent Outsourcing Deals Are Shaking Up Career Paths."
2 Successful subjects, I strongly caution, only represent a fraction of the outsourced professionals I spoke with for this study. The majority of professionals, to reiterate, had not found the outsourcing environment professionally beneficial or to their liking. As a result they either moved on to other employment opportunities out of their own volition, or they had subsisted in degraded outsourcing jobs until the time they eventually were dismissed by employers.
3 Paul left his position at Circuit three years after our 2005 interview. Following his departure, he moved up in marketing and then sales positions within a consumer products company. In 2017, Paul became a regional administrator for a professional service organization. Indeed, after outsourcing Paul had career growth "moving up" and across "unrelated professional fields."
4 This synopsis is from a personal conversation with a friend who has worked extensively in PM.

References

Barley, Stephen R. and Gideon Kunda. 2004. *Gurus, Hired Guns, and Warm Bodies: Itinerant Experts in a Knowledge Economy*. Princeton: Princeton University Press.

Blau, Peter. 1962. *Formal Organizations: A Comparative Approach*. San Francisco, CA: Chandler Publishing Co.

Braverman, Harry. 1972. *Labor and Monopoly Capital: The Degradation of Work in the 20th Century*. New York: Monthly Review Press.

Burawoy, Michael. 1979. *Manufacturing Consent: Changes in the Labor Process Under Monopoly Capitalism*. Chicago: University of Chicago Press.

Burris, Beverly H. 1998. "Computerization of the Workplace." *Annual Review of Sociology* 24: 141–157.

Clawson, Dan. 1980. *Bureaucracy and the Labor Process: The Transformation of US Industry, 1860–1920*. New York: Monthly Labor Review.

DiTomaso, Nancy. 2001. "The Loose Coupling of Jobs: The Subcontracting of Everyone?" In *Sourcebook of Labor Markets: Evolving Structures and Processes*, edited by I. Berg and A. Kalleberg, 247–270. New York: Kluwer Academic/Plenum Publishers.

Edwards, Richard. 1979. *Contested Terrain: The Transformation of the Workplace in the 20th Century*. New York: Basic Books.

Eyre, Harris A., Rob D. Mitchell, Will Milford, Nitin Vaswani, and Steven Moylan. 2014. "Portfolio Careers for Medical Graduates: Implications for Postgraduate Training and Workforce Planning." *Australian Health Review* 38: 246–251.

Gladwell, Malcolm. 2008. *Outliers: The Story of Success*. New York: Back Bay Books.

Granovetter, Mark. 1974. *Getting a Job: A Study of Contacts and Careers*. Chicago: University of Chicago Press.

Griffin, Ann. 2008. "'Designer Doctors:' Professional Identity and a Portfolio Career as a General Practice Educator." *Education for Primary Care* 19: 355–359.

Halle, David. 1984. *America's Working Man: Work, Home, and Politics Among Blue-Collar Property Owners*. Chicago: University of Chicago Press.

Handy, Charles. 1991. *The Age of Unreason*, 2nd ed. London: Century Business.

Hicks, Maureen Soyars. 2017. "Flexible Jobs Give Workers Choices." *Monthly Labor Review (May)*. U.S. Bureau of Labor Statistics.

Hodson, Randy. 1995. "Worker Resistance: An Underdeveloped Concept in the Sociology of Work." *Economic and Industrial Democracy* 16(1): 79–110.

Hodson, Randy. 1999. "Organizational Anomie and Worker Consent." *Work and Occupations* 26: 292–323.

Kalleberg, Arne. 2011. *Good Jobs, Bad Jobs: The Rise of Polarized and Precarious Employment Systems in the US, 1970s to 2000s*. New York: Russell Sage Foundation.

Kalleberg, Arne L. and Peter V. Marsden. 2005. "Externalizing Organizational Activities: Where and How US Establishments Use Employment Intermediaries." *Socio-Economic Review* 3: 389–416.

Meiksins, Peter and Peter Whalley. 2002. *Putting Work in Its Place: A Quiet Revolution*. Ithaca, NY: Cornell University Press.

Mirvis, Philip H. and Douglas T. Hall. 1994. "Psychological Success and the Boundaryless Career." *Journal of Organizational Behavior* 15(4): 365–380.

Outsourcing Institute, Fall. 2003. "Preparing for Lift Out: How Recent Outsourcing Deals Are Shaking Up Career Paths." *Outsourcing Essentials* 5–8.

Overby, Stephanie. 2013. "New Onshore IT Outsourcing Centers Outnumber New Offshore Locations." *CIO*: July 26.

Platman, Kerry. 2004. "'Portfolio Careers' and the Search for Flexibility in Later Life." *Work, Employment, and Society* 18(3): 573–599.

Shaffer, Leigh S. and Jacqueline M. Zalewski. 2011. "Career Advising in a VUCA Environment." *NACADA Journal* 31(1): 64–74.

Sullivan, Sherry E. 1999. "The Changing Nature of Careers: A Review and Research Agenda." *Journal of Management* 25(3): 457–484.

Tucker, Robert C. (ed). 1978. *The Marx-Engels Reader*, 2nd ed. New York: WW Norton and Company.

Van Horn, Carl E. 2013. *Working Scared (Or Not at All): The Lost Decade, Great Recession, and Restoring the Shattered American Dream*. New York: Rowman & Littlefield Publishers, Inc.

Weber, Max. 1947. *The Theory of Social and Economic Organization*. New York: The Free Press.

Williamson, Oliver E. 1975. *Markets and Hierarchies: Analysis and Antitrust Implications*. New York: The Free Press.

Zabusky, Stacia E. and Stephen R. Barley. 1996. "Redefining Success: Ethnographic Observations on the Careers of Technicians." In *Broken Ladders: Managerial Careers in the New Economy*, edited by Osterman, Paul. New York: Oxford University Press.

Zalewski, Jacqueline M. 2007. "Discretion, Control, and Professional Careers With Outsourcing Companies." *Sociological Viewpoints* 23: 121–137.

Zalewski, Jacqueline M. 2015. "Work, the Job, and Professional Careers With Outsourcing: Theorizing About Job Quality and Loss." *American Sociological Society Conference*, August 23, Chicago, IL.

Zuboff, Shoshana. 1988. *In the Age of the Smart Machine*. New York: Basic Books.

6 Conclusion

The research findings on inO

At the beginning of my study in 2005, advocates of outsourcing such as the Outsourcing Institute promoted the outsourcing concept and their employment relationships to prospective professionals. They said that rebadging to outsourcing companies would benefit employees because they were moving to a firm that specialized in the latest technology, process tools, and other business services within their professional fields. This would revitalize professional careers by providing more breadth and depth in jobs, career structures, and a strong possibility for mobility. This would be especially the case for those making the transition to outsourcing during its growth phase around Y2K, according to the Outsourcing Institute (2003). However, in this study of subjects in 20 outsourcing cases – spanning the years of 1996 to 2012 – outsourcing did not deliver on its promises for the majority of people. Based on my analysis of professional careers with outsourcing over time, I refute the promise of career revitalization and challenge outsourcing's logic with the findings of what really happened in the inO cases here.

At the conclusion of this study at year-end in 2017, only five of the 42 subjects in this sample who were directly affected by outsourcing were still continuing careers with outsourcing companies over a significant period of time. The roles and assignments these professionals often completed strongly suggest a narrowing of the types of work available and especially work that yielded long-term tenure with outsourcing. Specifically, typical roles in outsourcing include the transformation of 1. customers' business processes and systems to the outsourcing company's standard ones and 2. project management. In 2017, Fran and Tanya continued to work in jobs at Tech Leader. They had respective careers there of 21 and 17 years. Fran was in a leadership role doing the transition and transformation of the work to Tech Leader's standard technologies and business tools in new outsourcing deals. Tanya had continued managing high-profile projects at Tech Leader. A third professional experiencing longevity at her outsourcing company employer was Christina. Christina had moved from one comparable IT management role to another and constructed a career over 14 years at Digitize. Like Fran, at different customers, Christina's role had been transitioning the work at new clients to her employer's standard systems. The fourth professional Brad has been providing IT security solutions and transformative processes to clients of Master Technologies for over 12 years. Finally, the fifth professional Doris has kept her manager role for 20 years supporting technology systems onsite at the same client for Right Technology Solutions. The remaining 38 subjects in this sample with employment experience in outsourcing no longer worked in these labor markets by 2017 calendar year-end. The lack of long-term work was due to one of three reasons: the termination of their jobs, voluntary quitting of jobs, or the nonre-newal of deals and the insourcing of their jobs by the customer firm.

The reasons that few professionals here experienced the revitalization of careers mostly relates to why the work and jobs got outsourced in the first place. In all the cases here, the rationale for outsourcing – which corresponds with most business analysis, logic, and reporting over the past 12 years – were cost reduction reasons and the expert business processes that outsourcing companies provided to custom-ers' noncore operations. Unfortunately for labor, this rationale from customers in deals mandated that outsourcing companies immediately began working to lower the cost of producing the work. Per experienced executive-level account manag-ers like Fran and news reports on the deals here, outsourcing contracts were writ-ten in language that guaranteed cost saving to customers for producing this work either immediately, in the short term, and/or periodically over the contract term.

The outsourcing companies in this study aggressively rose to this financial challenge by instituting flexible specialization in their social organization and using lean production strategies on customer accounts. Soon after deals began, most subjects described immediate attrition from employees who quit jobs there. Professionals quit because of immediate work speedup and the greater complexity in the work from added procedures, politics, and the additional projects in con-tracts. Because outsourcing companies' primary human resource (HR) goal was lean staffing by reducing the number of full-time employees (FTEs) located onsite at customers, to the chagrin of IT professionals like Maria, professionals who quit jobs there were not replaced. Employees who quit jobs, fortuitously, helped outsourcing companies achieve the lean, then leaner, social organization that they sought to make the work more profitable for the company.

Along with this non-replacement of labor practice, outsourcing companies also applied numerical and functional flexibility that helped them reach their goals of doing the work for less cost. Per subjects, outsourcing contracts usually described regular resource actions (i.e., job losses) over their term. In large part, the number of staff on a customer's account was reduced through the process of standardiz-ing and automating the work, often by the outsourced professionals themselves. From the labor perspective, their end goal was to work themselves out of work and maybe a job (if they could not find another one in the outsourcing company, which was a likely outcome). In addition to their work onsite for a customer, out-sourced professionals were also strategically networked into job silos spanning geographical regions. Satisfying their need for functional flexibility, when prob-lems and extra-ordinary work needs arose across customers in the expanded juris-diction and immediate solutions were needed, outsourced professionals could be summoned from the appropriate job silo to tackle them in a just-in-time manner.

Finally, sharing information about standard tools and systems between professionals in the same job silo helped them work more quickly toward the goal of the complete transformation of customers' unique business processes into the standard, centralized, and mostly automated ones at outsourcing companies. Brilliantly constructed, lean and flexible staffing systems at outsourcing companies, in sum, enabled outsourcing companies to purposefully work towards and eventually produce work at a lower cost.

Market logic (Thornton, Ocasio, & Lounsbury 2012) predominates in the culture of outsourcing. Work and labor become hyper-commodified in "numbers" that signify and substitute for work in interactions with others. In the inO cases here, with the exception of special projects, work in job areas was constructed with numbers in service level agreements (SLAs). SLAs were designed to quantify, measure, and to hold outsourcing companies and their employees ("the vendor") accountable for the work in contracts; they represent new market controls in the labor process. Thus subjects in inO, like Don from the Bravado Hospital case, lamented that most workplace conversations revolved around "making the SLA and, if we didn't make the SLA, doing some CYA to cover ourselves." Bonuses for onsite managers at outsourcing companies heavily incentivized the upselling of work and services to customers, focusing attention to increasing the sales and profitability numbers being produced onsite. But mostly, from subjects' perspectives, outsourcing companies were relentless about reducing costs through labor actions. Periodic job losses were especially the case in the large contracts involving the largest outsourcing companies and in the more recent deals. Long-term employees like Tanya referred to this recurring practice at Tech Leader as "cutting heads." Their repeated labor actions underscore that markets effectively deny humanity by refusing to recognize that their labor actions throw human lives into chaos. Outsourcing companies pursued more efficient, standard, and automated business processes that most aggressively reduced the cost of producing work for customers.

As work on an inO account became more automated, the possibility that jobs and employment would come to an end for outsourced professionals darkly loomed overhead. Herein lies the second and third reasons why employment with inO failed to produce revitalization in professional careers: its emphasis on standardizing and automating work in most jobs in this industry with the future goal of eliminating them; and the physical obstacles to mobility and ongoing job tenure with inO when staff are working onsite at the customer company (Kalleberg & Marsden 2005; Weber 2017). Today, and for several years now, outsourcing advocacy firms like the Institute for Robotic Process Automation and Artificial Intelligence have regularly promoted the labor saving benefits of "disruptive technology" and "intelligent automation." For example, one recent email (posted on February 23, 2018) from the OI contains a link to obtain a free white paper that describes "The Five Best Practices for Building an Intelligent Automation Center of Excellence." Public news stories, like a recent one entitled "Contracted: The End of Employees" in the *Wall Street Journal* on February 2, 2017, also forewarn ominous labor outcomes as companies increasingly use third party suppliers to produce the work in their noncore functions (Weber 2017). This study finds that outsourced subjects strategic work consists of remediation and the end result desired by outsourcing companies is complete routinization and automation of the work.

With inO too, the hyper-commodification of work and culture reduced their mystical qualities and meaning for professionals. Numbers did not provide the same meaning to IT and HR professionals as a technical discussion, for example, with colleagues did. In several hospital cases, where the work and people got insourced when contracts were not renewed with outsourcing companies, subjects enthusiastically said the switch made their work relationships more integrated with hospital staff and much more collegial and "honest". For IT workers like Lisa, the interactional work in the outsourcing job consisted less of the dialect of technicians which involved "solving a puzzle" and using technical language that tended to confound and amaze outsiders to the profession. In comparison, with insourcing, Lisa said her internal customers at Bravado Hospital (they declined to renew their outsourcing deal and insourced everyone in 2007) interacted with her now as if she were a "mastermind!" Other outsourced subjects described their lack of attachment to a customer's physical environment "that was not my own" (Fran). Still others, such as Dominic at Sourcing Central, described a disconnection to outsourcing employers' "distant organization." As both scholars and journalists have noted (Kalleberg & Marsden 2005; Weber 2017), temporaries, contractors, and outsourced workers exist in a "parallel workforce." From a peripheral position to both customers, vendors, and the defining features of their work, it was harder for outsourced professionals to decipher who they worked for or to have strong identifications with both employers and the technical aspects of their jobs.

Finally, a dominant finding of this study of inO revolves around the market effects on social relations in the workplace. Fundamentally, customers and vendors have incongruent proprietary (or financial) goals in the market relationship. Because the ownership and control over the work transfers to the vendor in outsourcing, there are also new work processes. Both circumstances underscore each company's different goals and necessitate actions reflective of market logic (Thornton, Ocasio, & Lounsbury 2012). Thus, the market organization structures the social organization of the work, professional approaches to it, and its relations along adversarial lines. Managers on both sides of the market organization emphasized differing roles and relationships and the need to protect the proprietary interest of direct employers. The resulting interactional challenges were fostered because people were not educated on the changed nature of the work, market relations, and the new business processes. Most professionals commented on the heightened political nature to their relational work in markets and described instances where they were "chewed-up!" or treated in an undignified (e.g., demanding and inhumane) manner by former colleagues and employees of customers. Many subjects said the added political work was the biggest drawback in their experience with inO.

The greater political nature, I argue, represents invisible work with markets. In business analysis, there is little discussion of the greater politics in working-out the new arrangements with inO. Management in deals here did not acknowledge the more adversarial organization of work, prepare for, or educate their employees about it before deals begin. Through their non-recognition, employers just expected their employees to handle the politics in markets as necessary, with no commensurate added pay for this difficult interaction work. This research recognizes this significant new work in markets and makes it visible in subjects' narrative. I call the added political work in outsourcing "market labor." By their failure to acknowledge the new work climate, I found companies often did not recognize what outsourcing a job function meant at the level of the shop floor, what processes would be added to make the work more complex, nor did they acknowledge the new adversarial political labor for working things out in markets. Outsourcing created new arrangements where people purposefully confronted unequal goals and problems in markets. Customers and vendors expected workers to figure it out with no preparation or training. Political work was invisible and, because of this, professionals on the front lines of the market organization were not recognized for this labor in any way.

So, what is the future of outsourcing? There are signs of cracks within it currently. For example, since 2017 calendar year-end and the beginning of 2018, the United Kingdom has witnessed the bankruptcy of Carillion, a large outsourcing firm that had contracts with the central government for various work including maintaining prisons, maintaining homes for military families, and providing meals to seniors in government-sponsored nursing homes (see, e.g., Lynam 2018). Furthermore, there have been several other newsworthy nonrenewals of outsourcing deals and the subsequent insourcing of workers. General Motors insourced most of their IT staff back in 2013 after problems surfaced in their deal with IBM (Baldwin 2013). Periodically, similar instances are reported that indicate outsourcing deals that are likely going awry; e.g., on February 19, 2018, computing.co.uk reported on an IBM outsourcing deal with Aecom explaining that it is "a mess" (Sumner 2018).

Yet, these same types of deal cancellations and news on the problems with outsourcing companies were also happening long before the conclusion of this study. For example, in 2005 Hewlett-Packard (one of the largest outsourcing companies at the time) was experiencing significant financial trouble and faced a massive reconstruction of their global operations that included job losses for tens of thousands of their employees. Recurring conflicts in deals reaffirm that customer companies often do not understand the transfer of ownership and control over the work and its new organization with outsourcing. And, some outsourcing companies find they cannot deliver the services they have been contracted to deliver at the cost they have promised to their customers. This results in financial problems and, like the case of Carillion in the UK, sometimes bankruptcy.

Business analysis, reporting, and the cases here over time find that outsourcing deals are getting smaller, and the work that is commonly outsourced is changing. For example, application hosting on "the cloud" has been a significant growth area for outsourcing with some analysts predicting it may eclipse "traditional outsourcing" in the near future (i.e., the type of outsourcing represented in cases here) (see, e.g., Bradbury 2015 and consultancy.uk/news 2018).

Yet, other economic signs assure that traditional outsourcing continues to grow. Large companies are increasingly outsourcing their noncore work like IT and HR work. For example, a Society for Information Management survey reported in *Computerworld* found that in 2012 companies spent 36% of IT budgets on average on outsourced services. This increased from 28% in 2011 (Thibodeau 2012). The *Wall Street Journal* explained that an analysis of 2,000 companies showed their reduction in direct labor costs over time (13.6% in 2009 and 12.5% in 2011) and explained it with the consistent logic for outsourcing (Chasan 2013). "There's a lack of desire from companies to invest in noncore activities, according to Matthew Eatough (CEO) from Proxima Group." Finally, as reported in a *Wall Street Journal* article and other public sources, compared to past industrial giants on the list like Ford Motor Company, some of the largest US companies today are outsourcing companies like IBM (PYMNTS 2017; Weber 2017). In the near future, per these business reports, outsourcing companies are betting on leveraging automation to reduce headcount and labor costs and increase revenue. For example, a recent story proudly stated that the "outsourcing giant Cognizant blazed an important new trail in outsourcing, solving the existential question of how to leverage automation and digital technologies to maintain growth whilst shrinking costly headcounts" (see "Cognizant: Decoupling Revenue and Headcount" on sourcing-focus.com, February 13, 2018). As further explained, this outsourcing company has increased the rate of profitability on each of their employees while decreasing their overall number.

Against this business news backdrop, the more tenuous nature of work and the common elimination of jobs I found over time in the cases here is strongly supportive of the fissuring theory Weil (2014) describes. Not only are hierarchical organizations unraveled with outsourcing, but entire professional fields may be facing similar issues as more work gets "fissured" and contracted to third party providers and undergoes aggressive standardization and automation with digital technologies. Growth in outsourcing will contribute to the structural reasons for the gig economy, greater contingencies in jobs or nonstandard employment, and income inequality. With the growth of its short-term nature, work may no longer be the integrating social force it has historically been. Instead work is becoming stressful for many in the job force as fear from economic uncertainty in markets is placed directly on the backs of laborers with outsourcing and other nonstandard employment forms. If for-profit companies have their say, contingencies in other jobs will grow and they – like the outcome in the IT and HR outsourcing cases here – will produce a spinning wheel of lean, flexible, and contracting labor markets that slowly move up the labor value chain, as Weil implies with the fissuring concept.

Implications of this research

One of the most disappointing results over the span of this study is that there was not a clear understanding of the numbers of US people affected and employed in the outsourcing industry. Overall, there continues to be a lack of reliable public information on the number of people who have been affected by the inO of jobs or figures on the economic value of the outsourcing of their work. Measures by firms that do research and analysis on outsourcing are disparate. Some reports might discuss the total contract value of inked deals in a quarter while others outline the number of employees of large outsourcing firms. Additionally, the numbers attributed to companies and industry sectors or to the outsourcing industry as a whole are inconsistent from year to year. There have been periodic examples of government and scholarly research estimating or examining the growth of outsourcing, the greater flexibility in some jobs, and other aspects of nonstandard, contingent employment (e.g., Brown & Siegel 2005; Cappelli & Keller 2013; Fisher 2017; Kalleberg 2011; Smith 1994). But clearly more research can be done and should be completed on inO and outsourcing of work. My earnest hope is that this study gives valued information to fill this gap in knowledge, and the findings here contribute to the growing recognition and public conversation about the increase in the outsourcing of work and jobs and their real effects on people.

As this research has shown, outsourced professionals were primarily recognized by customers and vendors as commodities. In outsourcing markets, people were conceived of as a product and, as such, the conditions of work and the treatment of people became degraded. Outsourced professionals were expected to give more of their time, do more work, emotionally handle the added politics of markets, and endure greater job insecurity all the while maintaining their cooperation and commitment to the goals of outsourcing companies and their contracts with customers. As Dwayne aptly stated in our interview, the conditions of work at outsourcing companies "create desperate people." Outsourcing companies fostered a real culture of fear, heightened competition between colleagues, undignified treatment, and estrangement between professionals across cases in this sample.

Increasingly and over time, the outsourcing deals here became more despotic. By significantly reducing most of the benefits of jobs with outsourcing, employers simply did not care if people took jobs in the later inO deals in this sample. The general treatment of outsourced professionals, after rebadging, did not generally improve either. And so, most often, outsourced professionals eventually withdrew their consent to the job and its degraded, divisive social relations and working conditions. The implication here is that showing outsourced professionals an overall lack of respect is not a positive model for how to treat others. Non-humane treatment does not promote self-confidence or better work, nor does it promote positive interactions with other workers or a positive outlook more generally. The degraded treatment and desperate working conditions for employees of outsourcing and other nonstandard employment arrangements likely contribute to the divisiveness in public discourse today, both here in the US and in other parts of the globalized world.

From a sociological perspective, work has traditionally provided a socializing and stabilizing anchor for social groups and societies (Durkheim 1969). DiTomaso (2001:265) reminds us – declining job security, poorer working conditions, and more social conflict in jobs "raises concerns about the disconnection of people from long-established patterns of social stability" (i.e., stable employment in work). As DiTomaso asked in 2001 and still is appropriate to ask today, "What is likely to replace the institutional forms that [used to] create the sense of identity, exchange, and investment"? (265) . . . "in a world of loosely coupled jobs in loosely coupled organizations, no one is safe or secure" (267).

Today, to a great extent, jobs in the janitorial, cafeteria, and logistics sectors have shifted to third party suppliers. As this research has shown, outsourcing work and jobs to another company who provides them to customers at a lower cost has been increasingly affecting white-collar jobs in IT, HR, and other fields. Per executives here (e.g., the former CIO for Sourcing Central), predictions by the large competitors in the field and people on the inside of the industry, outsourcing companies, the use of third party vendors, and their reliance on standardized and automated technologies to reduce labor costs are being aggressively applied to more skilled labor markets. For example, the outsourcing competitor Accenture and staffing executives at the largest US companies claim that in the next ten years some of the largest companies will employ only the most essential employees or – from their perspective – only those in the C-suite (Weber 2017). They claim 20 to 50% of the total workforce at the largest US companies – e.g., Verizon, Bank of America, and FedEx Corp. – is already outsourced (Weber 2017). Bendor-Samuel (CEO of Everest Group) was recently quoted in a sourcingfocus.com news report entitled "Cognizant: Decoupling Revenue and Headcount" (February 13, 2018):

> As the industry moves from the labour arbitrage factory model to the technology-based digital model the revenue per person rises and fewer people are needed. . . . Cognizant is one of many firms which is driving hard into the new digital marketplace and this effort is showing results both in their increased growth and the improved revenue per person and falling headcount.

The rationale for companies that outsource has been and remains the lowering of operating (and especially labor) costs. From the perspective of industry enthusiasts and the employee staffing signs at the largest US companies, full-time employees doing work amenable to outsourcing – and especially noncore work – should beware. Wherever the next layer of expensive full-time employees is, the work has the potential to be outsourced next.

Because of the strong possibility for growth in the types of work and the proportion of people affected by outsourcing to increase, labor protections will be increasingly necessary to help leverage against the proven negative outcomes for job tenure with outsourcing. In the context of the "loose coupling of jobs," DiTomaso (2001) has called for more institutional responses that help fill the void of work's general social integration function when work and jobs were more permanent in nature. Greater membership in organizations such as professional associations, unions, and other labor advocacy groups could help fill this void.

Future research directions

It is painfully clear there is a lack of public understanding of the outsourcing phenomenon. The vast majority of public discourse on outsourcing is developed and promoted by advocates of the outsourcing or sourcing industry. The data points on how many people work in outsourcing employment are mixed. Outsourced and other contingent workers do not fit neatly into job categories of nonstandard employment (Cappelli & Keller 2013). For example, in the past, the Bureau of Labor Statistics has gathered data on the number of people in contingent or alternative work arrangements (including those employed by contracting firms) in a Current Population Survey Supplement in 1989, 1996, 1998, 2001, 2005, and 2017 and found some growth in jobs. But they still only constituted small fractions of working people; around 4% work in alternative work arrangements and .6% of those working for contracting firms (BLS 2005 & 2017). In the 2001 National Employer Survey, "40% of establishments reported a vendor on premises, although this only added up to .86% of all onsite workers" (Capelli & Keller 2013: 882). Foremost, we need more hard, objective, and scientifically reliable government data on outsourcing and other forms of nonstandard employment. Employment is core to economic livelihood and social well-being. Reliable data needs to be gathered and analyzed on the outsourcing of jobs and it needs to be reported in and circulated within the public sphere. This will make the general population aware of and understand the actual trends in outsourcing, the causes of it, and how it affects people in their daily lives. This information will enable professional people to make more informed choices as the economic environment may become increasingly conducive to a breadth of work and job changes.

More research and analysis needs to be completed on how markets effect social relations in work and workplace culture. Very little research exists that specifically focuses on the interactional aspects of work in markets and the added market labor that employees described here in this study; subjects say they did not expect the labor because employers did not prepare them for it. Many subjects claimed the greater political work in markets was the biggest drawback to outsourcing for them. More studies can be designed to examine how professionals approach and rework new arrangements in markets. Outsourcing is likely to grow. How can the effects of this growth be more thoughtfully construed for the human people subjected to it? Markets should not and do not have to be worked out in social conflict, as a minority of the cases here suggest. In this regard, the outsourcing case of Rapture Hospital and Right Technology Solutions was the successful inO archetype here. To help advocate for more recognition, preparation, and compensation, companies who outsource successfully and also the people involved should be investigated and rewarded with recognition.

Finally, there is a strong tradition in sociology for seeing a correspondence between the economy and economic changes to other institutional, cultural, and other ideological changes. For example, Karl Marx gave the economy and its systems of production primacy, stating that all other social constructions and institutions were shaped by it (Williams 1973). Similarly, Emile Durkheim (1969) suggested that work has traditionally been an organizing and socializing force in earlier and industrializing societies. Work is being increasingly governed with market logic and the loss of social protections for labor. Work's stabilizing core is being aggressively usurped. As DiTomaso (2001:265) argues, loosely coupled labor markets are breaking "long-established patterns of social stability that creates the potential for substantial social disruption and widespread distress." This close and personal examination of the inO of work and jobs on a sample of IT and HR professionals finds that work becomes more adversarial with inO and politics and undignified treatment too often result. It encourages companies and people to perceive things through the lens of self-interest, job insecurity and fear, and competition with others. It denies humanity by constituting all human behavior in terms of commodification. Something significant has been happening in the US economy – the workplace has been growing less humane and meaner, especially in outsourcing. Given these significant economic and social changes, from a sociological perspective, it is fundamentally important to theorize how changes in work and the effect of markets may be helping shape the adversarial nature and approaches many people take in public life today.

References

Baldwin, Howard. 2013. "Outsourcing Adieu: Companies Retake the Reins on IT Services." *Computerworld*: July 18.

Bradbury, Danny. 2015. "IT Outsourcing Remains Healthy, but the Functions Being Outsourced Are Changing." *ITworldCanada.com*: August 31.

Brown, Sharon P. and Lewis B. Siegel. 2005. "Mass Layoff Data Indicate Outsourcing and Offshoring Work." *Monthly Labor Review*: August.

Bureau of Labor Statistics. 2005. "Contingent and Alternative Employment Arrangements." February.

Bureau of Labor Statistics. 2018. "Contingent and Alternative Employment Arrangements." June.

Cappelli, Peter and Joseph R. Keller. 2013. "A Study of the Extent and Potential Causes of Alternative Employment Arrangements." *ILR Review* 66(4): 874–901.

Chasan, Emily. 2013. "Outsourcing Labor Continues, Poses Risks for Some." *Wall Street Journal*: August 5.

Consultancy.uk/news. 2018. "Growth in UK Outsourcing Industry Nears 20%, Cloud Main Driver." January 22.

DiTomaso, Nancy. 2001. "The Loose Coupling of Jobs: The Subcontracting of Everyone?" In *Sourcebook for Labor Markets: Evolving Structures and Processes*, edited by I. Berg and A. Kalleberg. New York: Kluwer Academic/Plenum Publishers.

Durkheim, Emile. 1969 [1893]. *The Division of Labor in Society*. New York: The Free Press.

Fisher, Lisa. 2017. *Flexible Work Arrangements: Embracing the Noise to Understand the Silence*. New York: Lexington Books.

Kalleberg, Arne L. 2011. *Good Jobs, Bad Jobs: The Rise of Polarized and Precarious Employment Systems in the United States, 1970s to 2000*. New York: Russell Sage Foundation.

Kalleberg, Arne L. and Peter V. Marsden. 2005. "Externalizing Organizational Activities: Where and How US Establishments Use Employment Intermediaries." *Socio-Economic Review* 3: 389–416.

Lynam, Joe. 2018. "Carillion Collapse: UK Puts Up 100m to Back Carillion Contractor Loans. *BBC.com*: February 3.

Outsourcing Institute. 2003. "Preparing for Lift Out: How Recent Outsourcing Deals Are Shaking Up Career Paths." *Outsourcing Essentials* 5–8, Fall.

PYMNTS. 2017. "Gig Workforce Swells As Companies Shed Headcount." *PYMNTS.com*: December 29.

Smith, Vicki. 1994. "Institutionalizing Flexibility in a Service Firm: Multiple Contingencies and Hidden Hierarchies." *Work and Occupations* 21(3): 284–307.

Sourcingfocus.com. 2018. "Cognizant: Decoupling Revenue and Headcount." February 13.

Sumner, Stuart. 2018. "IBM Outsourcing Deal With Aecom 'a Mess' and the CIO Is 'On His Way Out,' Claims Insider." *Computing.co.uk*: February 19.

Thibodeau, Patrick. 2012. "2012 36% of IT Budgets on Average Spent on Outsourcing, Up From 28% in 2011, Society for Information Management Survey." *Computerworld*: October 10.

Thornton, Patricia H., William Ocasio, and Michael Lounsbury. 2012. *The Institutional Logics Perspective: A New Approach to Culture, Structure, and Process*. Oxford: Oxford University Press.

Weber, Lauren. 2017. "Contracted: The End of Employees." *Wall Street Journal*: February 2.

Weil, David. 2014. *The Fissured Workplace: How Work Became So Bad for So Many and What Can Be Done to Improve It*. Cambridge, MA: Harvard University Press.

Williams, Raymond. 1973. "Base and Superstructure in Marxist Cultural Theory." *New Left Review* 82: 3–16.

Index

Note: Page numbers in *italic* indicate a figure and page numbers in **bold** indicate a table on the corresponding page.